CLOWNS and CANNONS
The American Circus During the Civil War

by William L. Slout

An Emeritus Enterprise Book
2995 Ladera Road, San Bernardino, California 92405
REISSUED IN THE YEAR 2000

Copyright © 1997 by William L. Slout

All rights reserved.
No part of this book may be reproduced in any form
without the expressed written consent of the publisher.
Printed in the United States of America by Van Volumes, Ltd.

Clowns and Cannons: the American circus during the Civil War
ISBN 0-8095-0304-2 (cloth). - ISBN 0-8095-1304-8 (pbk.)

An Emeritus Enterprise Book
REISSUED IN THE YEAR 2000

TABLE OF CONTENTS

Preface	vii
1860	3
1861	39
1862	83
1863	125
1864	155
1865	181
Bibliography	221
Index	231

I wish to express my gratitude to Fred Dahlinger, Jr., Director of the Robert L. Parkinson Library and Research Center, Circus World Museum, Baraboo, Wisconsin, and to Stuart Thayer, distinguished circus historian, for their generous and helpful support during the preparation of this book.

PREFACE

This is a story of the survival of the American circuses throughout one of the most perilous periods in our nation's history. The events encompass the years from 1860 through 1865. The 1860s was a decade of transition for these traveling exhibitions. By this time the size, both in equipment and personnel, had leveled off. The *modus operandi* from one show to another was similar. Performances were fixed and showed little variation. And the number of proprietors in the business had reached a peak. These elements would remain relatively stable until the early 1870s.

There was only a handful of large shows. A comparison can be made by an 1859 estimate from the New York *Clipper*. Spalding & Rogers carried 220 horses, 200 people, the boats *Floating Palace*, *James Raymond*, and *Banjo*, with a daily expense of $700; VanAmburgh & Co., 150 horses, 130 people, at $500 per day; Sands, Nathans & Co., 120 horses, 110 people, at $400; Nixon & Co., 90 horses, 80 people, at $300. Others, such as G. M. Eldred & Co., Levi J. North's, Antonio & Wilder, Rivers & Derious, L. B. Lent's, Mabie's, Sloat & Shepherd, George F. Bailey & Co., and Yankee Robinson's were estimated as having about 90 horses, 60 people, at $250. There were nearly a dozen other lesser companies in the $10,000 investment area that had an operating expense of $150 per day.

Horses were one of the major expenses for shows. In the spring of the year they came out of the barns fat and fresh; but after a few weeks of country roads they began to wear down. Some would break down completely during the season and have to be replaced. A large crew of hostlers were required to drive and care for them. And, of course, they had to be fed and shod and given the special care that such work animals require. Without horses, circuses of that day would not have been able to leave winter quarters.

The breakdown of personnel traveling with a first-class concern included the manager, treasurer, a contracting agent, an advertising writer, two to four men in the paste brigade, a layer out, ringmaster, equestrian director, boss canvasman, boss hostler, a doorkeeper, any number of canvasmen and hostlers, and a watchman who sat up all night to protect the stock and to wake up the company at the hotel to insure breakfast was prepared on time to make ready to move on. Often the division of labor overlapped, with people doubling up on their expected duties.

The treasurer was responsible for selling the tickets, keeping the books and paying the hotel and other local bills. He was the last person to leave town, since there was little for him to do before the ticket wagon opened for the afternoon performance. And, traveling in his own light conveyance, he was usually the first to arrive at the next stand.

At the outset of the season, the agent started in advance of the company by fifteen or twenty days, traveling in his own light buggy. His responsibilities were to contract the lot, secure the city license, arrange for board of the company and the horses, and deal with the newspapers. He was followed within a day by the advertising wagon, carrying the paste brigade who hung the pictorial posters at every available spot within a comfortable radius of the stand. The writer appeared a week or ten days ahead of the show to create a public excitement through his flamboyant releases to the newspapers.

There were fifteen to twenty male and female performers— equestrians, gymnasts, leapers, tumblers, vaulters, posturers, clowns, contortionists, tight-rope walkers, jugglers, wild beast handlers and tamers, and sideshowmen.

On the morning of the show's arrival, the layer-out came an hour or so before the others. His duties were to book the company into the hotel, assign the rooms, with the performers receiving the best accommodations, and arrange for the bedding of the horses at the stables. The telegraph wagon arrived next and in no time the tent was in the air and the ground broken for the placement of the ring.

By now the company had assembled at the outskirts of the town and a procession into it was in preparation. The band chariot was cleaned off, pads were put on the horses, band members donned their uniforms, and performers got into their spangled and plumed costumes. The grand entree usually began around 10:00 a.m. A designated member went through the streets in advance to find the best route for the parade. The same individual led the assemblage along the route, followed by the bandwagon, the performers in light wagons, and then the luggage vans and closed cages. The company was met at the edge of town by a horde of excited youngsters, who tirelessly followed the caravan to the vacant area where the big top was to be raised. The more experienced circus watchers were situated along the way where a clear view allowed counting the wagons to confirm there were as many as had been depicted on the bills.

This done, the performers went to the hotel and slept until noon. Within a half-hour of noon, dinner was on the tables. After eating, the performers walked to the lot for the afternoon show, which began at 2:00 or 2:30 and lasted about two hours. Supper was held at 6:00 and the evening performance began at 7:00. The company then had time for a little sleep.

The start for the next stand depended on the distance to travel. If the jump was a long one, breakfast was served at 3:30 a.m. and the company was on the road an hour later. If the roads were bad or the journey extremely long, a "circus jump" of fifty miles or more, the troupe might start out as soon as the night performance was finished. Col. James H. Sprague, a cornet player in L. B. Lent's band for the 1860 season, recalled that before the nightly performance ended the sidewalls were down, part of the stakes removed, and the loose baggage packed. In less than an hour after the tent was cleared of audience, the show was ready to move out. The canvas wagon and pole and chain wagons were particularly heavy and traveled only four miles an hour, so those vehicles usually started out at midnight. This also applied to the elephants if the show had any.

Circuses usually set up their tents on a lot located at the outskirts of the city. The main tent, generally a round top of some 100 feet to 120 feet in diameter, was surrounded by sideshows, candy stands, etc. Within the canvas was a 42 foot earthen ring besprinkled with sawdust and surrounded by tiered boards for seating the audience. Here one might encounter a young man hawking peanuts, candies, and lemonade, and another selling the clown's song books.

At performance time the band struck up and the entire costumed *ensemble* formed the grand entree by mechanically circling the sawdust ring, as someone once described it, "solemn as owls, their faces as long as a fiddle." This required pageantry was followed by the entrance of the ringmaster, arrayed in spangled coat, vest, ruffled shirt and striped pants, carrying in his hand a large whip. In a most elegant manner, he announced the appearance of the principal equestrienne.

Starting from the right of the arena opening, where subordinates stood ready to hold the garters and paper balloons, the horse was trotted out carrying the young lady. She was accompanied by one of the clowns, who bumblingly assisted her act, as he carried on an inane discourse with the ringmaster. After which, the rider guided her horse over banners held by the assistants to the delight and admiration of the auditory. The act was concluded by the clown singing a comic song.

There was usually a "Pete Jenkins" act involving a performer dressed as a rube who would stumble about the ring to the merriment of the audience. Finally, after throwing off his rustic attire to reveal his glittering equestrian tights, he would display his artistry as a bareback performer.

The program continued with more equestrians interspersed with gymnasts and other entertainers until the ringmaster made a final appearance to thank the audience for their kind attendance and announce that the performance would conclude with the trick mules. A young man from the audience was selected to ride them, who, upon mounting one, was unceremoniously pitched back into the crowd. Another youngster then came forward and ended the program by riding the mule successfully, to the delight of everyone.

With the show over, as the audience spilled out of the main tent they encountered a man standing upon a high box in front of a smaller tent urging them to see the fat woman, the boa constrictor, and the educated hog for the small price of 25¢. Their curiosity accommodated, they then traipsed homeward, their dreams well satisfied until the next circus came to town.

This period was within the heyday of the talking and singing clowns. The one-ring format under the main circus tent created an intimate arena where they could exhibit their intellectual prowess and vocal talents. At this time they were receiving their greatest prominence in the circus show bills and programs and were taking away larger salaries than other more physical, or knock about, jesters. Among the favorites can be included Dan Rice, Sam Lathrop, Nat Austin, Johnny Patterson, John Davenport, Tony Pastor, and John Lowlow. Along with this popularity came the sale of clown songbooks, collections of favorite numbers—"Joe Bowers," "Dixie," "Camptown Races," "Jordan is a Hard Road to Travel," "The King of the Cannibal Islands"—or originals, both comic and sentimental. The books also included stories, jokes, and biographical information of the featured artist, who, by their sales, reaped additional income.

By 1859 there were some fifteen to eighteen wagon shows on the road and a few more traveling by boat or rail. These included the

Metropolitan Circus, which toured the mountain and mining country of California and Nevada Territory; VanAmburgh & Co.'s Eastern Menagerie in the northeastern states; VanAmburgh & Co.'s Western Menagerie in Illinois, Wisconsin, Indiana, and Ohio; Antonio & Wilder's Great World Circus in Ohio, West Virginia, Pennsylvania, Indiana, and Michigan; Nixon & Co.'s Mammoth Circus in New Jersey, New York State, New England and Canada; Sands, Nathans & Co.'s American and English Circus in New England, New York State, Canada, Pennsylvania, and New Jersey; Harry Whitby's New York Circus in New York State; Kimball's Oregon Circus; Oliver Bell's Railroad Circus with a steamer on the Great Lakes; Yankee Robinson's Great Double Show in the South; G. M. Eldred & Co.'s Circus in Texas, northern Mexico, and the South; Levi J. North's Circus in Ohio, Kentucky, Tennessee and Georgia; Sloat & Shepherd's "Joe Pentland" Circus in New York State and Massachusetts; O. W. Hyatt's Great Railroad Circus in Ohio and Indiana; and Lee's California Circus.

If the 1860s was a decade of transition, it was also a period of survival. Right from the beginning there was a universal premonition of trouble. By mid-1860, amusement companies and performers were migrating northward, fearful of being stranded in the midst of civil conflict. Whereas circuses had previously roamed the full length and breadth of the settled areas of the United States, only two managements—Robinson & Lake and Dan Rice's Great Show—ventured into the South that year. The former moved back into Northern territory by August; the latter remained several months longer, ending up at the Academy of Music, New Orleans, in February of 1861, leaving safely in advance of the hostilities.

After the declaration of war, the South was closed to traveling amusements. With the number of circuses on the road throughout the conflict remaining steady, and nearly half of the country taken away from their itineraries, the problem of over-crowding occurred, a condition which often led to severe competition. A few shows left the country for the West Indies and South America, others eased across the northern border into Canada, and still others extended their movements farther west into Iowa, Wisconsin, and Minnesota.

Adventurous circuses followed in the wake of the Northern armies, performing for the encamped soldiers and the civilians of the liberated territories. At the outset of the fighting the major rivers were closed to traffic other than military. But, as the war progressed and the

Union forces overran the Confederate strongholds along the water routes, circuses were again able to visit the river towns by boat.

The Northern economy was as sensitive to the quivers of social and political influences as in any other period. At the start of the war, public uncertainty created a climate of hard times for amusement enterprises; but once industry and agriculture began meeting the demands of the military, money was plentiful. After the initial patriotic gusto dissipated, Northerners were in need of diversion from the horrors of war. The theatres, the concert saloons, the minstrel halls, and the circus arenas were the beneficiaries.

A major source for this volume was the New York *Clipper*, the only continuous reporting organ of nineteenth century circus activity. But, as the bibliography reveals, I have made use of newspapers of the period, articles by or about people connected with the narrative, books of nineteenth century biography and circus activity, etc. Credit must be given to the director and staff of the Robert L. Parkinson Library and Research Center at the Circus World Museum in Baraboo, WI, for the fund of material—both textual and illustrative—made available to me. I am also indebted to the staff at the California State University, San Bernardino, library for the generous assistance, most particularly through their efforts in securing inter-library loans. I have tried to be scrupulously accurate with my selections, although challenged by the pitfalls one encounters in researching nineteenth century popular amusements—conflicting dates, variations in the spelling of surnames, apocryphal accounts, etc.

William L. Slout

Clowns and Cannons

The Hanlon Brothers
1. George 2. Frederick 3. William 4. Edward 5. Alfred

1860

John Brown was dead but, as in the song, his truth was marching over the political face of the nation. There was trouble with pesky Mexican border marauders who were attempting to usurp control of the Rio Grande country. The best known of the pony express agencies started running between St. Joseph, MO, and Sacramento, CA, a distance of 1,980 miles. Oregon was in its first year as the Union's thirty-third state. The famous overland mail service from Missouri to California, but two years old, was affording travelers a journey of three cramped, sleepless weeks or more on discomforting Concord coaches. The country's first oil well opened in Titusville, PA. The homestead act was vetoed by President Buchanan, which alienated small farmers and immigrants alike. The country was canvassed by that periodic breed we call census takers, who found the nation's population had reached nearly thirty-one and a half million, including the four million enslaved Americans. The Prince of Wales, visiting the United States, could observe the young ladies wearing beaver hats trimmed with ostrich feathers and hoop skirts so expansive as to cause accidental fires. Their unique waterfall hair style, created over a frame of horsehair, lasted in vogue throughout the decade. The popularity of the new song, "I Wish I Was in Dixie," would soon be split in half.

The Harper's Ferry invasion by John Brown and his supporters had shaken the confidence of the South in the good faith of the North, convinced as they were that the rhetoric of the abolitionists reflected the full sentiment of the northern population. After Brown's capture, there was panic over rumors of an expedition to rescue him, which resulted in creating a concentration of troops at Charleston, Virginia, where the extremists were incarcerated. As the day of execution approached, the excitement intensified. Charleston was placed under martial law and the nation held its breath.

In New York City the autumn weather had been mild but there was promise of winter bluster as the 1860s began; still, the popular places of amusement—the major dramatic houses, negro minstrelsy, and the concert saloons—were doing first-rate business. There was public satisfaction with the several theatres as far as the plays were concerned. A new credibility and acceptance was occurring, brought about by a contemporary manner of staging, which resulted in longer runs for each well acted piece. As a consequence, productions were individually better presented than when a change of title took place every night or two, tiring out the actors with learning new roles and exhausting the treasury with a constant and almost fruitless outlay for new scenery and expensive costumes.

The popularity of negro minstrelsy is almost as inexplicable as the creation of the universe; nevertheless, Ethiopian entertainments were enjoying a vast audience. Not only in New York City was it one of the favorite amusements, but it was growing in popularity everywhere—east, west, north, and south. Americans were laughing at the comic antics of the mock black man while the real Negro was the pawn in a national battle. Holding first place in this city was undoubtedly Bryant's Minstrels, ensconced within Niblo's Saloon, housed in the same building with the popular Niblo's Garden theatre. In Philadelphia, Sandford's Opera Troupe had firm hold; and Morris Bros., Pell & Trowbridge's Minstrels were a favorite of the Boston public.

The concert saloons were sharing a sizable part of Broadway night life as well. The entertainments were performed in converted theatres amid a barroom atmosphere and where the patrons were attended by "pretty waiter girls" who dispensed drinks and engaged them in conversation and, in the less desirable places, made private "arrangements" with customers who had money to squander on such things. The offerings were of a varied and somewhat pleasing character with each act on the program lasting about ten minutes. One could drop in and while away an hour or so and leave.

January, 1860! Barely before New Year's Eve hangovers were bestilled came the announcement of the auspicious arrival to America of William Cooke and what was advertised as Cooke's Equestrian Troupe from Astley's Royal Amphitheatre, London. Cooke! Astley! What a joyous sound to those familiar names and what an exciting circus tradition they represented.

William was a third generation of the famous Cooke dynasty which began in Scotland with old Thomas Cooke in the 1750s. Overshadowed by his younger brother James' equestrian virtues, he became a clown, rope-walker, and strong man. He formed his own circus company in 1834 and eventually gave up performing to direct equestrian dramas and train ring animals. He took over the management of Astley's Amphitheatre, London, in 1853 with assets of £50,000 and laboriously managed that famous arena until his seven-year lease and much of his wealth ran out in 1859. During the length of this tenancy he had been kept afloat by his touring tented attraction; so one can only speculate that, like others before him, he came to America to enlarge his depleted treasury.

The circus with Cooke's name opened on January 16, 1860, at Niblo's Garden and, as George C. D. Odell put it, the company "took possession and startled the most blasé." Niblo's Garden! This gracious old venue had its own colorful tradition. Originally the site of the old Bayard farm, located away out of town on Broadway, or what was generally known as the Albany Post Road, it became a drill ground for militia officers shortly after the War of 1812. Later, a celebrated breeder of race horses, Charles Henry Hall, secured the property and built for himself a two-storied, slate-roofed mansion of solid brick, and for his prized quadrupeds a shingled palace of wood and glass, the sum of which rested on grounds lined by an avenue of poplar trees and enlivened with decorative floribunda. Here, sometime shortly after 1823, William Niblo took memorable possession.

Niblo, "an active little man with keen, shrewd money-making eyes," was the industrious proprietor of the old Bank Coffee House, named after its neighbor, the bank administering to the financial wants of New Yorkers, located in the business quarter of downtown Gotham. There, for some years, Niblo successfully served up such gastronomic delights as turtle soup and salmon from Boston until, ambitious for greater glories, he transformed the old Bayard farm site into a summer garden spot, wherein ice creams and other delectables were served up. Amid a setting of latticed arbors, ornamented by gorgeous illuminations, and within the sound of tireless musicians, devourers of such delicacies could lounge or stroll about the Edenic grounds on torpid summer evenings, interrupted merely by such novelties as balloon ascensions and pyrotechnic displays or periodic flights of tight-rope performers.

At the outset, the gardens were located far up town, a milestone from City Hall, and beyond the service of the city stage lines. Undaunted, Niblo ingeniously created his own stage line, equipped with new and innovative vehicular design. In 1828, as the resort had grown in popularity, the training stable was converted into a concert saloon, Theatre San Souci, wherein Madame Otto warbled "Meet Me by Moonlight Alone" and Gambati launched his solos on the French horn. Then, sadly, on the morning of July 18, 1846, the little theatre was destroyed by fire. But a house with such precious memories could not be easily consigned to ashes. The place was re-built in a manner that surpassed in elegance and utility the previous structure and opened for trade on July 30, 1849; after which, the theatre housed a continuous offering of high-class performers and performances.

At this time, 1860, Niblo's Garden was under the management of James M. Nixon. He was a showman of the nineteenth century mold, with a career that was comparable in length to many of the great proprietors of that period—John F. Robinson, S. P. Stickney, George F. Bailey, and Adam Forepaugh. Under the influence of the indomitable P. T. Barnum (and what showman was not at that time), he used innovative tactics, issued what was described as "flaming, regardless of expense advertisements," engaged much of the finest talent available, and spread his managerial interests into various niches of public amusement. Odell referred to him at various times as "elegant," a "power," and "a wielder of big interests."

He had worked his way from a mere groom with Aaron Turner's circus around 1836 to performing with various troupes in the 1840s and 1850s as acrobat, ringmaster and equestrian director; and then in 1856 he entered management by investing in the James Myers' circus. At season's end he joined with William H. Kemp, the English clown, and in 1857 and 1858 put out a show under the title of Nixon & Kemp.

And now, in January of 1860, Nixon established himself at Niblo's Garden, taking over the proprietorship in preparation for the arrival of Cooke and a talented company. The place was specially prepared for circus performances, the ring being covered with a thick Canton matting, a decided improvement for indoor arenas, being at once a sure and elastic footing for the horses and entirely free from the dust and annoyances of the old system of tanbark and sawdust. All of the costumes and properties were tastefully selected. And, most important, thanks to James Nixon, the company was a combination of outstanding English and American performers.

James Robinson, premier, Boston-born bareback rider, was summoned home from his European tour. He had accompanied Howes & Cushing's Great American Circus to London in the spring of 1857 and throughout his stay established himself as a star performer in both England and on the Continent. The Hanlon Brothers, English gymnasts, were engaged. They had made their American debut at Niblo's in 1858 under Nixon's management. Joe Pentland, famous for his impromptu songs and portrayal of a drunken sailor on horseback, was the feature clown. Miss Sallie Stickney, billed as Mlle. Heloise, performed her equestrienne act of leaping, cutting, pirouetting, and one-foot riding which was to rank her at the top of her profession. There were also William Duverney, the "greatest dislocationist in existence"; Mons. F. DeBach, Parisian equestrian and juggler on horseback (and who had only recently performed at Metropolitan Garden, Second Avenue and Thirteenth Street); and, not the least, a Mr. Charlton, billed as the "oldest of gymnasts."

Mlle. Heloise! Why Mlle. Heloise, you may ask? Well, the answer was forthcoming in a letter to the *Clipper* dated March 13, 1860, from her father, S. P. Stickney:

> I noticed in the *Clipper* of March 10th that a correspondent asks the question why Miss Sallie Stickney should drop her own name and assume that of "Heloise." I will answer. When Miss Stickney arrived in New York this winter to fulfill an engagement at Niblo's, Mr. Nixon desired her to use her name "Eloise," the name she used when she appeared at the same house under Rufus Welch's management in the winter of 1851. Through an error on the part of the person who made out the bill, instead of "Eloise," her name was printed "Heloise," and it was not considered of sufficient importance to make the correction. Her real name is Sallie Eloise Stickney.[1]

The observer for the New York *Times* found the opening performance an achievement which had elicited abundant applause from one of the most crowded houses he had ever witnessed. He was impressed with the riding of the leading equestrians; for, as he expressed it, "in New York, as in every other city of the Union, good circus riding is thoroughly understood and appreciated." He went on to comment:

> Mlle. Ella Zoyara, the principal lady of the company, is a very remarkable performer, and the graceful daring of her "acts" brought down the heartiest applause of the house.[2]

Thomas Hanlon's *l'échelle périlleuse* was found to be stimulating and unique. After going through a sequence of gyrations on a swing attached to the ceiling at one end of the proscenium, the gymnast suddenly released himself from it and, flying some twenty or thirty feet through the air, grabbed onto a rope on the other side. "The feat is terrible to behold, but beautifully performed."[3]

Thomas Hanlon's *L'échelle Périlluese*

The lollipop of the evening, taking the spotlight and making a New York debut, was decidedly Mlle. Ella Zoyara, whom Nixon had enticed from England with the offer of $500 a week, free passage for self and two servants, all medical bills, and use of a horse and carriage when required.[4] The rider's beauty and grace upon the back of a mount at once aroused an impressive response of adulation from the Niblo Garden patrons.

But within a few weeks the charade was challenged and the truth emerged. Ella Zoyara was in reality Omar Samuel Kingsley, a Creole from Louisiana. While a circus managed by Spencer Q. Stokes and Signor Louis Germani was playing in New Orleans, the boy was apprenticed to them by his parents at seven years of age. His Christian name is unknown but everyone called him "Sam" or "Little Sam." By the time he was eleven he showed amazing skills as a rider. Because of his physical beauty, Stokes dressed him in complete female attire, which was worn in and out of the ring. It has been stated that once so appareled he did not wear male clothing again until he was nineteen. Caution was taken that his playmates were only girls his own age, developing in him the manners and grace of the female sex. Stokes' deception continued for eight years, even to members of the company in which Zoyara performed. In 1851, with Stokes as mentor, he sailed for England and a tour of the Continent, performing under the name of Ella and under the guise of a female rider. Story has it that while in Moscow a Russian count fell madly in love with him and men of nobility in the countries he visited flocked around him and bestowed unto him rich gifts.

A contemporary of the young equestrian described his appearance in this way:

> He had a faultless complexion of the fairest brunette type, his face never showing the slightest trace of a beard, and his features were perfect and of a most delicate, womanly character, as were also his hands and feet. His hair, of raven blackness, hung in luxuriant masses almost to his waist.[5]

The young man had created quite a stir before the question of his sex arose; then the stir became a storm. Once discovered, there was resentment by the press, unhappy as they were at being hoodwinked. "If the person is a man, the humbug is a very dishonest one; if a woman, for the sake of all parties, the point should be settled."[6] It was conceded that Zoyara's novelty as a rider had lost its charm; and the attending public, particularly the male section, many of whom had sent the boy bouquets and tender notes and other expressions of adoration, were disillusioned.

Before the reality of his sex was established and while the question was yet in doubt, it was suggested that a committee of "strong-minded" women be selected to "wait upon" him and look into the facts of the case; but, understandably, Zoyara was not inclined to be examined. It mattered little, for in no time the truth was out and the whole secret exposed. "Humbug is the order of the day and he who is the cleverest at imposing upon his fellows is sure to draw the dollars," wrote an irate journalist.[7] "If this person is a boy as represented, then a most barefaced imposition has been practiced upon the American public by the management of the concern and the sooner the public resent the fraud the better," wrote yet another.[8]

A competing diversion for Nixon's circus at Niblo's was Van-Amburgh & Co.'s Mammoth Western Menagerie and Zoological Establishment that had commenced an exhibition in the new Zoological Hall at Palace Garden, Fourteenth Street near Sixth Avenue, on November 21, 1859. The doors were opened at 1:30 and 6:30 p.m. Admission was 25¢, children under nine years of age 15¢. The publicity promised a varied collection of animals, birds and reptiles and featured the elephant Hannibal, "securely bound in large chain cables" and put through its paces by B. F. Thomas. Prof. Langworthy entered the dens and exhibited to the audience "the wondrous power he exert[ed] over his tenants of the forest." The celebrated trick pony, Black Diamond, was introduced along with the pony-riding monkey, Jocko. However, if one preferred his animals dead, he could attend Dr. Chaillu's African collection, 635 Broadway, and find specimens of "the great and powerful gorilla," along with other curiosities, uncaged, unfettered, and inanimate, domesticated by the nimble hands of a taxidermist. Admission 25¢.

The so-called Cooke's Equestrian Troupe terminated its run at Niblo's Garden on March 3, 1860, and moved to the Boston Academy of Music (formerly Boston Theatre). The troupe had drawn well and could have remained in place and enjoyed respectable business. Nevertheless, the horses and acrobats gave way to Mr. and Mrs. Barney Williams, who opened at the Garden of Niblo on the 5th in a new piece called *Patience and Perseverance*. It was a return engagement—the couple having performed there to crowded houses the previous October and November.

The circus opened at the Boston theatre, also on the 5th, to what was near a house record as Mlle. Zoyara, still being the attraction, caught bouquets tossed from the audience. After the opening week the houses began to slack off, the Bostonians showing more restraint than their New York cousins. Also, the original levels of admission were found to be too "pricey" for the general public, so a reduction was soon made. And, after all, only across the way the Morris Bros., Pell & Trowbridge Minstrels were offering a new burlesque with the alluring title of *Macbeth, or, the Downfall of Gilson's Beanery*.

After five weeks, the circus took back Niblo's on April 9 with Ella Zoyara, James Robinson, the Hanlons, Joe Pentland and company—Cooke having departed—and began offering a series of spectacles.[9] A new version of *The Bronze Horse*, with musical and dramatic features and an equine ascension as a grand climax, was produced in April and extremely well received. There followed *Merry Sports of England* and *Blue Beard*, the latter being cleverly mounted and featuring the singing of Miss Marian Macarthy, who had joined Nixon's company in early May. The troupe was also enhanced at this time by a renowned Italian equestrian, Signor Sebastian Quaglieni, who performed unique Pickwickian impersonations on horseback.[10] Although the houses continued to be well filled, the engagement terminated on May 26 with *Cinderella*, enacted almost entirely by children.

The attention of New Yorkers was divided during the circus' second stand, distracted in part by the political stirrings for the upcoming Republican convention. General Tom Thumb was back in town and appearing at the Exhibition Rooms on Broadway, his drawing capability still exemplifying the power of human curiosity. John C. Heenan had won the belt from Tom Sayers on April 17 and was champion of the world; but no belt was forthcoming and no decision was determined either, as the British referee refused to give one. For a fight that lasted through thirty-seven official rounds and an inspired five more of unofficial fisticuffs, over a period of two hours and twenty minutes, one would have hoped for more satisfying results. Only days later, Mrs. John C. Heenan, better known as Miss Adah Isaacs Menken, notorious among New Yorkers for her risqué performances and, one might add, even more notorious for her sensational off-stage behavior, opened at the old Bowery Theatre in a piece justifiably called *Satan in Paris*.

At this time, one could go to Frank Rivers' Melodeon, billed as the cheapest place of amusement in the world, and enjoy Miss Fannie Forrest, "the charmer whose dulcet strains subdue all hearts." But, most particularly, amongst the new features, the management announced the

"ELLA ZOYARA," EQUESTRIAN.

actual presence in flesh and blood of the original Mlle. Ella Zoyara Boyzenarius, the oriental myth, "whose being has entranced the sense of the Old World and whose fame has so addled the brains of rival managers as to make each of them fancy that they had separately created and were alone able to show this wonderful personage."[11] What this version of Zoyara did to enchant the audience is unexplained. It certainly did not race around a ring on the Melodeon's music hall stage.

The Republican National Convention held in Chicago on May 16 was far removed from the Gardens of Niblo but the outcome was as meaningful to New Yorkers as to the populous in all parts of the country. The plank of the party pledged opposition to further extension of slavery. The leading candidate for the Republican nomination, William H. Seward of New York, was defeated on the third ballot by Abraham Lincoln of Illinois. Southern reaction was violent: "It makes little difference whether we are governed by a gentleman or ruled by a baboon, but with Lincoln comes something worse."[12]

Although there was an abundance of crop production, the western farmers complained about a shortage of money, causing local authorities and self-appointed community guardians to become more and more uncomfortable with the annual invasion of outside entertainments. This was emphasized by an increase in license fees. While touring Kentucky, the Antonio Bros.' circus was forced to pay $38 for a sparsely populated rural location and $50 for a city stand. The license in New Hampshire was $30 a day, and Tennessee and a few other southern states levied taxes as high as $100 for each performance.

Vermont prohibited circus (not menagerie) exhibitions entirely. George F. Bailey & Co. risked performances at Burlington, Wells River, and Brattleboro, where the ban on circuses was enforced by a $300 fine, and apparently got away Scot free. The first two places are located just across the border from New Hampshire and the third across from Massachusetts; so it would have been fairly simple to sneak in and out without drawing too much attention.

The *Clipper* editor was vehement in his railing against the unfair treatment of itinerant companies by the "puritanical and narrowminded" local officials:

> There never was a more reviled, slandered, and generally abused professional class than show people; nor did a more outraged, cheated, plundered, persecuted and, at the same time, enduring set of victims ever invoke public justice or appeal to popular sympathy. In their

perambulating excursions through the country, showmen always and everywhere seem as if by common consent to be legitimate prey to all with whom they have dealings. Everybody wrongs them, from the stable boy who cleans the horses up to that sublime dignitary, the village trustee.[13]

An exception to such local attitudes occurred when the Connecticut legislature, which had previously banned traveling amusements, passed an act allowing them to show within its borders. It took no time for Niblo & Sloat's organization to move into the state, as Sloat immediately booked Hartford for the Fourth of July date. Unfortunately, this example of geniality was not all-pervading. Still, circuses paid the fees or strong-armed the dates and showed sparingly in states that banned exhibitions.

It was rumored in February that Barnum was negotiating for a share of old Grizzly Adams' California Menagerie, which was then en route from San Francisco. Actually, Barnum purchased a half-interest in it from a man who had preceded Adams' arrival. On hearing of this, the California menagerie owner claimed that the man had only advanced him money and had no right to sell a share of the exhibition; but he ultimately consented to the arrangement, figuring the experienced Barnum could more ably manage his New York engagement.

James Capen "Grizzly" Adams, California hunter and trapper and exhibitor of wild beasts, was born in Medway, MA, in 1812. When the gold rush fever struck, he migrated to California, ultimately moving into the mountains to live. At some point, he killed a female bear, then captured and trained her two cubs. He acquired other animals native of the region and began a menagerie collection. The bears were trained to walk on their hind legs, talk on cue, wrestle, etc. A nasty encounter with one in the Sierra Nevadas in 1855 resulted in Adams sustaining severe wounds to the head and neck, leaving an indentation in his skull the size of a silver dollar. Shortly after that incident he moved out of the mountains and began exhibiting his collection, first in San Jose and then San Francisco. In 1856 he entered the circus business with Joseph Rowe, until Rowe left with his troupe of performers for Hawaii. Before moving his menagerie east, Adams again had an encounter with one of his bears, which opened the injury on his skull.

Barnum and James Nixon erected a tent at Broadway and Thirteenth Street in which to house the menagerie; and on opening day, April 30, a blaring band paraded the animal cages down Broadway and up the Bowery with old Adams on a platform wagon in his hunting togs, mounted atop the largest of three grizzlies. Within the tent were displayed several wolves, a half-dozen different species of California bears, California lions, buffalo, elk, twenty or thirty large grizzlies, and "Old Neptune," a sea lion from the Pacific Ocean.

The California Menagerie continued to exhibit until July 7. Then, after a doctor's suggestion that injuries would soon cause his death, and wishing to leave his wife with financial security, Grizzly Adams sold his share of the menagerie establishment to Barnum, who then combined with James M. Nixon to take Cooke's Royal Circus with Old Grizzly Adams California Menagerie on tour. Adams struck a deal to go along for ten weeks at a total salary of $500. After fulfilling most of the contract, he left and retired to his daughter's home in Neponset, MA, where he died a short time later.

With horses and riders gone, the Niblo's Garden theatre underwent refurbishing for a summer re-opening on June 4. Nixon's "flaming, regardless of expense advertisements" announced the arrival of such featured entertainers as the Nelson Sisters, plump Polly Marshall, and the Hanlon Brothers. Niblo's Saloon was also opened and under Nixon's management for mid-summer entertainment. But the dramatic season did not go well with the public and thus ended on June 28.

The equestrian troupe, after completing their summer tour—what the *Spirit of the Times* called "one of the most successful campaigns to the principal towns, cities, and villages of the West ever achieved by a traveling company"—moved back in on Monday, July 30. Nixon's advertising bills, labeled by the *Spirit* writer as "something 'stunning' in their lengthened sweetness long drawn out," heralded the arrival of Mlle. Zoyara, the Hanlon Brothers, James Robinson, Duverney, Charlton, DeBach, Quaglieni, and Pentland, with "forty auxiliaries, each of brilliant talent," all opening for a short season. The company was greeted with enthusiastic applause as each artist respectively appeared before the audience. The press reported that the "performances were of the same varied, exciting, and excellent description as [had] already placed Mr. Nixon at the head of the managerial and equestrian profession."[14] What was called an historical pageant, *The Oriental Festival*, was restored to the Niblo stage; also the equestrian spectacle, *The Shield of the Cloth of Gold,* presented in tandem with *The Steeple-Chase; or Life in Merry England*, which was enhanced by the importation of six thoroughbred horses from the British Isles. Advertisements promised that all this would be produced in rapid succession, with original music composed by John Cooke (oh! oh! still another Cooke?), leader of the orchestra. Although the arenic action was impaired this time from lack of space, the ring being smaller than in the earlier stands, the houses were filled with country cousins and other summer visitors to the city. The run came to a close on Friday, September 14, and the stables were vacated to make way for a two hundred night tenancy of the great Edwin Forrest, who opened his stay with *Hamlet* on the 17th.

The tour of the California Menagerie through the New England States began around August 4. Performing variously under the titles of Cooke's Royal Circus, Nixon & Adams, and Cooke & Adams, the show moved through Rhode Island, Massachusetts, and New Hampshire until the end of September; after which, Nixon sold the equipment to Boston showman George K. Goodwin and put an outfit out on rails under the name of Nixon's Royal Amphitheatre.

The circus appeared in Baltimore for a week beginning October 2 at a lot on the corner of Calvert and Eager Streets. The ads professed "of Niblo's Garden; Astley's, London; and the Philadelphia and Boston Academies of Music, on its Southern Tour by Railroad." Thaddius Barton of Baltimore was listed as manager; T. U. Tidmarsh of New Orleans and Texas as advertiser; the clowns were James Ward and John Davenport; Robert Ellingham was the ringmaster; the brass band was led by Herr Kopp. The advertised roster of performers included Mlle. Ella Zoyara; the six Hanlon Brothers—Thomas, George, William, Alfred, Edward, Frederick; equestrians Signor Sebastian (Quigliani), George Ross, Mons. DeBach; stilt performer Herr Charlton; Duverney, the contortionist; Frank Stark, double somersaulter; William Kincade, general performer; and Master Willie Nixon.[15]

On leaving Baltimore the Nixonites were routed through the southern states—Virginia, North Carolina, South Carolina, Georgia, Alabama—and then opened a stand in New Orleans. It is assumed that local rail systems were utilized for a good portion of these travels.

By 1860 track mileage within the states east of the Mississippi totaled around 30,000. But full use of rail at this time was cumbersome. For example, eight changes of cars were necessary for a trip from Charleston to Philadelphia. No rail line entering either Richmond or Philadelphia made a direct physical connection with any other. Travel was further inhibited by a variance in gauge size from one rail line to the next. Circuses moving on cars designed to operate on the standard gauge (4 feet 8½ inches track width) had to unload and transfer equipment to cars compatible with, say, the southern gauge (5 feet track width), these two sizes being the most popular in use. At first look, one might assume diversity of gauge size created obstacles of movement too difficult for a traveling circus to overcome. Maybe not.

Stuart Thayer's routing for Nixon's Royal Circus begins at the nation's capital, a direct line on standard gauge track from Philadelphia and Baltimore, and continues to Richmond, Norfolk, Petersburg, Weldon, Raleigh, Goldsboro, Wilmington, Charleston, Savannah, Macon, Columbus, Montgomery, and finally New Orleans. Following Nixon's movement through the process of full-blown speculation, the circus could have jumped to Richmond on standard gauge; taken standard and southern gauge, or boat travel, to Norfolk; then southern gauge to Petersburg. Weldon, NC, a much smaller community, must have been a jump-breaker to Raleigh, both being on standard gauge. The same gauge could move the troupe to Goldsboro, intersecting with another standard gauge to Wilmington. From there the road to Charleston, SC, was fitted with the southern gauge, which continued into Georgia for the Savannah, Macon and Columbus dates. We are now on the Georgia-Alabama border and must use a standard gauge to get to Montgomery, the end of the line before reaching New Orleans. Here we find ourselves in a quandary. We can either move directly south on a southern gauge rail to Pensacola, FL, and thence by boat to New Orleans, go part way to Pensacola before hiring wagons to haul the show overland to Mobile, or use river boat transportation from Montgomery down the winding Alabama to Mobile and then to New Orleans. However the journey ended, primary rail travel was not only feasible for the Nixon entourage but, by all accounts, preferable.

Five days after leaving Montgomery, the circus opened on Saturday, November 19, at the St. Charles Theatre, New Orleans, and remained at this stand for three weeks before closing on Friday, December 8. Two days later the show opened in Havana, Cuba, at the Villanueva Theatre for the winter season, the Hanlon Brothers and Ella Zoyara still the feature attractions. Back home the breezes of national anxiety were accelerating. Only ten more days would pass before South Carolina seceded from the Union.

Americans were soon to be given the opportunity to view a rare hippopotamus, thanks to Col. Gerald C. Quick and Col. Joseph Cushing.

The beast was said to have been captured on the Ganges River and delivered to the London Zoological Gardens, Regents Park. According to the *Clipper*, Quick was invited to England by the Royal Directory to arrange an exchange for various species of American animals which were uncommon in England. A more reliable account by Stuart Thayer states that in March of this year the London zoo sold the hippo to Joe Cushing who exhibited it in England with his circus. Quick bought an interest in the property, at which time plans were made to ship it to America in the charge of Frank J. Howes.[16]

Howes was a native of Rochester, NY. He had entered show business in 1851 under the guidance of agent Charles Bristol and eventually became an equestrian director, ringmaster, and circus proprietor. At this time he was returning from European engagements with both Howes and Cushing's Great United States Circus and the Jim Myers' Circus.

After departing from Liverpool, October 3, the two-year old, 1,000 pound Bucheet docked in New York aboard the steamer *City of Manchester* on the 19th, accompanied by Howes and its Arabian attendant, Ali. The animal arrived with the distinction of being the first of its kind to make port on this continent. But before being viewed in the United States it was loaded onto the *DeSoto*, October 22, bound for New Orleans and exhibition at the Spalding & Rogers museum, an adjunct of the Academy of Music. The entourage docked in New Orleans on October 30. The doors were opened at the museum for public viewing on November 1. Then, in early January, the hippo was shipped to Havana where it was placed before the public under a canvas pavilion opposite the Tacon Theatre for a period of eight weeks.

The Spalding & Rogers' New Orleans Circus performed on the *James Raymond* steamboat throughout the 1860 season. They had no land show that year and their *Floating Palace* was laid up for repairs. River travel took the company to stands in Mississippi, Tennessee, Kentucky, Indiana, Ohio, Illinois, Missouri, and Iowa. Tom Watson, the clown, publicized the show by riding down the river in a tub drawn by four harnessed geese. The trick, originally performed in England some years earlier by Dicky Usher and later by Tom Barry, was facilitated by an underwater tow line attached to the tub which led to a row boat some distance down stream.

In addition to the clown, there was the little equestrienne and *danseuse*, Kate Ormand; riders Jean Johnson and Frank Barry, Hercules

John Glenroy

Libby, John Keefe, Charles Fish, etc.; along with the trick ponies—Aristook, Wildfire, and Big Thunder; the spotted mule, Jubelo; the dwarf mule, Phoenix; and the trained horse, Hiram.

The company was in Cairo, IL, in June at the time of the explosion of the steamer *Ben Lewis*. Watson, gymnast William Teal, and a deck hand rendered heroic assistance to the survivors of the tragic event. They launched a rescue boat and, after arriving at the flaming hull, picked up a number of people who were clinging to the ship's rudder. The old clown's familiar call, "Here we are!" was never more welcomed. At the end of the tour, in November, the *James Raymond* was sold to Dan Rice.

The Great Union Circus of 1860 was the first of thirty-three different circuses George W. DeHaven would put on the road during his career. DeHaven was born in Jackson, OH. When he was but twelve years of age his widowed father gave him $200 in gold and told him to shift for himself. The young man purchased a team of oxen and a plow and hired out for farm work. Through investment in labor and thrift, he was able to acquire a threshing machine with which to work in the wheat fields. In 1858, after having saved his money, he bought interest in a circus put out by Oliver Bell and R. G. Satterlee called Satterlee, Bell & Co. And now, this year, in partnership with Oliver Bell, he initiated his managerial career.

DeHaven's company moved about in Indiana, Illinois, Iowa, and Michigan. One of its features was an old act of equestrianism under the title *Mother Goose, or, The Man Who Lost His Wife*. By August, the show ran out of money and was forced to lay over until a backer could be found. In a short time, Sam Matthews entered into partnership and the circus continued on the road, abandoning rail travel and taking to the country towns until funds ran out on October 5 at Dowagiac, MI.

DeHaven was a man with big dreams and an uncanny ability to talk a circus into being. "Any man," he would say, "can start a circus with money, the thing of it is to put one on the road without any." Agent Charley Pell said of him:

> [He is] a hustler of indomitable perseverance, resourceful and restless, and if any man can organize a show and run it on wind, he can. The most successful of men have been laughed at and derided and George W. DeHaven may be in that class, and to prove to you the faith that is in me, I would engage to him tomorrow and take any chances.[17]

On closing in Michigan, DeHaven returned to Freeport, IL, and opened an interim circus there, giving two performances a week, Saturday afternoons and evenings. The operation continued until April, 1861. During this time, as an aftermath of the Zoyara notoriety, John Glenroy was occasionally billed as a French equestrienne, Mlle. Reine, a ruse seemingly carried off with success. As Glenroy stated it:

> In fact, I carried the deception so far and so well that it was a nightly occurrence for me to receive half dozen very loving epistles and bouquets. Many an hour's fun have the company had while I read my love letters to them, and on the Saturday afternoon and evening performances it was amusing to see the young men come and hang around the dressing-room door of the circus to try and get an introduction to the French rider, M'lle Reine.[18]

A new circus partnership was formed this summer when Dan Gardner and Richard Hemmings erected a tent in Comac's Woods, Philadelphia. Hemmings, born in Birmingham, England, was the son of an actor and member of Edmund Kean's company of players. He made his first appearance in the show world when only five years of age at the Queen's Theatre, Manchester, as a member of Goffe's Monkey Ballet. He later became a part of Andrew Ducrow's riding act. After training as an aerialist and tumbler, he joined his uncle's troupe of acrobats, billed as "Prof. Hemming and his Wonderful Infants." The last appearance in England was at Vauxhall Gardens' Winter Circus, London, in 1855, after which he sailed for America.

Dan Gardner, a native of New York City, was the patriarch of the performing Gardner family. His father was in the printing trade and wanted the son to follow him; but after working in the shop for a time, and not enjoying the profession, he left home around 1826 and became an assistant property man for the Mount Pitt Circus. He went on the stage for the first time there in 1828, singing "Push Along, Keep Moving" and playing clown for Archie Madden's equestrian act. During the early days of negro minstrelsy, Gardner performed as a wench dancer but gradually became more versatile, gaining a proficiency on the slack-rope and at juggling, tumbling, riding, and, most happily, performing as an old fashioned clown.

In the spring of 1860, Richard Hemmings arrived in New York; and while there, stopped at the Florence Hotel, which in those days was the headquarters of the circus profession. This was when he first met Dan Gardner, who had come to New York to look after his son, Billy, a run-away that had married without his parents knowledge or consent. The previous year both Hemmings and Gardner had been out with shows and had undergone the same experience—no salaries paid. They talked over their misfortunes of the past few seasons and determined the future of playing engagements didn't look bright because of the war scare. Hemmings had planned to take a trip back to England, but Gardner persuaded him against it; instead, they decided to put together a show and go into management for themselves—the beginning of the partnership of Gardner and Hemmings.

The two made arrangements for a place on the outskirts of Philadelphia, known as Comac's Woods, the old Comac estate, at the end of the Tenth and Eleventh Street railway. The idea was to turn the place into a summer resort with Gardner and Hemmings furnishing a circus to perform in the open and a daily tight-rope ascension to the top of a nearby building as an attraction to bring out the people. Their salary was to be $100 a day for each day they gave an exhibition. The land owner was to install a bar in the old mansion house on the property and furnish other kinds of concessions on the grounds.

The circus performances at Comac's Woods opened near the end of April, consisting of Richard Hemmings on the tight-rope; James Madigan, somersaulter; Tom King, leaper; and little Eliza Madigan, dancer; all under the ringmaster's whip of Frank Whittaker. But what appeared to be the most impressive act was *l'échelle périlleuse* of William Smith:

> This is by far the most wonderful display of intrepidity ever witnessed in this city. It is a great improvement upon Hanlon's performance. This is the unanimous verdict of all who have seen both performers. When jumping from the rack to the rope, instead of hanging by the hands, he clings by the feet. Indeed, the entire performance of Mr. Smith exceeds anything I ever saw.[19]

As this was the only resort of its kind in Philadelphia at the time, it was a big success. The circus did a phenomenal business up until the Fourth of July, at which time there were over 35,000 people on the grounds. But, as fortune would have it, on that day two rival volunteer fire companies were holding picnics. Toward evening things began to get heated between the intoxicated and combatant hosemen, then turned into a good, old fashion brouhaha. When the newspapers came out the next morning with headlines related to the riot, Comac's Woods was finished as a summer resort.

In the fall the company performed for five weeks at Gilmore's place on Walnut Street, Philadelphia, under the name of Gardner, Hemmings and Madigan. Their special feature for the engagement was Mons. Blondin, the great wire-walker and "Hero of Niagara," who proved to be an immense drawing card.

After closing, they went to Baltimore and performed in the old Front Street Theatre. Billed as Messrs. Madigan & Co., proprietors of The Great American Consolidated Circus, the company opened on Monday, December 3. F. W. Whittaker was equestrian director; T. Allston Brown, advertising agent; Dan Gardner, buffo clown; W. H. Gardner, Shakespearean clown; and John J. Foster, performing clown. Parquet and dress circle, 50¢ (no charge for reserved seats); family circle and gallery, 25¢; boys' gallery, 15¢. Of the performances, a Baltimore *Sun* observer wrote:

> Amongst the artists of the company, M. Moreste deserves particular notice for his performance on the horizontal bar. Anything more graceful in gymnastics, or more truly surprising, we have not seen. It is one of the most pleasing series of feats we have witnessed. Mr. James Madigan's equestrianism, *battoute* leaping, and somersaults, are among the very best performances in that department.[20]

Mons. Blondin was brought in for a week as a special feature. During his act he ascended from the stage to the upper gallery, one hundred feet above the parquet seats, in a sack and blindfolded. His feats were also varied with occasional somersaults and standings upon his head. The climax of the act occurred with his bearing one of the auditors on his back as he ascended the rope, much like he had done across the wide expanse of the Niagara. The advertising read: "He will also carry on his back any one of the audience who may feel disposed to accompany him."[21]

The "Hero of Niagara" was held over for a second week. Along with his feats on the rope were added a variety of pantomime performances for which he had acquired distinction as one of the principals with the Ravel Family, including the serio-comic piece *Jocko, the Brazilian Ape*.

On December 15, either because a local man failed to materialize for the trek up the cable or because there was need for a publicity event to bolster Blondin's farewell appearance, T. Allston Brown made the piggyback ascension, for which expression of bravery the press of

Baltimore designated him "Colonel," a title that has clung to him ever since.

Blondin's departure was filled by the Parisian equestrienne Mlle. Josephine Gagliani, whose first appearance in America occurred on Monday the 17th. The *American and Commercial Advertiser* noted that although less known in this country she was "perhaps fully his equal in dashing attractiveness and in intrepidity of style." But with their feature attraction departed, the circus company closed on Christmas night after a three-week stand.

Dan Rice's Great Show had opened a winter engagement at the National Theatre in Philadelphia on October 31, 1859. In February of 1860, Rice introduced a "female" rider billed as "Ella Zoyara." This was not Omar Kingsley of the Nixon/Cooke company at Niblo's Garden but another concoction of male/female deception. Following Nixon's lead, Rice encouraged public inference that the girl was really a boy in woman's attire. A short time later, he brought out a card confessing his Zoyara to be a female, the real Miss McCoy. This was probably the most truth to come out of the whole Zoyara charade.

In November the *Clipper* brought to light a rumor that Ella Zoyara had married an actor by the name of Frank Drew in St. Louis. This was later confirmed by Dan Rice's son-in-law, bareback rider Charles Reed.[22] If the rumor was fact, it would support the suggestion that Rice's Zoyara was indeed a woman. Eventually, the *Clipper*, tired of or resigned to ending the flap, conceded the matter a draw:

> Dan is a showman, and understands his business better than Barnum ever did his. All hail, Zoyara, and peace be unto the followers and admirers of this remarkable "dam-sell."[23]

Carlyon, in his fine doctoral dissertation, has speculated that Rice's Zoyara was Miss Estelle Barclay, the "daughter" of equestrian Fred Barclay, a young lady who had performed previously for Rice under the various names of "Mlle. Estella," "Mlle. Estrella," and "Mad'lle Estrello."[24] In supporting his claim, he observed that the name of Estelle Barclay and that of her "father" disappeared with the appearance of Ella Zoyara. The assumption has acceptable credence. My own sources suggest that both Estelle and Fred were apprentices to Rice and that Fred, born in 1850, was much too young to be a father to anyone. There was a Master Barclay who gave a spirited exhibition of hurdle racing with the Nixon/Cooke company at Niblo's in early January. Then, too, a Master Fred Barclay was on the roster with Rice's circus in

1863, described as "a precocious youth in a dashing act of Retro Equitation, introducing Bounds, Leaps, Pirouettes and Somersaults on his Golden Cream."[25] The term of apprenticeship may have ended for Estelle by 1860 or perhaps she did marry Frank Drew and leave the circus business.[26] There was a minor actor by the name of Barclay at the American Theatre, New Orleans, in 1837. Could Estelle and Fred have been his progeny?

Rice closed his show in Philadelphia on March 31, 1860. He then moved to Baltimore, opening April 2 at the Front Street Theatre "for two weeks only." The advertisements announced the appearance of the singing clown, Tony Pastor, and "the world renowned equestrienne," Ella Zoyara. Dress circle and parquet, 50¢; family circle, 25¢—no half price; colored circle, 25¢; boys' gallery, 15¢; children under 12 years of age to dress circle, 25¢. At this time an English steeple chase was enacted, using both the stage and ring. For the Wednesday and Saturday matinees, "grand family festivals" were given with "attractions of the most extraordinary character" presented.[27]

It was announced on April 9 that "a remarkable array of novelties" would be introduced, "nearly every act being new." Mlle. Ella Zoyara made her first appearance at this time; a grand Chinese spectacle, *Ward's Mission to China*, was brought forward; and Frank Drew, "the well known comedian," made his debut to Baltimorians as clown of the arena.[28] Ahah! Frank Drew! Soon to be a groom, not of the stable but of the altar?

The two week engagement was stretched another six nights, during which more novelties were unveiled. On the morning of the 16th a unique display was enacted when Madame Zoyara, "the mother of the great equestrienne," drove a bandwagon with a twelve-horse hitch through the streets of the city—Baltimore, Gay, Howard, Pratt, and Broadway being the route. A hostler in female get-up perhaps? On this same day the *American and Commercial Advertiser* declared that the great Dan Rice himself would "for the first time this season officiate in his original role of humorist." The spectacle *The Field of the Cloth of Gold* was introduced. And Mrs. Dan Rice brought out one of her highly trained dancing horses. On the 19th, the great leaper, Tom King, took a benefit, with his wife, the former Virginia Myers, making her first appearance. On Friday, the 20th, a black rhinoceros, "the only animal of the species ever tamed," performed in the arena. On Saturday the

DAN RICE.

Yankee Robinson

company made a grand parade through the city and in the evening closed the run with a benefit for Rice.[29]

On August 9, Rice announced that his elephant, Lalla Rookh, would swim the river from Cincinnati to Covington, KY. A sizable crowd gathered to watch the promotional stunt; during which, the clown waited on the Kentucky side while the keeper, C. W. Noyes, guided the pachyderm into the water. The animal found the river so to its liking that it swam around gaily, forgetting its assignment. Occasionally it would dive beneath the surface and then come up with a powerful surge that brought its body nearly out of the water. After some time, the star attraction made it to the opposite shore. On September 11, Lalla Rookh died in Indiana of "lung fever."

Starting in November, the show floated south on the *James Raymond*, which had been purchased from Spalding & Rogers, and then opened at the Spalding & Rogers Amphitheatre in New Orleans on December 10, one day following the Nixon circus closing. This marked Rice's first visit to the city in six years.

There was an announcement in the *Daily Delta* of December 9 that the show would begin the engagement with a grand procession, the marshals being "gentlemen from Kentucky, South Carolina, Tennessee, Georgia, Alabama and Louisiana," who would be followed by the band playing "Hail Columbia" and "The Marseillaise Hymn." The South had put new lyrics to the latter and was using it as an anthem. Rice was obviously catering to Southern sentiment. Newspaper items indicated that the circus was drawing well in their 1,800 seat theatre—filling it to the "utmost," the place being "overflowing."[30] The Southern audiences were well pleased with what the clown was saying. Northern audiences would not be pleased on hearing this.

Robinson & Lake's Great Southern Menagerie and Circus had been on the road continuously since starting out in Ohio in April of 1859, traveling through Kentucky, Tennessee, Georgia, South Carolina, North Carolina, and Virginia. The company began the year of 1860 in Florida and Georgia and then moved into South and North Carolina, followed by lengthy stays in Virginia and Ohio. Primarily a two family show—justifying the title, William Lake, Sam Long, and Archie Campbell were the clowns—all popular in the South; Lake's wife, Agnes, was a rope-walker and equestrienne; little Alice Lake sailed through banners and created pleasing poises on the back of a horse; old John Robinson and his boys contributed their feats of horsemanship; and there was a female wild beast tamer, Eugenie DeLorme. The ads promised the appearance of a "Horned Horse—The Last of his Race. The Perplexity of Naturalists. THE WONDER OF THE AGE."

Through a singularly unfortunate choice, the show moved into Port Royal, VA, on the 29th of May. What followed appears to have been a pre-planned attempt at harassment of the circus company, which resulted in the killing of one of the towners, Mark Boulware. According to an account submitted by Harry Keys, gymnast with the show, the local authorities started it all off by demanding an exorbitant license, which Robinson and Lake refused to pay. As a result, the outfit was taken down and packed for travel. But hoping to reap some kind financial gain from the dilemma, Jack Robinson, manager of the minstrel show, left his tent up and prepared to give a performance.

After most of the audience were seated and the entertainment was about to begin, a number of town hoodlums appeared at the door and requested entry without payment. Their demands being rejected, they grew noisy and obscene and again tried to force their way in and were again repulsed. Still another attempt was made, resulting in the leader of the bullies striking and knocking down the doorkeeper, Mr. Adams. Pistols were fired by the group, one round wounding one of the circus grooms in the thigh. Finally, the circus people drove the rowdies off the grounds.

Supposing the difficulty was settled, many of the company left for the hotel. Shortly after they had retired to their beds, the towners appeared outside the hostelry and again created a nuisance. Gibbs, the landlord, talked them into leaving as a fellow citizen and pleaded that his wife was ill in bed. Back at the lot, the circus cadre had gone off to get something to eat, leaving but three men to guard the belongings. Following the departure, the towners made an assault on the baggage wagons and cages. One of Robinson's men, in trying to remonstrate with the crowd, was beaten. It was during this last incident that Boulware, town drunk and troublemaker, was killed, presumably an accident by one of his own men.

The circus left for Fredericksburg and arrived about 11:00 a.m. of the following day. No show was given in the afternoon but at night the company began performing to a good house until the sheriff came to the lot with a military force, arrested them all, and marched them to the mayor's office where they were confronted with the murder of Boulware. Gibbs, the Port Royal innkeeper, came to Fredericksburg and generously testified in the company's behalf. The trial lasted two days and since no proof was forthcoming as to who killed Boulware the company was exonerated and allowed to move on. On the morning of June 1, Robinson & Lake's Circus quite willingly departed from Fredericksburg, leaving the nasty matter behind them.[31]

California was enjoying nearly ten years of statehood; yet circus activity was confined to its northern half where many communities had evolved to service the mining industry. But even these places could not have offered rich rewards to a circus manager. Southern California, with few commercial centers and great distances between them, was still too undeveloped to accommodate a profitable tour. Oregon had just become a part of the Union in February of 1859, but the thinly populated Washington Territory would have to wait nearly thirty years. Consequently, despite the vast space that was the West Coast, there was room for only a limited number of traveling exhibitions.

This year of 1860, an organization briefly existing under the title of Rocky Mountain Circus, with George Bartholomew as the proprietor, appeared in Los Angeles for a few days in January and then disappeared. Another attraction, the Pennsylvania Circus, with Frank Durand as proprietor, arrived in San Francisco May 27 on the steamship *John S. Stephens* and came to life for a short period in June before dissolving into oblivion.[32]

The Metropolitan Circus set up on the lot at Jackson & Kearney Streets in the bay city under the management of Lathrop, Peoples, Franklin & Co. It remained there from March 10 through the 19th. With the stand terminated, the company toured the mountain country of California and Nevada Territory, visiting the mining areas and agricultural fairs.

John Wilson's "Dan Rice's" Great Show booked the American Theatre, San Francisco, from April 26 to May 10 and exhibited greater sustaining powers than the aforementioned. The suggestion was that Wilson had obtained some of Dan Rice's trained animals and made arrangements to use the Rice name. This may or may not be true. Any pair of comic mules could be christened Pete and Barney. The admission prices, much higher than in the East, ranged from private boxes at $5 & $10 to the dress circle at $1; secured seats, $1.50; parquette, 75¢; orchestra seats, 75¢; family circle, 75¢; and upper circle, 50¢.

The Scottish born Wilson had migrated to America somewhere around 1849. In New York City he obtained employment with Beck's dry goods store as a clerk and then as a window dresser. A year later he left for San Francisco and took up the butcher trade. Then, in 1858 or 1859, with the help of William Hendrickson, he bought the Sands, Nathan & Quick elephants, Victoria and Albert, for $22,000. They were shipped west in 1859 in the charge of Dr. Charles Bassett, as agent for the owners. The elephants were the first to be exhibited on the West Coast and, as such, created quite a sensation.

During Wilson's run, a satisfied San Francisco *Evening Telegram* carried the following notice:

> Crowds still continued to flow into the American Theatre to witness the wonderful performances of the troupe brought to our state by the indefatigable John Wilson. The riding of Walter Aymar has never been excelled by any person. He not only is daring but is graceful while riding at full speed as if passing ices to a lady in a parlor. The perilous feats of Mr. Painter, on what he terms *l'échelle périlleuse*, have won the admiration of our best gymnasts and the applause of the thousands who have visited the theatre. It is one thing to be a clown and another to be a good one. Since the days of John Gossin we have never seen a person who combines so many of the needful requirements as Mr. Aymar. The best vaulter in the troupe—in fact the best in the United States—he keeps his audience in good humor by his witty sayings and doings. What we have already mentioned is sufficient amusement for the price charged; but Wilson seems determined to outdo all his competitors in quantity as well as quality. For the same amount of money can be seen the trained elephants, the knowing mules, the trick ponies and, as is announced in auction advertisements, many other articles too numerous to mention.[33]

The show left the American Theatre and went under canvas for four performances beginning May 11 and then commenced a tour through the interior of California, Oregon, Washington Territory, and lower Canada. But before the following month had run its course the headline "Victoria is dead!" pricked the hearts and souls of the circus community.

The tragedy occurred when the two pachyderms, Victoria and Albert, were being moved from Columbia to Murphy's Camp. In the course of travel, the company was ferried across a swift running river. However, the ferryman refused to take the two elephants because he feared his old boat would not stand the weight. While the elephant handler, John Peoples, was arguing for passage, Albert bolted into the stream and Victoria followed close on. The current was so strong it

AMERICAN THEATRE,

Corner Sansome and Halleck streets.

JOHN WILSON & CO.....................Proprietors
DR. CHAS. H. BASSETT............Equestrian Director

UNPRECEDENTED ATTRACTION!

DAN. RICE'S GREAT SHOW!

THE INTERIOR OF THIS TEMPLE OF the Drama has been entirely remodeled, refitted and converted into a magnificent

AMPHITHEATRE!

Which, for elegance and picturesque grandeur, far outstrips anything of the kind ever produced in California.

The First Performance will be given on
THURSDAY EVENING.........APRIL 26th,
When the following world renowned Artistes will appear:

MRS. WALTER HYMAN,	M'LLE LANGE,
MR. WALTER AYMER,	MR. WILLIAM AYMER,
MR. H. C. DURAND,	MR. WILLIAM PAINTER,
DR. C. H. BASSETT,	MR. D LONG,
MASTER LEROY,	MR. CHARLTON,
MR. HALSTEAD,	MR. J WINTERS,
MR. BLISS,	MR. CARR,

and Mr. J. PARSONS.

....ALSO....

DAN RICE'S TRAINED MULES,
PETE AND BARNEY.

The wonderful performing Elephants,
VICTORIA & ALBERT,
The highly trained Horse,
CRUSOE,
The beautiful Vaulting Courier,
WHITE SURREY,
The favorite Talking Pony,
CINDERELLA,
The Comic Elfin Pony,
SHELLBARK,
Together with a Magnificent Stud of
TRAINED HORSES.

This Colossal Exhibition is under the Management and direction of DR. CHAS. H. BASSETT.

HERR SWARTS will lead the Orchestra of the Arena.

GRAND EQUESTRIAN MATINEE

On Saturday Afternoon.........at 1 o'clock.
CHILDREN HALF.

N. B.—For the better accommodation of the patrons of this establishment, the Manager takes pleasure in announcing that he has made arrangements with both Lines of Omnibusses from North Beach and South Park, to pass the American Theatre after 7 o'clock on each evening during the continuance of this performance.

PRICES OF ADMISSION:

Private Boxes......$5 to $10		Dress Circle..........$1 00
Secured Seats.........$1 50		Parquette............. 75
Orchestra Seats....... 75		Family Circle......... 75
Upper Circle.......... 50		

Box Book will be opened on Wednesday morning, at 10 o'clock, when seats may be secured, and afterwards, one day in advance.

Doors open at 7½ o'clock. Performance to commence at 8 o'clock. ap21 carried both beasts a mile down stream and over some rocky falls. Victoria managed to float ashore and, on finding Albert missing, threw her trunk in the air and bellowed so loudly the noise could be heard for two miles around. Ultimately, Albert was landed and the troupe continued to Murphy's Camp. Within a few days, Victoria began showing signs of illness. Then, at Iowa City, she fell and was unable to rise up. Albert tried to help her with his trunk but to no avail. Sadly, the company was forced to leave her behind in the care of the keeper, and on June 28, 1860, she died. The loss to the owners was estimated at $15,000. The Wilson circus returned to San Francisco for an October 5-17 stand at the Jackson & Kearney Street lot. From October 30 to November 12, the group occupied the Hippodrome (formerly Mechanics Pavilion), modeled on the lines of the famous *Cirque Olympus* of Paris. According to the *Alta Californian,* this was the largest and best show ever seen in the state. Still featured was the performing elephant Albert and the trick mules Pete and Barney. With the run finished and the threat of unpleasant times ahead, the show sailed for Honolulu on the vessel *Yankee*, departing on December 26 with a complement that included the elephant and mules.

Election day came. Throughout the fall campaign Lincoln had stayed quietly in Springfield, directing party activities from his modest office. To avoid stirring up controversy and perhaps splitting the Republican vote, he did not make a single political speech. The strategy worked. On November 6, 1860, "Honest Abe" became the first Republican president. Alarm spread through the southern states. In the North, too, many Americans were disappointed with the outcome and fearful of the future.

Two circuses removed to the southern hemisphere as the year came to a close, perhaps foreseeing difficulties facing amusements in the coming months. Niblo & Sloat's New York Circus and Performing Elephants (From Cooke's Amphitheatre, London) left New York City on November 13 for the West Indies, with L. B. Lent as manager; Thomas Niblo, treasurer; and J. G. Sloat, one of the partners. After a seventeen day passage the company arrived safely in Bridgetown, Barbados, West Indies. Three weeks later, on December 6, Lenton, Nichols & Co.'s Circus left for South America in the bark *Utah*. Arrangements were made for the purchase of the stud at their destination since they were hesitant to subject horses to the perils of sea travel.

The few circus managers who customarily performed in the South headed north at the end of the summer. The dark clouds of national disunion dimmed the prospect of returning below the Mason-Dixon line for the following season. After Spalding & Rogers sold their river boat, *James Raymond*, they forsook their usual New Orleans venue, the Academy of Music, and moved north to the safety of New York's National Theatre. Only Dan Rice's Great Show would remain and then not for long. His eventual departure left New Orleans devoid of arenic performances until nearly a year after it was re-taken by the Union forces in April of 1862.

South Carolina seceded from the Union on December 20. In so doing, state leaders claimed that secession entitled them to all government property within its boundaries. This included the forts Sumter and Moultrie. President James Buchanan refused to give up government property but promised not to send reinforcements to protect it. On the 27th, Major Anderson, with two small companies of men, transferred his command from Fort Moultrie across the bay to the unoccupied Fort Sumter, situated on a ledge at the mouth of Charleston harbor. This was construed by the South to be an act of war.

In Springfield, IL, at this holiday time, the frightful prospects of such a calamity were not apparent.

> [Mr. Lincoln] takes it easy, allowing nothing to upset his quiet sway, and passes through the streets as if he had nothing on his mind more than any ordinary business man. The city is unusually gay on account of the many strangers daily arriving; the hotel keepers are pleased, and the saloons all doing a good business. Christmas day was duly observed, business being generally suspended, and everyone appearing in their Sunday-go-to-meeting attire. Sleighs were flying in all directions, boys shouting, and men drinking. At night the whole city appeared illuminated, and many a joyful family gathering took place.[34]

CIRCUSES AND MENAGERIES, 1860: Antonio Bros.; Bartholomew's; George F. Bailey & Co.; Cooke's Royal Circus (winter); George W. De-Haven; Gardner & Hemmings; George K. Goodwin & Co.; Great Buckley Show; Lathrop, Peoples, Franklin & Co. (California); L. B. Lent; E. F. & J. Mabie; Madigan & Gardner (Baltimore, winter); Miller & Lovell; Niblo & Sloat; Levi J. North; Orton & Older; Pennsylvania; Reynolds' Menagerie; Dan Rice; Robinson & Lake; R. Sands; Spalding & Rogers; Stow & Co.; VanAmburgh & Co.; Rufus Welch (Philadelphia, winter); John Wilson & Co. (California).

NOTES

[1] New York *Clipper*, March 24, 1860, p. 390. The explanation came in a letter from Boston dated March 13. The 1851 engagement at Niblo's for manager Rufus Welch occurred from April 4th to the 26th under the guise of *Cirque Français*. In the troupe with Mlle. Eloise were Mr. Lee, Mlle. Caroline Loyale, François Loisset, C. Rivers, Richards, Master Derious, Eaton Stone, etc.

[2] New York *Times*, January 17, 1860, p. 5.

[3] *Ibid*. Hanlon is credited with developing the act termed *l'échelle périlleuse* (hazardous ladder). In its standard form, the gymnast worked from a horizontal ladder, swinging from rung to rung before leaping some distance to a hanging rope. For the feat at Niblo's, the reviewer mentions a "swing attached to the ceiling." It may be that the act was varied to accommodate spatial or other program necessities.

[4] Thayer, III, p. 116.

[5] Heck, pp. 45, 48.

[6] *Spirit of the Times*, February 11, 1860, p.12.

[7] New York *Clipper*, February 11, 1860, p. 342.

[8] New York *Clipper*, February 4, 1860, p. 334.

[9] Other members of the troupe included E. Rivers, Foster, Nagel, Davenport, Ruggles, Ellingham, Andrews, Cooke, Whitby, DeBach, Stickney, Mrs. Rynar, and Mrs. Nixon. William Hanlon was also scheduled to join his brothers but his appearance was delayed. He had been unable to perform because of an injury sustain some months earlier.

[10] Usually billed as Signor Sebastian, Quaglieni (d. 1882) performed in America for about 25 years and was considered excellent in somersault and carrying acts and as a bareback rider. Had just closed an engagement with Dockrill & Leon, Iron Amphitheatre, Havana, when he was stricken with yellow fever and died. His son, Romeo Sebastian, was also a circus rider.

[11] New York *Clipper*, April 21, 1860, p. 6.

[12] Smith and Judah, p. 1.

[13] New York *Clipper*, September 9, 1860, p. 191.

[14] *Spirit of the Times*, August 11, 1860, p. 328.

[15] Baltimore *American and Commercial Advertiser*, October 2, 1860, p. 3.

[16] Stuart Thayer, e-mail, November 22, 1996. In what is probably an apocryphal story, the exhibition was cut short by the "clouds of secession." Howes was alerted by Mayor Monroe that it might be a propitious time to leave the city. Accordingly, the exhibitor, laden with his ponderous cargo and accompanied by Robert Heller, musician, magician and second-sight artist, who apparently had not foreseen the danger, stowed away on the ship *Havana*, bound for the city of the same name. This was related by Charles H. Day, *Billboard*, December 29, 1906, p. 32. The *Havana* was soon re-christened and became the famed vessel *Sumter*.

[17] Henderson, pp. 17, 28.

[18] Glenroy, p. 122.
[19] From a Philadelphia correspondent for the New York *Clipper*, November 3, 1860, p. 30.
[20] Baltimore *Sun* as reprinted in the New York *Clipper*, December 22, 1860, p. 287.
[21] Baltimore *American and Commercial Advertiser*, December 1, 1860, p. 3.
[22] Townsend Walsh, p. 65.
[23] New York *Clipper*, March 10, 1860, p. 375.
[24] Carlyon, p. 349.
[25] MacAllister, *People in the Circus Business*, p. 7. Fred Barclay performed with various circuses until at least 1887. He was a volunteer in the Spanish-American War with the First Florida Infantry, Company E. While in Cuba he contracted malaria and never really recovered. He died in 1907.
[26] There is a Frank Drew listed in Brown's *History of the American Stage*. He was an Irish actor who came to this country with his parents in 1837 and made his debut at the Olympic Theatre, New York City, at the age of eight. This Mr. Drew married Mrs. C. I. Stone in 1850 and as far as I can tell was quite satisfied with that arrangement.
[27] Baltimore *American and Commercial Advertiser*, March 31, 1860, p. 3.
[28] Baltimore *American and Commercial Advertiser*, April 9, 1860, p. 2.
[29] Starting a summer tour, the company exhibited at Annapolis, April 23; Laurel Factory, 24; and Washington, 25-27. It then made its way into Maryland, Virginia, North Carolina, back into Virginia, Tennessee, Kentucky, Ohio (Cincinnati), Indiana, Illinois, Arkansas, Mississippi, and Louisiana.
[30] Carlyon, p. 254.
[31] New York *Clipper*, June 23, 1860, p. 78, from a letter to the editor dated June 6.
[32] Thayer, *op. cit.*, pp. 279-83. The Rocky Mountain Circus was discovered by researcher Michael Sporrer. The troupe was absorbed by Wilson's circus in San Francisco on October 30. Joseph Rowe returned financially thinned from Australia at mid-summer after three years of touring in the South Pacific and was welcomed with a complimentary benefit.
[33] New York *Clipper*, July 7, 1860, p. 95.
[34] A letter from W. H. P., Springfield, IL, December 28, 1860, published in the *Spirit of the Times*, January 12, 1861, p. 586.
[11] *Spirit of the Times*, June 30, 1860, p. 452.

DEATHS IN 1860: Joseph W. Brewer, gymnast, known for his work on the horizontal bars and bottle act, at St. Helena, CA, April 23, age about 38; **Harry Huntington**, agent, at Elmira, NY, in June; the elephant **Victoria**, in California on June 28; **Col. Hugh Lindsay**, a showman for nearly forty years, at his Berks County, PA, residence on August 3; James Capen "Grizzly" **Adams**, October 25, at the home of his daughter in Neponset, RI, age 55; **Joe Sweeney**, Ethiopian entertainer and banjoist, at Appomattox, VA, October 27.

1861

The year welcomed Kansas as the thirty-fourth state on January 29, but the songs being sung around the country reflected the division of the nation—"Glory, Glory, Hallelujah!," "Maryland! My Maryland!," "John Brown's Body," and "The Vacant Chair, or We Shall Meet but We Shall Miss Him." It began with a premonition of bad times. The outcome of the presidential election had created a level of uncertainty regarding the nation's stability; with showmen, the financial prospects of amusement enterprises looked dim. Although many managers had held on with some satisfaction throughout the winter months, the political climate was clearly worsening.

The year of 1861 began with unavoidable steps toward war. In January alone, South Carolina seized Fort Johnson in Charleston Harbor, which had been abandoned by Federal troops; Mississippi became the second Southern state to secede; Alabama took over the U. S. Arsenal at Mount Vernon, as well as the Forts Morgan and Gaines which guarded Mobile harbor; Florida troops easily took possession of the United States fort at St. Augustine and became the third state to secede; on January 11, the state of Alabama also elected to secede; on the 19th the state convention at Milledgeville voted for the secession of Georgia; Louisiana seceded a week later and closed the mouth of the Mississippi to Northern shipping. The sides were clearly drawn. What a way to begin the new year!

As the time for Lincoln's inauguration neared, threats of an assassination plot in Baltimore put the authorities on the alert. Lincoln was persuaded to leave his special train at Philadelphia and ride into Washington in a heavily guarded sleeping car. In his inaugural address the President assured the South that he would respect its rights, that there was no need of war. "We must not be enemies."

The declaration fell on deaf ears. Following South Carolina, Georgia, Florida, Alabama, Mississippi, and Lousiana, Texas went out on February 1. The states declared there was no legality that bound them to the Union; rather, they were voluntarily associated and, like foreign nations, could act independently for their own well-being. The Southern population, then, did not consider themselves "rebels"; they were defenders of the rights of sovereignty against interference, intrusion and conquest. The North, on the other hand, without disputing the constitutional implication that the thirteen original states were "thirteen independent nations," assumed that by 1861 the body of states constituted a single entity, a single Union. The North, almost as a whole, was determined to hold that union together. The difference between North and South was irreconcilable.

On the 9th of February the organization of the Confederate States of America was created, with the Mississippian, Jefferson Davis, elected its president. The consolidated power of the southern states into the Confederacy enabled South Carolina to affect a much stronger posture in its efforts to gain possession of Fort Sumter.

The secession of the truly southern states occurred without equivocation, but the sentiment of the border states of Kentucky, Tennessee, Virginia, Delaware, Maryland, and Missouri was less clear and, for some, remained in question for a period of time. On January 3 the state government of Delaware elected not to secede. On February 9 a majority of Tennessee citizens voted against secession; but this expression of democracy proved to be worthless, for politicians later reversed the decision. On April 4 the Virginia state convention voted down a motion to put the secession question before the voters and waited for circumstances to decide their action.

The citizens of Maryland were determined to remain loyal to the Union. On the 29th of April the vote against secession in the state's legislative body was 53 to 13. Still, there were many who were strongly pro-Confederacy, particularly on Maryland's eastern shore, and they would aid the Southern cause throughout the war.

Attempts to carry Missouri into the Confederacy were resisted by men loyal to the Union and by a small force of regular soldiers in the region led by Captain Nathaniel Lyon. The battle of Boonville on the 17th of June decided the fate of Missouri in favor of the North. Still, this did not leave the state free of conflict; for by war's end Missouri was surpassed by only Tennessee and Virginia in the number of battles fought.

Kentucky endeavored to carry out a policy of neutrality. Nevertheless, by the beginning of May, volunteers within the state made up fourteen companies for the Confederacy. On the other side, William Nelson, a native Kentuckian and a friend of Lincoln's family, volunteered to secretly supply arms to the pro-Unionists in the state. Through his efforts 5,000 guns were shipped to men in sympathy with the Northern cause. It is safe to say that in all the border states, whether with the South or with the North, there was a noticeable split in loyalties, a condition which created difficulties for both sides.

The winter circus scene in New York City was highlighted by the arrival of Spalding & Rogers' Great New Orleans Circus. Following their summer boat tour, reluctant to return to the South, the company moved into the Old Bowery Theatre for an indefinite stand. At this point, Spalding and Rogers had been joined in successful management for over a dozen years.

Dr. Gilbert R. Spalding was born in Coeymans, Albany County, NY. He acquired the title of Doctor from being the proprietor of a drug and paint store in Albany from about 1840 to 1845. Near the end of those years he used Sam H. Nichols' circus as security of a loan. The show continued under Nichols' management until Spalding realized he was not about to recoup his money that way. So he visited the circus with the intention of bringing it to Albany and disposing of it but, finding his own management was paying off and since he was enjoying the circus business, he determined to keep the property for a while longer.

Charles J. Rogers was the son of English performer John Rogers, who came to America in 1816 with James West's circus company. Young Rogers was introduced to the ring at age eight in Baltimore while with Price & Simpson on the occasion of his father's benefit; at which time he performed on the trampoline and turned a somersault over four ponies. In 1826, Charles was apprenticed with the combined shows of Quick & Mead and Fogg & Howes; after which, he was connected with various circuses until 1847 when he joined Spalding's company as principal rider. He bought an interest in the show the following year and so began the successful career of their proprietorship.

The state of the Union discouraged Spalding & Rogers from returning to their New Orleans quarters for a winter season. Instead, they took what was said to be a three-year lease on the Old Bowery, commencing for the 1860-61 winter season, with the idea of replicating the success of their New Orleans amphitheatre. The place was redecorated and re-designed and equipped with a moveable stage to accommodate both equestrian and dramatic entertainments on the same evening. Performances were given nightly with Wednesday and Saturday matinees. Admission for the dress circle and upper boxes was 25¢; the

Marietta Zanfretta

gallery, 10¢; the pit, 12½¢; "colored boxes," 25¢; and private boxes ranging from $5 to $8.

America at this time was not wanting for outstanding performers and Spalding & Rogers had several in their employ. One of the features was the team of François and Auguste Siegrist and Marietta Zanfretta. François, after beginning his career in Germany, was engaged as chief clown for the Paris Hippodrome where he remained for several years. He traveled throughout Europe under Franconi's management before coming to America with his brother, Auguste, for the establishment of Franconi's Hippodrome in New York City in 1853. Together the brothers did the trapeze, the *perche-équipoise*, and the Brothers act on the four globes which, it is claimed, was first introduce to America by them.

Marietta Zanfretta was married to François. A Venetian by birth, she was one of the greatest female tight-rope dancers in the world, daring and graceful, extremely attractive with "black, lustrous Italian eyes that pierce[d] like an arrow" and an exquisite form. T. Allston Brown was expansive in his tribute to the lady:

> Her movements are as lithe as those of a panther. She never uses the balance pole but poises herself on the rope without any advantageous aid. She performs the same feats on the *corde tendue,* which I think surprising in a dancer on the firm floor. She runs backwards and forwards, turning with incredible rapidity, dances on the rope, stands on the point of one toe, descends the angle of the rope into the parquet, and re-ascends unfaltering and fearless. Indeed, her doings are unexampled.[1]

Kate Ormond, whose real name was Kate Simpson, was a young woman with raven black hair and coal black eyes, attractive both in and out of the ring. She was the adopted daughter of Francelia Delsmore Ormond, who had been an outstanding equestrienne and member of the Spalding & Rogers company for several years. Apprenticed to Charles J. Rogers at this time, Kate was to become an excellent pad rider and a specialist of single equitation. Later, when she toured the coastal cities of South America (1862-63), it is said that men crowded around the circus entrance to fawn on her and escort her to her hotel.

The circus had one of the great leapers of the day in Tom King. While performing in California in 1856, the twenty-four year old athlete leaped 31 feet 7½ inches over nine horses. He married equestrienne Virginia Myers—daughter of clown and showman James Myers and the former Rose Madigan—in 1859 while with the Joe Pentland Circus. The couple then worked together throughout most of their married life.

Master Charles Fish, "the paragon of equestrian precocity," was another of Rogers' apprentices. At age nine he had been placed under the care of James McFarland, then traveling with Spalding & Rogers, until around 1864 when McFarland was killed during a domestic quarrel. The following year Fish was indentured for seventy-eight months to Rogers. Fish was lithe and slight of frame and blessed with agility and grace. It is claimed that he was the first to do a somersault on a horse and land on a single foot. "Robinson was declared the more dashing rider," Fish once remarked, "but I was declared the champion trick rider of the world, a title I am ready and willing to defend against all comers." The reference, of course, was to James Robinson, the great bareback rider.

The Spalding & Rogers company was well fortified with Messrs. Merrymen. Dan Castello, one of the principal clowns, was back from an 1859 London appearance with his trained bull, Don Juan. Sam Long, who sang a good song, told a clever joke, and was eager to make his audience laugh, had returned from an engagement on the West Coast. Julian Kent, with Dan Rice's show as early as 1852 and later with Madigan's before joining Spalding & Rogers, completed the trio of funny men.

It was unfortunate that the company followed on the departure of Cooke's Equestrian Troupe which had dominated New York circus activity while at Niblo's Garden only months before. On hand at the Old Bowery for the November 5 opening, the *Clipper* editor could not restrain from making a comparison by suggesting that the Cooke/Nixon circus was far superior. William Smith had moved over from the Continental Theatre, where he had been lauded by the *Clipper's* Philadelphia correspondent; but at the old Bowery his *l'échelle périlluese* was compared unfavorably to Thomas Hanlon's—the length of his performance being shorter and his leap to the rope less perilous and only half the distance. Kate Ormond was judged to be a capable rider for her age but undeserving the praise that had been given her. The Siegrist Brothers, with their performances on the globe and their trained canines, stood out. The clowns Castello and Kent were assessed "fair to middling."[2] It may have been this kind of reception that prompted the management to bolster their numbers with the addition of the little giants of equestrianism, James Robinson and Levi J. North, who joined on December 10.

When ring performances began to wear thin, and with the addition of North's stud of horses and ponies, a dramatic company combined with the circus performers to produce such pieces as *Putnam* and *The Warlock of the Glen*. Added to these was a Christmas harlequinade brought out on December 24, *The Monster of St. Michael; or, Harlequin and the Golden Sprite of the Sulphur Mines*, advertised as costing over $5,000 to produce. A new piece was inaugurated January 10, *Manfredone; or, the Monk, Mask and Murderer*, the main circus force remaining. This was followed by *The Terror of the Road; or, the Race for Life* on January 14, also with the full dramatic and equestrian corps.

On the 21st Spalding & Rogers put up the extravagantly staged *Tippoo Saib; or, the Storming of Seringgapatam*. The many scenes with their trick transformations filled a huge space in the very large program. They included such effects as a vast army encampment, an Indian jungle near the Taj Mahal, a grand review of British troops, illuminated gardens, the entrance to the Cave of Torture, and many more, ending with a view of a fortress—"a scene of vast grandeur, extending to the extreme height of the theatre"—where a bombardment by British forces, in a charge of horse and foot, wreaked the destruction of the citadel and the death of Tippoo Saib.

In spite of apparent laborious preparation, the Spalding & Rogers extravaganza faded out on January 28, when, with a benefit to E. L. Tilton, the stage manager, the equestrian and dramatic company said farewell. The stand had not been successful, so the circus departed for Boston's Academy of Music and another two weeks of poor business, after which the season was terminated. It had been a dismal winter for the proprietors. Public apathy exhibited by New York and Boston audiences was also apparent at their amphitheatre in New Orleans, where Dan Rice's Great Show was performing. The circus there, which had opened to encouraging attendance on December 10, later played to grosses of as little as $30 on some nights. Everything seemed at a standstill.

Elements of James M. Nixon's circus arrived in New York City from Havana on March 23, 1861, and opened at Niblo's Garden on the 28th where, in combination with the Ronzani ballet, the troupe filled out the remaining off nights until the end of the theatre season. Ella Zoyara and Mlle. Heloise were augmented by bareback rider Signor Sebastian; rider and leaper Tom King; rider and acrobat William Kincade; and other American performers whom the creative Nixon presented under

NIBLO'S GARDEN

James M. Nixon..Sole Lessee and Manager
Acting Manager...Mr. T. Barton
Stage Manager..N. B. Clarke
Scenic Artist..G. Maeder
Musical Director..John Cooke

RETURN HOME OF

NIXON'S ROYAL CIRCUS

After an absence of six months, making a tour through all

The Southern States and the Island of Cuba

and achieving the greatest successes ever made by any

EQUESTRIAN ESTABLISHMENT ON THIS CONTINENT.

Thursday Evening, March 28th, 1861

PROGRAMME:

1. CHINESE FESTIVAL.—with Gymnastics by the Equestrians and Dances by the Roman Ballet Troupe—Galletti, Tophoff and Corps de Ballet.
2. Equestrian Feats............by....................Mlle Victoria
3. Stilt Equilibriums............by....................T. Armstrong
4. Exercises in Tumbling.......by the................Company
5. Somersault Act of Horsemanship.. by..........Master Roberts
6. L'Echelle Perilleuse..........by....................W. Smith
7. The Olympians...............by............Kincade and Sebastian

INTERMISSION OF FIFTEEN MINUTES

8. Perch........................by....................King and Smith
9. Horsemanship Extraordinary...by..................Sig. Sebastian
10. Les Poses...................by the..............Lawrence Brothers
11. La Trapez...................by the................Cline Brothers
12. Picquette Equitation.........by....................Ella Zoyara
13. Slack Rope..................by....................J. Ward
14. Concluding with the comic Piece...........MONS. AND MADAME DENNIE

Trick Clown...SIGNOR FELIX CARLO
Jester..JAMES WARD
Ring Master...R. ELLINGTON

TO-MORROW, FRIDAY,

MR. EDWIN FORREST

AS.................................VIRGINIUS.

SPLENDID

EQUESTRIAN MATINEES

Will be given on

Mondays, Wednesdays and Saturdays,

COMMENCING AT HALF-PAST TWO O'CLOCK.

MR. FORREST'S NIGHTS

MONDAYS, WEDNESDAYS and FRIDAYS.

THE CIRCUS TROUPE

Will appear on TUESDAYS, THURSDAYS and SATURDAYS.

Spanish names. A repeat staging of the spectacle, *Cinderella,* with a cast of seventy-five children, was a companion attraction. On April 27, Nixon took a well deserved benefit. The theatre closed its doors two days later, an occasion that ended Nixon's management of Niblo's Garden. War prevailing, this grand old house would remain dark for a period of eight months.

The first shots of the long-feared civil war were fired by the South on Fort Sumter. On April 11, Gen. Pierre Beauregard, commanding the Confederate forces, demanded the surrender of the fort. Captain Anderson refused. The following day the bombardment began; and faced with overwhelming odds, Anderson was forced to surrender on April 13. On Sunday, the 14th, the gallant officer saluted his flag with a fifty gun barrage and, with his men, was conducted to a boat which would take them to New York City. As the siege ended, the war began.

> Until Friday the war fever had little effect upon our theatres; on that evening and the following, every place of amusement felt the pressure. Nothing else is now thought of but war. Everybody is talking "fight." We can think of but little else to talk about but "fight." It is "fight" in the theatres, "fight" at the opera, and "fight" in our concert saloons.[3]

Strengthened by the prevailing mood, President Lincoln put forth a call for troops, 75,000 three-month volunteers, drawn from militia of the various states of the Union. The gesture drew immediate anger from the governing halls of Virginia, North Carolina, Arkansas, and Tennessee, which promptly passed ordinances of secession and joined the Confederacy. Maryland, Kentucky, and Missouri remained loyal to the Union.

There is no denying the resolve the fall of Sumter engendered in the Northern public. The pervading sentiment was that their patience and tolerance had been repaid with violence. They were now ready for war, whatever the consequences. In Lebanon, OH, an enthusiastic meeting was held where speeches were made pledging unqualified support to the Federal government during the present crisis. The enlistment of volunteers in Philadelphia quickly filled the quota; and the volunteers who were too old to be accepted formed reserved guards for the protection of the city. In Boston, at a meeting held by the Irish citizens, patriotic resolutions were unanimously adopted expressing unflinching devotion to the Federal government. The state legislature of Rhode Island passed a bill authorizing the raising of a regiment with $500,000 being appropriated. At Reading, PA, the Ringgold Flying Artillery, under Capt. James

McKnight, received a requisition from the government for their 180 men and four field pieces to set out at once for Harrisburg. The governor of Maine issued a proclamation convening the legislature to determine measures in response to the President's call for troops. A large and enthusiastic meeting was held in Michigan City, IN, with Democrats and Republicans alike uniting for a defense of the constitution and the Union; and where strong anti-secession resolutions were adopted, denouncing all as traitors whose voices were not heard in support of the government. At Lafayette, IN, volunteers left for Indianapolis, escorted to the depot by the Lafayette Artillery and two companies nearly filled that would follow in a few days. General Cass made a speech at the Board of Trade in Detroit, MI, unfurling the Stars and Stripes over their rooms. The excitement increased at Richmond, IN, as companies drilled all day, with all the manufacturing establishments closed because of the volunteering. And at Madison, IN, as the volunteers prepared to leave, the scene at the depot was heart warming, with men shedding tears as they said farewell; a salute was fired for the volunteers, the Union, and the constitution.

John Glenroy, in his memoirs, recalled arriving in Chicago to find the "excitement intense," with "people enlisting everywhere and pushed forward to the front." Southern sympathizers found it wise to keep their views to themselves; otherwise, "their lives would not have been worth one hour's purchase."[4]

Washington, DC, as the United States' capital, was extremely vulnerable to attack, located as it was, surrounded by the rebel state of Virginia and the partially hostile state of Maryland. It was therefore necessary to fortify the city as swiftly as possible. On April 18, five companies of recruits from Pennsylvania arrived, untrained and unarmed. The 6th Massachusetts Volunteer Infantry was soon to follow; but not before encountering a hostile mob in Baltimore on the 19th.

The railroad travel to Washington required this military unit to debark at Baltimore's Philadelphia Station and take horse cars across town for boarding another train to their destination. Before all of the cars had made their way, Southern sympathizers barricaded the route by placing heavy anchors across the rails, forcing the soldiers to leave the cars. In so doing, it was apparent that very few carried arms of any kind. Shortly, made bolder by this observation, stones began to fly, clubs were flailed, and shots fired from the facelessness of the crowd. The soldiers had to fight their way through the hostility to join the rest of their outfit;

after which, the mob got completely out of hand, firing the station and running locomotives into the stream. Before the ruckus subsided, four soldiers were dead, another seventeen wounded, and twelve civilians were killed by return fire. The incident caused Maryland officials to refuse the transportation of Northern troops through Baltimore for a time. As an alternative, units headed for Washington came by ship from Philadelphia to Annapolis and then by rail to the capital.

It wasn't long before Washington was inundated with military. On April 25, the 7th New York and the Rhode Island Militiamen set up camp within the city, as well as more men of the 6th Massachusetts, who had been delayed repairing the railroad between Baltimore and Washington. Soldiers were encamped everywhere, including under the uncompleted capitol dome. The 7th New York was housed in the chamber of the House of Representatives. Public buildings became barricaded fortresses. Guests fled the city in anticipation of a rebel attack. On May 24, to protect against bombardment, Northern forces occupied nearby Arlington Heights and Alexandria, VA. There was no opposition at either place.

With the new Confederacy establishing its capital at Richmond in May, the opposing centers of government were barely one hundred miles apart, making the capture of either a paramount necessity to military strategists. On the 2nd of June, General Beauregard was given command of the Army of Virginia, with expectations of shortly going on the offensive. The Southern generals had three objectives—to protect Richmond, to capture the Union capital, and to defeat the opposing army. In this regard, Washington was situated right on the boundary line of Virginia; batteries from the nearby Arlington Heights could easily render the Northern seat of government untenable. In addition, the approaches to the city from the south contained no natural barriers. On the other hand, Richmond was secured on the north and east by the Chickahominy River, bounded on either bank by dangerous unfordable and extensive marshes; and no army could approach the city from the west without exposing its communications. The city's soft belly was from the south; but to accomplish an offensive from that direction would require the support of a sizable fleet of ships, which the Union did not possess at the outset of the war. The geographical features quite clearly favored the South.

But Virginia was divided into two sections by the Allegheny Mountains, with people of distinctly differing attitudes and objectives.

The western counties had a greater affinity with their Northern neighbors across the Ohio River than with their fellow statesmen to the east. As a consequence, counties loyal to the Union met in Wheeling on the 11th of June, the result of which established the new state of West Virginia as a member of the Union.

The citizens of Wheeling were accustomed to an annual visitation of one or more circuses and the war did not appear to interrupt this pattern. The city, sitting alongside the Ohio River, is located on a finger of land jutting up and away from Virginia proper and nestled between the boundaries of Ohio and Pennsylvania, states that saw a good deal of circus activity at this time. Consequently, shows routing from Ohio eastward or from Pennsylvania westward could handily schedule a stand in that city. And they did. Dan Rice's Great Show, on his way up the river, stopped on May 27, being the only arenic visitor for 1861. Although no shows were listed for 1862, Robinson's Great Combined Circus and Menagerie and Thayer & Noyes' United States Circus were there in the spring of 1863; and in 1864 four shows passed through.[5]

Secession! The dissolution of the Union was now recognizable to everyone. As might be expected, the amusement business was much better in the North than in the South and Southwest, where salaries were cut and traveling stars were canceling their dates and buying out their contracts. A correspondent in Louisville wrote, "The present theatrical season throughout the South has been, I'm sorry to say, disastrous; and in many cases a ruinous one, thanks to our Black Republican disorganizers of the North."[6] This kind of sour news was mimicked by others:

> Charleston is a "dead cock" in the theatrical world; Mobile no better; New Orleans is trying to keep a stiff upper lip, but it is a sad case and the end is fast approaching; Richmond, Virginia, we hear has gone up; Montgomery, Alabama, company dissolved and several of the members arrived here last week; Baltimore was ruined by the attack made upon Northern troops and its halls of amusement can scarcely recover from the effects of the blow.[7]

The Baltimore theatres were soon closed when the authorities put a ban on large assemblages. The citizens of the city were fearful, the streets were barricaded, the shutters of the houses "loop-holed" for musketry, and every gun store was emptied. Unionists were fleeing to safer climes.

"Secession, snow, squalls, slosh, and New York mud, all combined to tax the patience and the pockets of the gentlemen who cater for our amusement," wrote the *Clipper* editor.[8] The country's political instability caused the winter circuses to be short-lived. "The secession fever is now at its height in this city and the 'times is mighty hard' in consequence," wrote a correspondent from Richmond.[9] As the new year began the music of "Yankee Doodle" was hissed at the Mobile and Memphis theatres. A dramatic troupe at Lynchburg, VA, was reported to have joined the Minute Men of Virginia with avowals to fight for Southern rights. This was the same company labeled Northern abolitionists during an earlier week stand at Charlottesville. In New Orleans a variety troupe of mostly Northern performers, in an outburst of enthusiasm, organized themselves into a military company and readied to do battle for the South.

It was a Union imperative from the outset to form a citizens' army. At the beginning of the war, the regular military consisted of 1,098 officers and 15,304 enlisted men available for duty. By 1865, through the process of recruitment, the Army of the North had the strength of 1,052,038 men. Of this total, only 46,347 were obtained through the draft. The remainder were volunteers. Although most of the latter accepted bounty payments for their enlistment, the majority were there to fulfill a call of duty, express a patriotic impulse, or pursue the path of adventure and ultimate glory. A politician could become a regimental commander simply by rounding up a complement of 1,000 men. Cities and towns alike were quick to fill their early quotas, accelerated through spirited town meetings, the waving of flags, and the blaring of bands. No slackers tolerated.

Performers, too, were expressing their patriotism by joining military units in answer to President Lincoln's entreaty for three-month volunteers. For example, several members of the Arch Street Theatre, Philadelphia, formed a company known as the Wheatley Guard—using the name of the theatrical manager, William Wheatley.

The well known comedian and manager, George L. Fox, joined the New York 8th Regiment as a "three-monther" with the rank of lieutenant. On his last appearance at the New Bowery Theatre, April 22, a crowded house expressed their respect through lengthy applause. At the end of the play the curtain was again raised discovering the entire company, at which time the "Star Spangled Banner" was zestfully sung. The scene was then changed, revealing a view of Fort Sumter with the American flag flying from its summit, as Fox sang "Yankee Doodle," followed by the entire assembly singing "Aulde Lang Syne." At the

George L. Fox

finale, the house rose as a body and bestowed their approval in the way of deafening applause. The ladies waved their handkerchiefs, the men cheered, and the gallery gods emitted "cat calls, whistles, and various other outstanding demonstrations particular to the east side habitués." And, as a final gesture, Fox appeared before the curtain and made a speech profoundly patriotic.

It didn't take long for a universal show of patriotism within the amusement industry. By the end of April, E. M. Leslie's Union drama entitled *Anderson, the Hero of Fort Sumter* was being performed in at least four theatres around the country. Not to be outdone, Barnum brought out *Anderson; or, the Patriots at Sumter in '61*. "Cheer upon cheer has greeted the representatives of the various characters," he is quoted, "and the enthusiasm with which the glorious Stars and Stripes are greeted would strike terror to the heart of every traitor." Another new play was presented at the New Bowery Theatre, *The Stars and Stripes*, written by circus press agent Charles Gayler. A song, "Our Good Ship Sails Tonight," dedicated to the departure of volunteers, was composed by Stephen C. Massett. The Union flag was being raised over many of the theatres and other places of entertainment. In Philadelphia, the proprietor of McDonough's Olympic concert saloon offered the place as a militia training site and Captain Bill McMullin's Independent Rangers were drilling at the Continental Circus building on Walnut Street. The veteran manager of the Boston Academy of Music, Thomas Barry (not the clown of that name), who had served as an officer in the British 1st Royal Dragoons, volunteered his services in training troops and offered the use of the theatre stage as a drill room. And throughout the Union there were numerous theatrical performances where all or part of the proceeds were donated to the Volunteer Relief Fund.

The reported effect of war preparation and the generally unsettled political conditions on the amusement world was more apparent in the theatricals of the larger cities, primarily because that is where the majority of reportage focused. However, these institutions—the dramatic houses, negro minstrel halls, and concert saloons—fairly reflected the fate of circuses and other public exhibitions:

> We're in the midst of a war excitement, and the week closed heavily in the amusement world. Every place of amusement felt the depressing effects of the fearful news daily received from the seat of hostilities; in some of the theatres the falling off in the attendance being very large. The war, the mustering of soldiers, and the leave-takings of relatives

and friends, swallowed up everything else, and the people had enough to engage their time and attention without going to the theatres.[10]

The entire amusement world was turned "topsy turvy" over the war preparations. New York City became inundated with show people who had come from all parts of the country where theatres had closed or cut back, seeking employment where there was little to be had. Many would have preferred to stay on the road and work for merely room and board if the choice were theirs. Some were sadly destitute. Those who could afford the trip transported their talents to England and Canada for the duration.

At the end of their engagement, the remaining Havana contingent of Nixon's circus company left St. Jago de Cuba on March 24 aboard the *Black Squall* (H. W. King, Captain; Welch & Brothers, owners) to return to the mainland. Alas! After a stormy sixteen days, the ship was wrecked at Ocrakoke Inlet, near Cape Hatteras, on April 19 with a total destruction to the vessel and cargo. Two men, William Nixon and one of the crew, were drowned. All horses except one and all property and wardrobe were lost. Nothing was covered by insurance. And thus, sadly ends a chapter in the professional ledger of James M. Nixon.[11]

The Dan Rice rumors started as early as April. "He's talking secesh in the South and Union in the North." Much has been written about Rice's loyalty and disloyalty to the Union but no one has convincingly resolved the argument. In all probability it will always remain an enigma. The unsettled conditions within both Northern and Southern boundaries fomented rumors galore. Politically motivated antics designed to create dissension between peoples were recklessly indulged in. And those who harbored old animosities found new outlets for their dormant venom. Certainly Rice, as a highly visible public figure and a man of determined ideas, had many enemies as well as many friends. The clown's words of political jest within the arena could easily have been interpreted into whatever meaning befitted one's personal views. All these elements may have contributed to the Rice dilemma. But the stories continued.

Rice was accused of forming the Dan Rice's Zouaves out of his circus company during his stay in New Orleans. Allegedly a meeting was held by Rice where papers were drawn up and agreed to, tendering the services of the troupe to the State of Louisiana for defense of the

Confederacy. Rice was also accused of having copies of these papers made up for distribution along the route.[12]

His friends in New Orleans refuted the notion that he had expressed anything but Union sentiments. They stated that during a performance of the circus there on January 26 the audience became offended by an act of horsemanship in which the rider dashed around the ring waving the Stars and Stripes while the band played the "Star Spangled Banner." The swelling uneasiness within the auditory forced Rice into coming before them. Particularly addressing the man who was believed to have started the unrest, Rice went into an eloquently framed speech, relating to a time when standing on a dock at Liverpool he observed a vessel approaching the harbor with the Stars and Stripes flying above, and the sight of this symbol of his homeland gave him a feeling of security on a foreign shore. Then he went on to proclaim that he would defend the flag whether it be in a foreign land or on the stage of a New Orleans theatre. Impressed by such bravado, the audience cheered the clown and the performance continued.[13]

Rice closed his New Orleans stand at the Academy of Music on February 3; and, leaving aboard the *James Raymond*, steamed up stream, stopping to perform at cities adjacent to the great Mississippi River. Stuart Thayer has pointed out that early Rice biographers misstated that in departing from New Orleans he took the "fastest boat he could find to get up North" and "raced northward without exhibiting at many towns where he was billed once the war was declared." On the contrary, Thayer's investigation found that February and March were spent in "rather leisurely movement through Louisiana." And on the date of the declaration of war the show was in Metropolis, IL.[14] This does not conform to the picture of panic flight.

We do not mean to imply, however, that the "leisure" tour was without incident. When the company was booked into Memphis on April 2-6, a restraining order was issued on the closing day, designating the show a nuisance and enjoining it. How this writ came about is unclear. Quite likely it was instigated by a Southern sympathizer who was piqued at the sight of the Stars and Stripes wafting atop the tent or the strains of "Yankee Doodle" coming from within. Nevertheless, the show performed that night and left unmolested to pass into the Ohio River and down the Cumberland to Nashville; where the troupe, arriving two days after the surrender of Sumter, played to good business without incident.

The show, which was to appear in Cincinnati, had difficulty in procuring a lot. A petition to use a portion of the Orphanage Asylum grounds was tabled in council; but the circus came and set up on a lot on Court Street, between Elm and Race, beginning Monday evening, May 13, with afternoon and evening performances given on the 14th, 15th and 16th. The admission to the cushioned-seat dress circle, 50¢; children, 25¢; social stalls 25¢. With the usurped name of Ella Zoyara still on the bill, the stand was rewarded by a large attendance for the four days. Although the *Commercial* gave no indication of public animosity toward the show, the Rice boat was searched for contraband on the 16th.

This incident created fodder for the rumor mill. Word out of Cincinnati told of the Rice boating party being threatened by a mob of Northern sympathizers who demanded that the clown hoist the Union flag in place of his own. Rice responded by brandishing a gun and heading for the Kentucky side of the river, where he moored.

Upon hearing this report, a *Clipper* reader quickly rallied in support of the clown:

> To those who know the strong Union feelings that hold possession in the breasts of the people of Covington and Newport, Kentucky, the absurdity must be amusing; and all who know Dan Rice are satisfied that the report is a base fabrication. Mr. Rice has no flag of his own, no specific banner, but he sails under the glorious emblem of our free and happy country, the federal government—the United States, as it was given to us by our ancestors.

The writer went on to explain that the story was concocted by some "wag" attempting to gain notoriety by practicing "over vigilance." The "wag" contended that Rice had arms on board that might be intended for the Confederate cause. A party boarded the boat and found nothing.[15]

An article from the New Orleans *True Delta* called Rice the "Chameleon Clown." The complaint was that Rice showed "intense Southernism" and hatred of Northerners during his stay in their city but upon leaving was "cutting up all sorts of Black Republican capers in the West."[16]

At Erie, PA, on April 31, Rice put on his Northern makeup and delivered a speech to the Volunteers who were preparing to leave for war activity. The New Orleans *Crescent* was quick to respond:

Robert Stickney

Dan Rice, well known in this city, made a speech to some soldiers the other day in Erie, Pennsylvania. We find this speech published in the Cincinnati *Enquirer*. He told the volunteers that they were going "to annihilate treason, to subdue rebels," etc., etc. That was not the way Dan Rice talked when he was here last winter, but—never mind.[17]

Was this a matter of making amends for the secessionist reputation and of regaining public support? Chameleon-like? Perhaps. But we are now at war and the South is no longer show territory. In all fairness to Rice and other performers in similar straits at this moment in history, the sides had not been distinctly drawn. There was still anti-abolitionist sentiment in the North and open discussion of secession by Southerners residing there. In Rice's case in particular, it is sometimes difficult to distinguish when Rice the clown and Rice the man are speaking. And too, there is an inherent necessity within performers of most any form of public amusement to please its audience, not only for financial gain but to be "like" by them, to receive their spirited approbation. With no second-sight available to them, could men like Rice have truly realized the seriousness of their deportment as it related to the human suffering that followed? Whatever else he was, Dan Rice was no coward. He would not be driven from the arena. And he was a star performer, a celebrity. Time has shown that the public forgives its idols.

The summer season started slowly, owing to wet weather and the precarious nature of the times, with circuses playing to only fair business or less, instigating the frightful words of "salaries being cut." The public was diverting its attention from amusements to concerns about war preparation, and the drilling of local militia became compelling entertainment in itself. The blockade of the Mississippi River at Cairo, IL, reducing the amount of boat travel, slowed distribution of corn and other farm goods and caused such produce to be placed in temporary storage. There were demonstrations over the appraisal of currency and the banks' willingness to give par value. The abundance of circus activity in the central states and in Canada increased inclinations of civic officials to raise license fees even more. In addition, said officials frequently exacted sizable numbers of "family tickets" for the performances.

With war at hand, it is not surprising that amusement companies made a show of patriotism in their ads and in their programming. For this tenting season Sloat's New York Circus combined with Nixon's Royal Circus to form the First National Union Circus, billed as "adapted to the exigencies of war." The Car of Freedom led the parade, drawn by ten horses under the rein of Madame Mason clothed to resemble the Goddess of Liberty; and atop the car was a military band attired in the flashy uniforms of Zouaves. Spalding & Rogers' Railroad Circus used a grand entry which featured an allegorical presentation of "The Sons of Freedom and Daughters of Liberty" and the bills heralded the "Great Union Speech and National Songs" of Sam Long.

Notwithstanding the uneasiness and uncertainties that abounded, the general attitude prevailed that the war would be of short duration. "Our good, old pilot, General Scott, is gradually closing his grasp upon the traitors, and it cannot be long ere that grasp will tighten on the rebel crew, and crush them out of existence forever," the *Clipper* editor wrote.[18] A member of the New Jersey Brigade, corresponding from Camp Princeton, was equally confident: "When the Union guns begin to belch forth their fire and grape, the land of 'secesh' will become so all fired hot that the spirit of disunion will end its foul existence—burnt out—to be seen and heard no more."[19] Such optimism would soon be quashed.

By the month of May, both sides were experiencing an urgency for more troops and a need to push them into service with little time to prepare for military engagements, many being totally untrained and undisciplined. One company of Massachusetts militia was rushed to Fort Monroe with less than a day's notice. The decision occurred so quickly that some in the unit were left behind, there being no time to contact everyone. Following the first battle of Bull Run, members of the 79th New York Volunteer Regiment mutinied near Washington when they were denied furloughs. The entire outfit was placed under guard and the man responsible for fomenting the insurrection arrested. A few days later disgruntled men of the 2nd Maine Volunteers mutinied as well, which resulted in sixty of their number being sent to a camp off Key West, FL, for fatigue duty.

Most of the circuses were encountering bad business and other difficulties caused by war and congestion. The R. Sands company opened in Chicago on May 2 for three days on the lot opposite the Court House at Washington Street and played to surprisingly good houses; but after leaving the city they encountered discouraging conditions in their Illinois, Iowa, Wisconsin, and Minnesota territory, leading to one-third salary cuts and untimely forcing an earlier than usual closing in Chicago where they winter-quartered.

VanAmburgh & Co., with animals only, open in Chester, PA, at the beginning of April. The first week's business averaged $700 per day, the second week $600, considered a decent return for early in the season. But about this time Fort Sumter was fired upon and business fell off to a losing level. Then, the management's expectation to go into Maryland was thwarted by a letter from Easton, Talbot County, dated April 24, 1861:[20]

> Gentlemen: You are hereby notified that a mass meeting of the citizens of Talbot County on yesterday resolved that your exhibition should not be permitted to take place in this county as advertised by you. There is general excitement among our people and they require the civil authorities with the aid of the military (if necessary) to prevent your coming here at all hazards. I therefore give you solemn warning not to come at all through the country, and have directed the sheriff to summon the *posse comitatus* and the military companies to be ready at a moment's warning to use any force that may be found necessary to enforce the demand of the community and preserve the public peace. You will therefore understand that your exhibition cannot take place under any circumstances in the county and you will not be permitted to pass through our limits. Very respectfully, J.C.M. Powell, State's Attorney.

The company wisely turned back to Pennsylvania, not wanting to run the risk of losing horses and equipment. This change of plans resulted in an estimated $5,000 loss.

With no chance of trouping in the South this year, the prospects of crowding all of the traveling shows into the limited territory of the northern and western parts of the country led some managers to move into Canada. Routing shows across the border had been on the increase for the last several years—the panic of 1857 created an incentive to leave the country—but the amount of activity for 1861 seems to be influenced by war conditions at home, some shows spending a good part or most of their season there.[21] With over-crowding in the New York and New England territories, the simple decision was to expand the travels northward. E. F. & J. Mabie's Menagerie and J. J. Nathans' American Circus Combined was there under a new, patriotically designed, canvas of red, white, and blue. Levi J. North, after encountering weather at Utica, NY—so frigid it was necessary to light fires underneath the canvas to melt the snow—moved over the border and, finding Union sympathy intense, devoted the entire season there (performing in Toronto on the Queen's birthday). George F. Bailey & Co.'s French and American Circus, L. B. Lent's National Circus, George DeHaven's Union Circus,

WAMBOLD & CO.'S
DOUBLE SHOW.

MENAGERIE
AND CIRCUS COMPLETE,

Will exhibit at New Bedford,

ON SATURDAY AND MONDAY,

May 11th and 13th.

AFTERNOON AND EVENING.

This Mammoth Establishment includes a Menagerie, (full in every department) a splendidly appointed Equestrian Troupe, and a stock of highly trained Horses Ponies, Mules, and Trained Animals of various kinds.

THE WORLD-RENOWNED

WHITBY FAMILY,

AND A HOST OF STARS,

Appear in their elegant Entertainments, for full particulars of which see mammoth posters.

Tickets 25 cents. Children 15 cents.

my2-10t   FLINT PEASLEE, Agent.

Levi J. North

and VanAmburgh & Co.'s Menagerie moved in and out for short periods, while Alex Robinson's Circus was there for most of the season.

A new organization, Wambold & Co.'s Menagerie and Whitby's New York National Circus, operated by George K. Goodwin, made a Canadian visit while in their maiden season in the New England States. Goodwin came into show business in 1856 when he toured the panorama of "Italy" by Henry W. Waugh and for the next five years was engaged in this form of entertainment. He is said to have owned more panoramas than any other man in the business.[22] In January of 1860 he purchased John Sears' menagerie and went out that summer with G. K. Goodwin's Royal Menagerie and Great Moral Exhibition. Along with the animals the show had a stilt-walker, a juggler, a trick drummer, and a minstrel troupe. Then in October he acquired James M. Nixon's wagon circus which, combined with the menagerie, became Wambold & Whitby for the 1861 season.

On the return to the United States, the Goodwin party were victims of a public reaction illustrative of the extreme patriotic sensitivity prevailing in the Union. The company was accused of being a "secesh" outfit merely because, while traveling in Canada, it was their custom to raise both the Union and the British flags above the tent. A comparison was made to Lent's circus, which had flown only the Stars and Stripes. The fact that the Wambold title was advertised (recognizably an English concern) may have augmented the suspicion.

Such over-crowding in both countries created local outcries against traveling shows. The usual complaint of itinerant companies taking money out of the city and of them being the instruments of juvenile depravity were cited. Consequently, local authorities attempted to make it more difficult for amusements to set up in their communities. When Montreal banned circuses within the city limits, shows were forced to use a space in Guilbault Gardens outside of municipal boundaries.

To avoid congestion, some circuses ventured further west than had been their earlier practice. Minnesota, just admitted into the Union in 1858, was seemingly explored this year for the first time—George W. DeHaven, Dan Rice, and R. Sands & Co. being examples.

John V. O'Brien, whose managerial career stretched into the 1880s, had his first connection with a circus this year. He rented horses to Gardner & Hemmings and went along as boss hostler to keep an eye on his property, albeit one observer found their wagons and horses "sorry looking concerns." The company, somewhat enlarged from their initial year, moved about in Pennsylvania, New York and New Jersey. Near season's end, the show returned to Philadelphia and spread canvas on a lot on Twelfth Street below Spruce for an indefinite stay.

Madigan's Great Show in the northeastern states was probably the largest and best on the road this year. The circus featured the elephants Antony and Cleopatra and Victoria and Albert (not the Victoria and Albert sent to Wilson in California). Under the eye of George Hall, they went through their tricks of dancing, playing the hand organ, standing on their heads, and mounting pedestals. The sideshow consisted of a cage of animals, a Swiss stone eater and sword swallower, and the Gypsy Queen, all under the management of sleight of hand performer Spaf Hyman. Col. T. Allston Brown, the company's mouthpiece, made frequent pronouncements of good business; which created the necessity to enlarge the tent with a 44 foot middle piece, making it a 128 foot round top with two center poles.

A state law prohibited circuses from performing in Vermont under penalty of a fine of $300 and imprisonment to the manager and every person connected with the circus organization, as well as the landlord housing the troupe and the land owner leasing the lot on which the show set up. In spite of this, Madigan secured the services of a Mr. Philo A. Clarke, an advertiser, to pursue the issue with the state's Attorney General at Montpelier. Quite surprisingly, a consent was obtained for the Madigan circus to perform throughout the state. The company's reputation of quality and respectability may have had something to do with the decision; or maybe money exchanged hands surreptitiously. Whatever, the first date was at Bennington, August 8, where the tent was "crowded to suffocation day and night." A circus-starved populous responded and the company encountered nothing but excellent business. At their Montpelier stand the combined matinee and evening attendance totaled $2,700.[23] From Vermont the circus moved into Canada for a short time before returning to the land of the Green Mountains.

Access to the state of Vermont does not indicate the lessening of the usual antagonism that traveling organizations customarily encountered. Not at all. In way of illustration, at one point, Madigan set up in the town of Greene, NY, on a lot situated between two churches. About the time the audience was entering the tent, the church bells began chiming loudly to announce an evening devotion intended to "preach down" the show people. Publicist T. Allston Brown retaliated by ordering out the band to "play down" the competition with a rendition of national airs. It was reported that the bells stopped ringing, the tent filled for the performance and the prayer meeting was called off because of the interfering sounds of music, laughter, and applause emanating from it.

In mid-July Gen. McDowell began to move his force of 30,000 men, mostly green and undisciplined recruits, from Alexandria toward Manassas, where he expected to confront a sizable Confederate army. Shortly after dark on the 20th the General ordered his troops to advance and meet the enemy. On the following morning the first battle of Bull Run, fought near a small river called Bull Run and the town of Manassas Junction, occurred.

This first major confrontation of the war took on a circus atmosphere. Civilian spectators, some of them congressmen and their wives, buggied from Washington with their picnic lunches to observe the crushing of the Southern forces and the quick termination of the war. Instead, to the interruption of their gala, the Confederates routed the Union troops, who fled in disorder back to Washington. Chaos followed as the startled civilians, high-tailing homeward, interfered with the free passage of retreating soldiers. The disorganized rush back to the capital bore with it the startling revelation that the war would not soon be over. The South rejoiced. The North was dazed. But in no time, Charley Gayler's new play, *Bull Run*, was taking the New York eastsiders by storm.

Lt. George L. Fox of the 8th Regiment returned from the front on July 26, his three-month enlistment finished. His appearance at the New Bowery Theatre the following night was welcomed by a large and enthusiastic audience. The play, *Split Fire*, was an appropriate vehicle for his return, as it gave him ample opportunity to "gag" on the affair at Bull Run. The opening curtain rose as the orchestra played "Home, Sweet Home," followed by a medley of national airs. As Fox made his appearance, he was greeted with a burst of applause which lasted several minutes, with ladies waving their handkerchiefs and the gentlemen their hats and everyone shouting themselves hoarse. When the crowd was finally subdued, Fox, introducing himself as an emigrant from Bull Run, proceeded to relate in detail that very battle. After which, he was presented with a gold medal, a token he accepted with due modesty. And the play continued.

"✗" Manassus

The battle for control of the western rivers was beginning to take shape by the end of July. Circus managers must have followed this with interest. Union control of the waterways south would re-open lost performing territory and provide greater access to soldiers encamped along it. On the 25th, Southern forces occupied New Madrid, MO, alongside the Mississippi River near the Kentucky-Tennessee-Arkansas borders. The following week the North placed a contingent of men at Cairo to combat the civil unrest in southwestern Missouri. Early in August, over the protestations of Southern sympathizers and neutral Kentuckians alike, the Federal government established Dick Robinson, a military base near Lexington, where hundreds of Union soldiers were stationed throughout the war.

Dr. James L. Thayer entered into management this year, putting out a small clown troupe with Frank Phelps of Elmira, NY, consisting of a minstrel company and the Motley Brothers (Tom Pepper, John Keefe, William Hogle) with their acrobatic and gymnastic feats. A former tinsmith, stage driver, and circus chandelier man, Thayer made his performing debut on the Dan Rice show in 1856 when he was not only boss hostler and twenty-horse driver but appeared in the ring as a strong man. The following year, still with Rice, he entered the arena for the first time as a clown.

One of Thayer's featured attractions was his pair of comic mules. He had wintered in Girard, PA, where he erected a large building for the purpose of training ring animals—two of them being the trick mules Uncle Sam and Dr. Jones. The former was named after Sam Miller, keeper of Miller's Hotel on Chestnut Street, Philadelphia, a favorite pillow rest for circus folks; the latter after Dr. Richard Jones, well-known journalist, actor, negro minstrel, and press agent.

With the Cuban exhibition finished, Cushing and Quick's hippopotamus was sent to the Guilbault's Garden, Montreal, Canada, where the management erected a large tank to allow it to be shown in its "native element." Frank Howes was still on hand to manage the exhibition. Bostonians were the next to be presented with this one-of-a-kind animal, housed in a store on Washington Street. Next stop, New York City. Barnum's white whale had succumbed to the rigors of show business, leaving the Great Humbug with an empty tank on his hands. So hippo and Arab made their debut at Barnum's Museum on August 12 and starred for six months at a compensation of $300 a week.

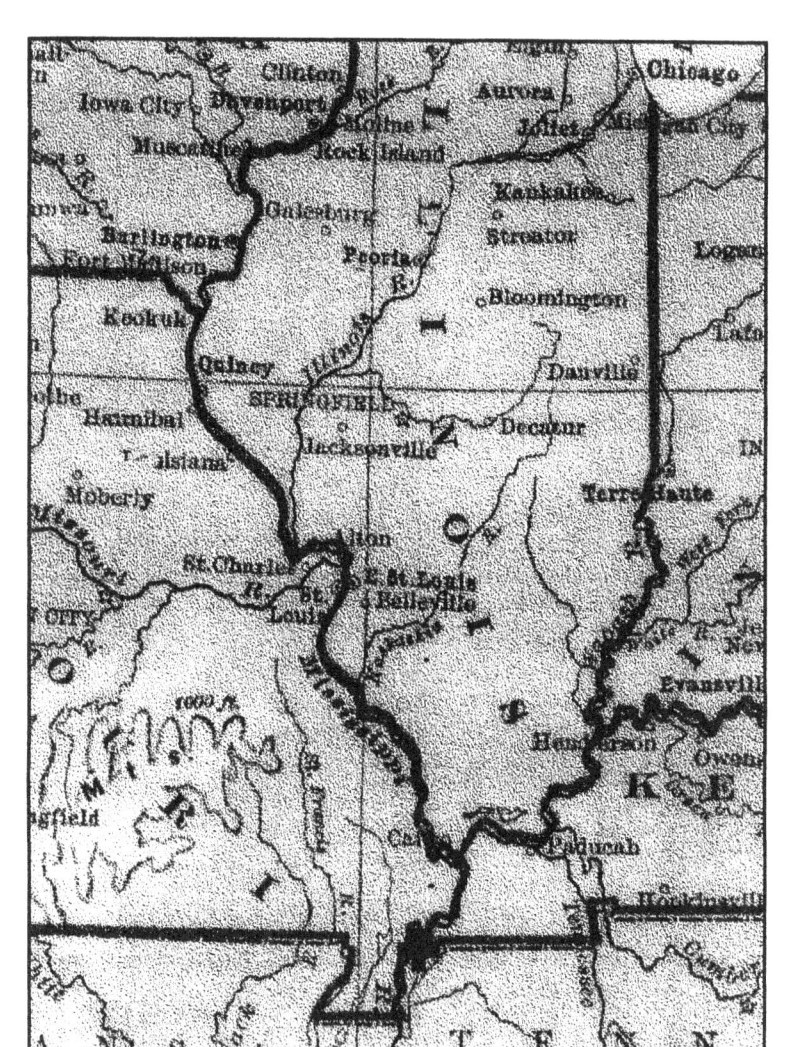

"✚" New Madrid, MO

Gen. George B. McClellan was now in charge of all the troops in and about Washington. By August he had restored order in the army and public confidence in the government's ability to accomplish victory. "The rebels have chosen Virginia as their battlefield," he wrote in a memorandum to the President, "and it seems proper for us to make the first great struggle there." The nation's capital was seen by circus managers as a potential bonanza. The 1860 census listed the population at 75,000; but now the town accommodated a glut of soldiers, government workers, and workers of the government. Washingtonians would soon be the beneficiaries of repeated arenic exhibitions.

The wreck of the *Black Squall* near Cape Hatteras on April 19, with a total loss of property, did not deter James M. Nixon. Nixon's Royal Circus Combined with Sloat's New York Circus performed primarily in New Jersey and the New England states throughout the summer and then moved onto the traditional South Fifth Street lot in Williamsburg in August before the tent was transported to New York City and pitched on the open grounds between the Palace Gardens concert pavilion and the Fourteenth Street Theatre, Fourteenth and Broadway. The circus opened there on September 2 for an indefinite stay and remained until the scorn of fall weather pronounced the season's end. During the run, Grizzly Adam's bears exercised their amazing acrobatics, Joe Pentland reappeared as clown, and Eaton Stone was there with his buffaloes driven in harness. Signor Zoyara, now of the male gender, the same Zoyara who had previously created such controversy at Niblo's the year before, drew the journalistic comment, "We must say, however, that Zoyara makes a much better looking woman than man."[24] But the rider did not abandon the skirt for tights exclusively; later in the run he performed as he had for the public on his New York debut—dressed in the feminine frills of Mlle. Zoyara.

By September the amusement business was gaining ground as the first shock from the hostilities had worn off. People in the North were beginning to take the war in stride—as much as one can take war in stride—and were now ready to seek escape from the daily reports of fighting. Show business, as it generally has, was about to profit during a period of conflict. New York City, the theatrical metropolis and entertainment center, was, it was suggested, wearing "quite a lively aspect, and the city presents a greater variety of amusements than we ever remember to have been presented for public patronage before."[25]

On September 1, Gen. U. S. Grant took command of Union forces in Cape Girardeau, in southeastern Missouri where the corners of Illinois, Kentucky, and Tennessee nearly meet, an area teeming with unrest. From his headquarters at Cairo, he learned that General Polk's Confederate forces had occupied Columbus, KY, and responded by sending a body of troops to Paducah, near the mouth of the Cumberland River, at the junction of the Ohio and Tennessee. The location was to prove strategically useful later in the war.

One might include here that Gen. Grant and his family were enthusiastic patrons of the circus. It was said that Ulysses' father, Jesse Grant, would walk farther to see a show than any man alive. The General was an admirer of Isaac VanAmburgh and was interested in the good horses that were often seen in the circus ring. "There was never a horse that 'Lys' couldn't ride," boasted his uncle, Samuel Simpson. Once a circus arrived with a trick horse which could throw everybody who got on. When people in the audience were invited to try their hand at riding it, Ulysses, then a mere boy, jumped in the ring and, as his uncle described it, "Lys held on and he rode that horse around the ring 'til it was tame as a cow."[26]

The George K. Goodwin menagerie, one of the most complete in the country, was destroyed by fire in Boston on the 12th of November. The flames originated on the ground floor of the building located on Portland Street and spread with such rapidity that nothing survived. The caged animals on the second floor, about one hundred in number, died of smoke inhalation. There were thirty-three cages in all, which contained, among other specimens, three lions, four leopards, a Bengal tiger, two African tigers, a hyena, two bears, an African goat, a Mexican wild hog, thirty to forty monkeys, and a large boa constrictor. On the lower story, five horses, three trick ponies, two trick mules, and seven watch dogs died in the flames. Fortunately, most of the show's horses were stabled elsewhere. In addition, two cabinets of wax figures, wagons, and sundry items were destroyed. The estimated worth of the entire collection was between $10,000 and $20,000 but the insurance covered only half its value. It was suspected that the blaze was ignited by an incendiary.

No theatre in New York City was suffering more from the conflict than the Old Bowery. It had been vacant all summer and early fall until October 7 when lights were lit again and the Great Orion Circus moved into place under the management of E. L. Tilton and H. Ashley.

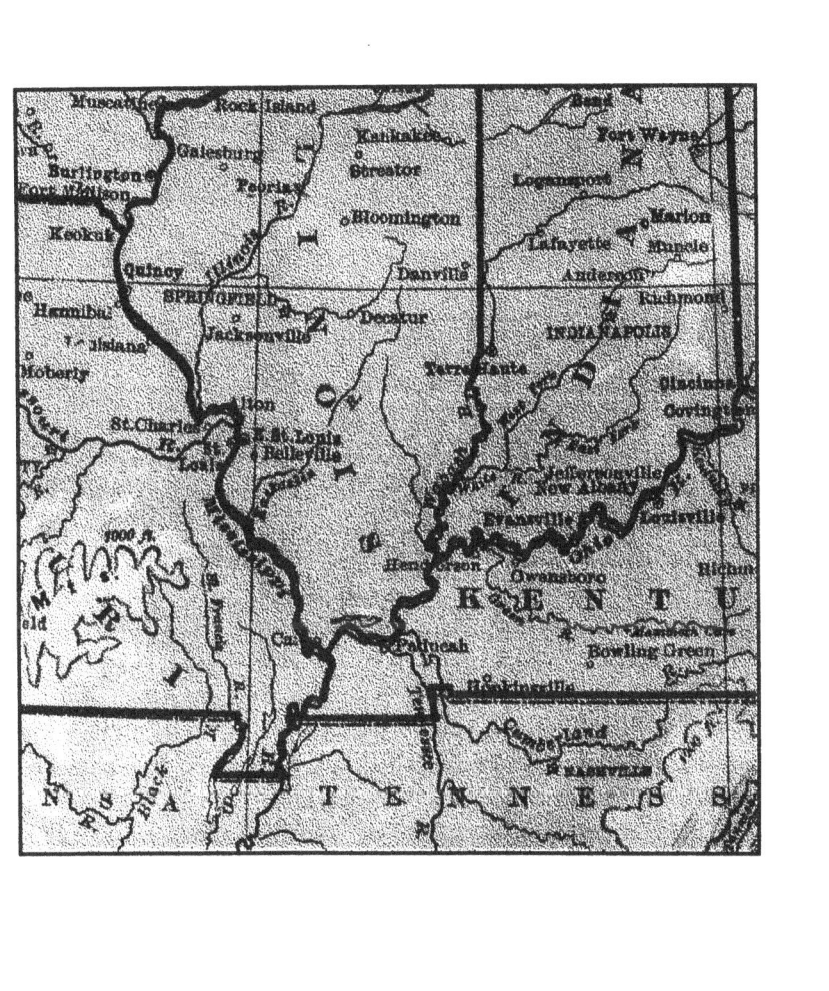

Tilton had been an actor of little merit at the Bowery; Ashley's name is totally unfamiliar. The proven circus entities here, however, were the equestrian director, John Tryon, Ella Zoyara and his pupil, "Little Gemma," and the clowns of the arena, Lee Powell and Charley Devere. Signor Sebastian's bareback riding, performed with ease and grace and daring, was generously applauded as well. Hogle and Keefe, masters on the trapeze, astonished audiences with their dropping feats.

A week after opening, the circus was enlarged by the addition of the Madigan company. James Madigan's double somersault was one of the outstanding items on the program. Running from the rear of the stage, he would leap with two complete turns in the air before alighting on his feet, and, on touching the ground, turn another one.

However, Tilton and Ashley faded quickly, for on the 28th of the month Samuel P. Stickney's National Circus was installed. S. P. Stickney! What history that name brings to mind! Although considered only a competent but not outstanding rider, he was one of the leading circus proprietors prior to the civil war. Called "Old Sam" or "S. P." by those in the profession, he began his career riding and training horses with Price & Simpson in 1823 and ended it with Stickney's Calisthenics Exhibition in 1876. In 1827, before twenty years of age, he was in partnership with Jeremiah Fogg when they crossed the Allegheny Mountains with a show. The troupe performed in Cincinnati and then took a flatboat down the Mississippi River to New Orleans, showing in towns along the route. Following this venture, the two managed circuses in Philadelphia and New York City. Stickney was in partnership with John Robinson in 1843 and, while with him, pioneered the four-horse act. He organized his own show, S. P. Stickney's New Orleans Circus, in 1844-47. One of his best acts was "The Courier of St. Petersburg" on eight horses. In addition to his riding, he was an able ringmaster, horse trainer, manager and tireless teacher of the equestrian art. He performed with various circuses and managed his own companies off and on until his death in New Orleans. With his wife, the former Christiana Wolf, he fathered five remarkable performers—Rosaline, Sallie Eloise, Emma Auline, Robert Theodore, and Samuel Jr. A Bostonian by birth, tall, gentlemanly, patriotic, and possessing a fair education, S. P. Stickney personified the real spirit of nineteenth century equestrian entertainment.

Stickney's opening company at the Bowery included his daughters Emma and Sallie and his son Robert. The respected clown, Joe

William Hanlon and His Zampillaerostation Act

Léotard's Act at *Cirque-Napoleon*

Pentland, was there along with Luke Rivers, William Smith, and Tom King. Gymnasts William F. Hogle & John Keefe, Zoyara, "Little Gemma," and Signor Sebastian were held over from their Orion engagement.

During November other featured performers appeared. Alonzo Hubbell, "the American Sampson," threw cannon balls about and exhibited his skills at heavy juggling. He pulled against two draught horses and displayed an ability to endure the weight of two men clinging to his hair while he hurled them around the arena until they lost their grips from exhaustion. Eaton Stone, the Vermont bareback rider, made another of his many appearances before New York audiences. Herr Andre Cline, the Englishman who preferred the German moniker, performed on the tight-rope with his usual grace and eloquence, unique from all other performers through his expressive pantomimic work. Mlle. Castilla, the wire ascensionist, came over from Levi J. North's Circus. The Matty Brothers, German imports, went through their gymnastic specialties. And young Robert Stickney revealed a talent that was to take him to the top of his profession, as can be seen from a *Clipper* observer's prophetic remarks:

> A mere boy as yet, he exhibits the points which older heads might profit by. His positions are not so free and easy as they will be as he increases in years, and the spectator at times fears that he will be unable to accomplish the difficult feats prepared for him; but he is true and steady and leaps the flags and goes through the balloons without a balk. His turning a somersault while on the horse is a remarkable performance and elicits the warmest applause. Young Bob is destined to make his mark in the wonder-world when he shall have attained to riper years.[27]

Then, within less than two weeks, on November 7 to be exact, the circus world was shocked to find that Sallie Stickney and Omar Kingsley (Ella Zoyara) were married and, it was said, withdrawn from the Old Bowery circus. One wonders why they would depart so suddenly, leaving S. P. minus two pleasing and popular performers.

Announcing the feat of the year! William Hanlon unveiled his Zampillaerostation! Performed in the manner of the acrobat, Léotard, Hanlon's act—with a name fit for a spelling bee—was observed to be more difficult and more finished than the Frenchman's. The modest and unassuming Hanlon Brothers had practiced for months before attempting a public exhibition. New York's Academy of Music was the venue selected for the debut. The opening night came on Thursday, December 12, with the theatre "filled to the utmost extent by a highly respectable audience." From the first tier of boxes a standing place had been erected with an iron ladder attached for mounting the perch. About twenty feet from this, in the parquet, an iron framework stood from which the first trapeze hung. Some fifty feet beyond was a second iron framework with its hanging trapeze. Another thirty feet further was a third such swing suspended from the proscenium. Eighteen feet beyond that was a wooden framework to serve as a landing place for the acrobat. All of the preceding were secured by iron wires of a half inch thickness to the boxes on either side. As the act began, William Hanlon positioned himself on the platform some twenty-five feet above ground level. The two other Hanlon brothers were stationed at the center trapeze swings to assist William in his flight to the stage. At a given signal the gymnast swung on the first trapeze, leaped to the second, sent up to meet him by a brother, and then the third, sent up by the other brother, and finally landed on the stage platform. The finish of the act was a repetition of this with the addition of somersaults as he passed from one trapeze to the next. The *Clipper* observer assessed it to be "the most surprising, graceful, and perfect acrobatic feat ever attempted," adding, "we have no doubt but that it will be the sensation of the season."[28]

It didn't take long for the war to find its way into pictorial exhibition. During Christmas week, when New Yorkers were celebrating the birth of the Prince of Peace, Goodwin & Wilder's "Polymorama of the Present War" could be viewed at Niblo's Saloon and Banvard's "Panorama of the War of the Mississippi" was being unveiled at the New Hall of Art, 652 Broadway.

CIRCUSES AND MENAGERIES, 1861: Antonio Bros.; George F. Bailey & Co.; Dr. Charles H. Bassett (California); George W. DeHaven (Sam Weaver); Dr. S. S. Foster; Gardner & Hemmings; Goodwin & Wilder, Howard's Athenaeum, (Boston, winter); Holland & Madden; Tom King (Washington, DC, winter); L. B. Lent; Mabie & Nathans; H. P. Madigan; James M. Nixon; Nixon & Sloat; Levi J. North & Co.; Dan Rice; Alexander Robinson; Robinson & Lake; Yankee Robinson (quasi-circus); R. Sands; Spalding & Rogers; Dr. James L. Thayer; VanAmburgh & Co.; Wambold & Whitby; W. W. White; John Wilson (California).

NOTES

[1] Brown, *Amphitheatres and Circuses*, p. 57.
[2] New York *Clipper*, November 24, p. 254.
[3] New York *Clipper*, April 20, 1861, p. 6.
[4] Glenroy, p. 123.
[5] Gardner, Hemmings & Co.'s American Circus, May 28, 1864; Lake & Co.'s Great Western Circus, October 6-7, 1864; Robinson & Deery's Metropolitan Circus, July 4-7, 1864; Thayer & Noyes' United States Circus, June 18, 1864; G. F. Bailey & Co.'s Circus, May 1, 1865.
[6] New York *Clipper*, March 2, 1861, p. 363.
[7] New York *Clipper*, May 4, 1861, p.22.
[8] New York *Clipper*, January 19, 1861, p. 319.
[9] *Ibid*.
[10] New York *Clipper*, April 27, 1861, p. 22.
[11] New York *Clipper*, May 11, 1861, p. 31. George Ross, equestrian, and Wessell T. B. VanOrden, advertiser, suffered broken legs from the falling of a boom, which forced them to stay behind when the company continued homeward. On their recovery they boarded the steamer *State of Georgia* at Fort Monroe and arrived in New York City on June 2.
[12] New York *Clipper*, June 22, 1861, p. 78.
[13] Polacsek, p. 4.
[14] E-mail letter from Thayer to the author, February 13, 1996, contesting the statements C. G. Sturtevant and John Kunzog.
[15] New York *Clipper*, June 15, 1861, p. 71.
[16] New York *Clipper*, June 29, 1861, p. 87.
[17] New York *Clipper*, June 1, 1861, p. 54.
[18] New York *Clipper*, June 22, 1861, p. 78.
[19] New York *Clipper*, July 20, 1861, p. 110.
[20] New York *Clipper*, May 4, 1861, p.22.
[21] One of the first American circuses to venture into Canada was the Olympic under the proprietorship of H. H. Fuller in 1838, which spent several weeks in New Brunswick. The next in line was the sparsely documented National Circus, which devoted the better part of the summer of 1840 to performing in Quebec and Ontario, entering from Maine and returning through New York State. June, Titus, Angevine & Co. was also there that year. Leaving from Buffalo, the show performed in Ontario and Quebec from mid-August to mid-October before returning to New York. The following year their eastern unit crossed over to play a few dates in New Brunswick during a tour of Maine; while the western unit picked up dates in Ontario en route from New York to Michigan. That same year a circus from the Bowery Amphitheatre, under the management of the Turner brothers, left New Hampshire in mid-July and apparently worked out the remainder of their season in Quebec and Ontario. Also in 1841, P. H. Nichols' Grecian Arena and Classic Circus, moving out of

and back into New York State, visited Ontario for a few weeks in August; and Nathan Howes and the Mabie brothers left New Hampshire in early August and remained in Canada for the rest of the season and the better part of the following one. Samuel H. Nichols' Victory Arena and Great Western Amphitheatre spent about a month in Ontario in 1842, coming and going from New York State. John T. Potter's Victory Arena and Great Western Circus touched into Ontario out of New York for a few dates in 1844. That same year Spalding's North American Circus crossed through Ontario on the route from Michigan to New York; and again in 1845 between stands in Michigan and Ohio and 1846 between Michigan and New York. Rockwell & Stone's circus was an exception to the general pattern. From 1842 through 1846, routing took the company in and out of Ontario, Quebec, and New Brunswick from points in New York, New Hampshire, and Maine. Other shows playing Canadian dates were: 1851, Welch's Grand National Circus; James M. June & Co.'s Oriental Circus; 1852, P. T. Barnum's Asiatic Caravan, Museum and Menagerie; Pentland's Dramatic Equestrian Establishment; 1853, Spalding & Rogers; R. Sands and G. C. Quick & Co.; 1854, Franconi's Hippodrome; Levi J. North's Colossal Circus; 1855, S. B. Howes; Ballard, Bailey & Co.'s French Circus; Chiarini's Italian Circus; Levi J. North's Colossal Circus; 1856, Spalding & Rogers' New Railroad Circus; Spalding & Rogers' Two Circuses; Welch & Lent; Joe Pentland Circus; 1857, Dan Rice's Great Show; Rivers & Derious; Joe Pentland Circus; VanAmburgh & Co.; 1858, L. B. Lent's National Circus; Rivers & Derious; Nixon & Kemp; 1859, Joe Pentland Circus; Nixon & Co.; 1860, L. B. Lent's; Levi J. North's; George K. Goodwin & Co. The above taken from Thayer, II, III.

[22] These included five of Dr. Kane's expedition to the North Pole, one of England, Chapprel's rendering of Cuba, etc., and later there were four of the Civil War.

[23] The remainder of the route included East Arlington, Factory Point, Dandby, Rutland, Brandon, Middlebury, Bristol, Vergennes, Hinesburg, Burlington, Milton Falls, Cambridge, Bakersfield, St. Albans, Bennington, Barton, Lyndon, St. Johnsbury, Barnet, Wells River Bradford, West Topsham, Barre, Montpelier, Northfield, West Randolph, South Royalton, Chelsea, West Fairlee, White River Junction, Woodstock, Windsor, Springfield, Proctorville, Saxton's River, Townsend, Brattleboro, Wilmington.

[24] New York Clipper, September 14, 1861, p. 174.

[25] New York *Clipper*, October 12, 1861, p. 206.

[26] Dingess manuscript, p. 247.

[27] New York *Clipper*, November 23, 1861, p.254.

[28] New York *Clipper*, December 21, 1861, pp. 286.

DEATHS IN 1861: Showman **Richard Sands**, rider and clown, died of yellow fever in Havana, Cuba, February 24; **Alex Rockwell**, clown, died in New York City in April, age about 50; **Richard Sliter**, jig dancer, died in Jackson, MI, May 21; **Charles Watson**, clown, July 13, in Plymouth, England; **James Hernandez**, real name Mickey Kelly, bareback rider, a native of Albany, NY, died in Singapore, East Indies, July 19, while with Risley's Royal Pavilion; **Ned Kendall**, famous bugler and bandleader, died in Boston, October 26, age 54; **Angelo Chiarini**, rope walker, fell from a rope in San Francisco, died November 28; **Stebbins B. June**, brother of John J. and James M. June and nephew of Lewis June, age 50; **Washington Chambers**, clown, fell from the flies in the St. Louis Theatre.

Upper Mississippi River Routes

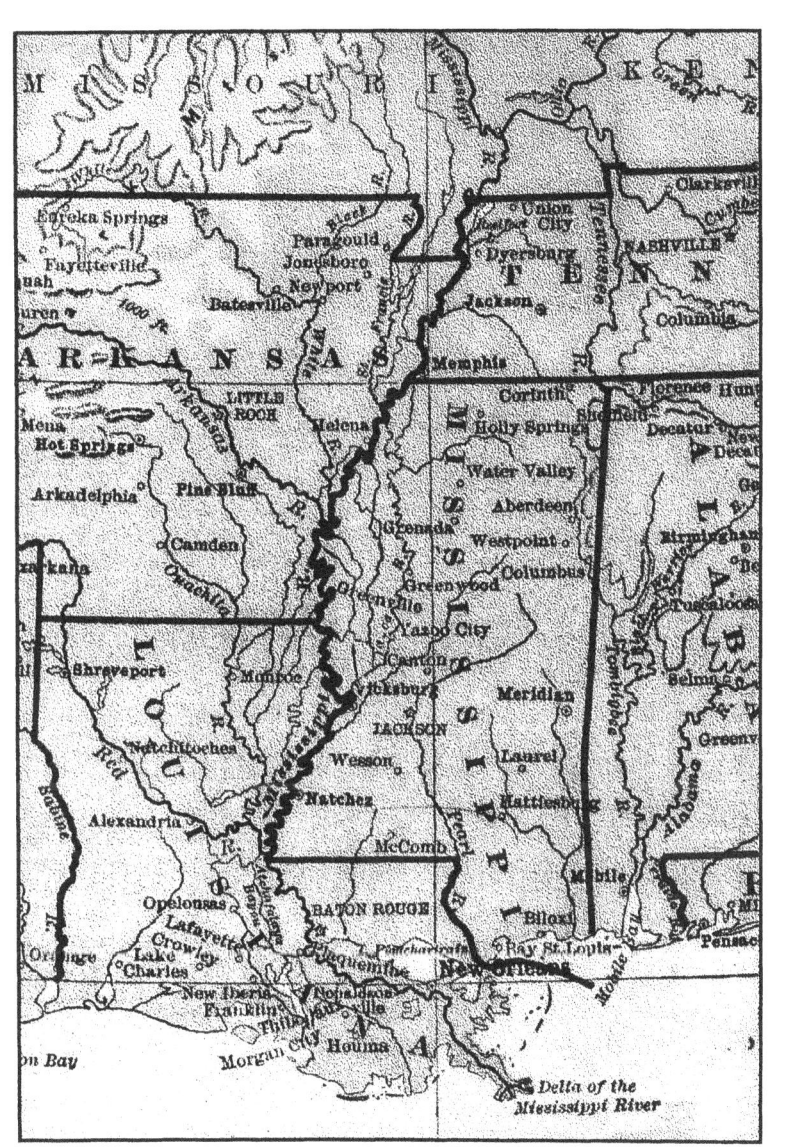

Lower Mississippi River Routes

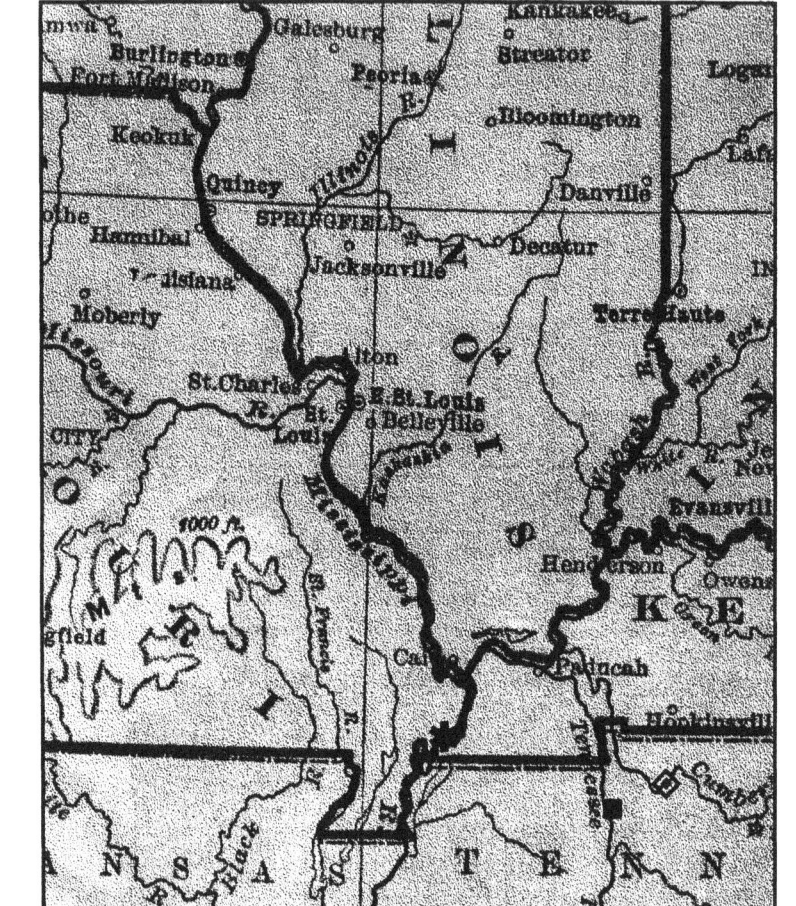

"✳" Island No. 10; "■" Ft. Henry; "◆" Ft. Donelson

1862

The war machinery moved relentlessly ahead. But bullets were not the only enemy; throughout the first year of fighting, two percent of Union troop deaths were caused by typhoid, dysentery, diarrhea, and pulmonary diseases. For the South the rate was even higher. This year treasury notes—"greenbacks"—were issued by the government as legal tender. For Northerners who felt like singing, Julia Ward Howe had written new words to "Glory, Glory, Hallelujah," transforming the piece into "The Battle Hymn of the Republic," first published in the *Atlantic Monthly* in February; while Southern voices had their own battle hymn in "The Bonnie Blue Flag." Visitors to Barnum's Museum could ogle at the Connecticut Giantess, "the handsomest Fat Girl and largest mountain of human flesh ever seen," eighteen years old and weighing 618 pounds. The last pirate was hanged in the country this year when Captain Nathaniel Gordon had his neck lengthened and his errant career cut short.

At the start of hostilities the Mississippi and its tributaries were closed to civilian traffic. The importance of these waterways for commerce and passenger service cannot be over-emphasized. They were connecting links to many of the major mid-western and western cities—Omaha, Kansas City, Pittsburgh, Cleveland, Chicago, Louisville, St. Louis, Terre Haute, Nashville, Memphis, Little Rock, Baton Rouge, Shreeveport, New Orleans and all the places in between. With the Mississippi as the major thoroughfare, there were adjoining rivers suitable for commercial navigation throughout nearly its full length. The Ohio River was 975 miles long from its formation by the confluence of the Monongahela and the Allegheny; the Tennessee and Cumberland met the Ohio, the Tennessee traversing a course of 650 miles from Knoxville well into Alabama, the Cumberland winding 700 miles from eastern Kentucky down into Tennessee and back again; the navigable streams of the Arkansas was an aggregate of 3,250 miles in length, including the White, the Arkansas, and the Ouachita; in Louisiana the Mississippi received 510 miles of the Red and 218 miles of the Ouachita; and the great Missouri connected the cities of Omaha, Kansas City and St. Louis as it opened into the Mississippi.

For circuses, the shutting off of north-south river travel was a sizable inconvenience. It should be emphasized that prior to the war shows had made good use of it. As early as 1822, Victor Pepin moved his circus by boat from Natchez to New Orleans. The following year Pepin, now Pepin & Barnet, went clear from St. Louis down to New Orleans. More extensive use of the rivers began in 1828 with J. Purdy Brown's circus and continued sporadically until the 1840s when several shows were traveling up and down stream seasonally, managed under such familiar titles as Stickney, Spalding, Rice, Spalding & Rogers, Showles, Rockwell, and Runnells. Some of these outfits used boats only at the end of a tour, moving primarily along the river from St. Louis to New Orleans for a winter engagement there, or, in reverse, returning north to begin their summer season. Although most of the shows were conveyed on wagons, there were occasions when the wagons were left ashore and the outfits loaded onto a leased vessel for longer jumps to towns along the shoreline. Then, too, there were circuses that were designed for the distinct purpose of moving by company owned river craft.

The most prominent circus boats were the *Floating Palace*, the *James Raymond*, and the *Banjo*. The first, although the best known, has little official information available. Still, from various pictures, one can assume it was a flat-roofed structure set on a keel-bottomed barge. It is believed there was a museum just inside the entry and beyond it, toward the bow, the arena, housing a full sized circus ring, surrounded by boxes and loge, together seating 800. The second floor gallery accommodated another 1,000. There was a stage at one end of the main hall and somewhere offices, dressing rooms and stables. The boat was used from 1852 to 1859. At the time of the secession of Louisiana from the Union it was tied up in New Orleans where it was seized by the Confederate authorities and made into a hospital.

In 1853, the Shields company of Cincinnati built the steamboat *James Raymond*. Like the *Floating Palace*, the *Raymond* was fitted up for exhibitions, having a stage for the presentation of minstrel shows. It also contained staterooms for the performers, crew quarters, a galley, mess hall and laundry. Some time this year the Federal government seized the boat for war use, paying the partners $32,000 for it.

The *Banjo* was a smaller version of the *James Raymond*, built in 1855 by the Shields people. Spalding and Rogers owned half of it,

John Mann one quarter and William McCracken the remainder. Seating 800 spectators, it was generally used for minstrel and variety shows.[1]

The ill-fated writer, Ralph Keeler, once recalled life on the *Floating Palace* with a negro minstrel company:

> I was engaged by Dr. Spalding.... He was then fitting out the *Floating Palace* for its voyage on the Western and Southern rivers. The *Floating Palace* was a great boat, built expressly for show purposes. It was towed from place to place by a steamer called the *James Raymond*. The *Palace* contained a museum, with all the usual concomitants of invisible ladies, stuffed giraffes, puppet-dancing, etc. The *Raymond* contained, besides the dining hall and state rooms of the employees, a concert saloon fitted up with great elegance and convenience and called "The Ridotto." In this latter I was engaged, in conjunction with "a full band of minstrels," to do my jig and wench dance.[2]

The clown, Pete Conklin, has written that he was on the *Floating Palace* showing in New Orleans when war was declared. The Confederate government seized the *Palace* and ordered all northern people to leave the South. So the performers organized a company under the commonwealth plan, called Dan Castello's Great Show, chartered a small steamboat, and "fought and showed" their way up the river, finding it necessary to exhibit under two flags. While making stands along the route from New Orleans to Cincinnati, the circus ran up the Stars and Stripes and the band played "Yankee Doodle" for towns on one side of the river and flew the Palmetto Flag and played "Dixie" for towns on the other side.[3]

In 1860, Lavinia Warren, the future Mrs. Tom Thumb, was being exhibited by Col. Joseph H. Wood on the *Floating Palace*, probably when it was docked at New Orleans before confiscation. Following the election, Wood felt it would be wise to abandon river travel and move north from their lower Mississippi location. They took the first train to Vicksburg, which was already being used for carrying munitions of war, making travel very uncertain. After many delays, they reached the city on the morning of December 2. They then attempted to book the last steamer going to Louisville. Although the boat was already overcrowded and after some difficulty in getting passage, the captain turned to Wood and said, "If you will quietly and speedily get your people to my boat, I will resign my cabin to Miss Warren and the other ladies; the rest must accommodate themselves as best they can on deck." They then proceeded on uneventfully to Louisville and northern safety.[4]

At the beginning of January the plan for Federal control of the rivers and the occupation of New Orleans was set in motion as Union forces advanced along the Mississippi, Tennessee, and Cumberland waterways. Gen. Grant and twenty-three regiments left Cairo for a march toward Columbus, KY, and Generals Smith and Halleck moved up the Cumberland and Tennessee toward the Confederate stronghold at Fort Henry. The *USS Lexington* and the *USS Conestoga* were sent up the Ohio River to help defend the area. Flag Officer Foote, with a new fleet of ironclads, moved along the rain-swelled Tennessee toward the fort, well ahead of Grants' 15,000 mud-mired soldiers. Meanwhile, the ships of Flag Officer Farragut tightened the blockade at the mouth of the Mississippi and began preparing for an assault on New Orleans.

Amusements followed the Union army wherever it went. In Cairo, theatres benefited from the activity created by the military campaign in the West. The Athenaeum, located on the east side of Commercial Avenue near Seventh Street, was built at this time to serve as an amusement place for the soldiers. Because Gen. Rosecrans and his army were stationed near Wheeling, readying for movement elsewhere, managers Edwards and Brownell opened a variety house at Washington Hall in that city to accommodate local amusement-goers as well as the entertainment hungry troops stationed nearby. The success of the venture prompted a move to the more commodious Athenaeum, which was rechristened the Gaiety Theatre. There was a troupe of circus and variety performers in Nashville, TN. And, farther south, the Academy Hall in Baton Rouge, LA, opened under the management of G. A. Pratt with a company selected from New Orleans. Still, the military situation made trouping precarious and greatly narrowed the breadth of travel.

George K. Goodwin, not to be discouraged by the burning of his menagerie, took James Waterman Wilder as a partner for a 1861-62 winter season in Boston. Wilder had come into the circus world through manufacturing a Drummond light and gasworks for Spalding & Rogers, with whom he remained from 1850 through the close of the 1857 season, executing various assignments from gas man to agent, to treasurer, and manager. He had interest in the circus of Antonio & Wilder for the years of 1858-59, managed Niblo & Sloat's company in 1860, was treasurer when Spalding & Rogers took over the Old Bowery Theatre, and was general agent for their railroad circus the following summer.

Goodwin & Wilder opened at the Howard Athenaeum on November 21, 1861, but shortly moved to the Academy of Music. Befitting

GOODWIN & WILDER'S
North American Circus!!
[From the Boston Academy of Music.]
COMBINED FOR THE SEASON OF 1862, WITH

Mrs. Dan Rice's Great Show!

A GRAND NATIONAL EQUESTRIAN CONGRESS!
No half Circus and half Menagerie combined, but two well-known Circuses consolidated in one.

LOOK AT THE ARRAY OF STARS!

MRS. DAN RICE, the Queen of the Arena.
M'LLE. JEANETTE ELSSLER, the Great Tight Rope Danseuse, from Franconi's Hippodrome.
MRS. J. SHOWLES, the unequalled Maitresse de Cheval.
M'LLE. ELIZABETH, the Beautiful Equestrienne.
NAT AUSTIN, the Australian Clown.
JACOB SHOWLES, Antipodean Equestrian.
JOHN BARRY, the Great Somersault and Trick Rider.
CHARLES SHAY the Japanese Juggler and Knife Thrower
THE WONDERFUL SNOW BROTHERS, in their Great Gymnastic Feats.
OLD BOBBY WILLIAMS, the well known Grotesque.
J. C. RIVERS, the American Clown.
MASTER WILLIAM AUSTIN, the Youthful Gymnastic Hero.
J. FOSTER, J. DOVISE, and others.
The wonderful Manege Horse, WHITE SURREY.
The beautiful performing Horse, AMERICAN EAGLE.
The Pugilistic Mules, HEENAN and SAYERS.
The Learned Ponies, ROBIN GREY and CUPID.

Together with other attractions too numerous to mention, a description of which, will be found in the splendid Bills of the Company, and in the Hand Book of the Arena.

Performance at 2 1-2 and 7 1-2 P. M.
ADMISSION 25 CENTS.   CHILDREN 15 CENTS
Will Exhibit at
LYNN, on TUESDAY, May 27th;
SALEM, on WEDNESDAY, May 28;
NEWBURYPORT, on THURSDAY, May 29.

the times, the grand entry was titled "Sons of Freedom and Daughters of Liberty." Zoyara, returning from an engagement in Washington, appeared in both petticoats and tights beginning on Monday, December 23. Private boxes were $3; dress boxes, box chairs, and parquet, 50¢; family circle and children, 25¢; gallery, 15¢. (colored persons admitted to gallery only). Prices on Wednesday and Saturday afternoons were 25¢, children 15¢, to all parts of the house.

S. P. Stickney's circus, which had taken possession of the Old Bowery in the fall of 1861, continued into this year with a series of spectacles. *O'Donoghue; or, the White Horse of Killarney* was the first presentation. This was followed by the pantomime *Baron Munchausen*. The stage manager, J. C. Foster, took a benefit on January 14, when his own piece, *McCulloch's Invasion of Missouri*, reflected the ever present consciousness of civil conflict. The month of January saw a new influx of arenic stars in the persons of Kate Ormond, Louise Tourniaire and Dan Rice. Eaton Stone reappeared for more bareback exercises and by February the clowning of Sam Lathrop was in evidence.

Foote's gunboats began a push on Fort Henry and, after hard fighting, the fort surrendered on February 6. The Union forces then moved on to Fort Donelson, which was the last obstacle before Nashville, attacking on the 14th. Two days later the fort's commanders asked for terms of surrender. Grant responded with, "No terms except unconditional and immediate surrender can be accepted." With this uncharitable retort, the Confederates acquiesced. Foote's gunboats now controlled the Cumberland River and the road to Nashville was clear. On the 25th the city was in the Union and remained so for the rest of the war. Situated as it was in north-central Tennessee, easily accessible by boat from the various river routes, Nashville was now another Southern stand for the hovering circuses.

The exploit of Fort Donelson produced instant public and political response. The success inspired the designation "Unconditional Surrender" Grant and a promotion to the rank of Major General of Volunteers. The successes on the river furnished the North with an important boost of morale and influenced the New York staging of the new drama, *Victory on Victory; or, the Capture of Fort Donelson*.

In New York City the growing popularity of concert halls created anxiety among managers of other competing amusements. At the beginning of the war, Broadway enterprises experienced an economic slump. But despite the dimming prospects for the entertainment

First Eads Gunboat, USS St. Louis

Armored Ram, CSS Manannas

dollar, more and more such places were opened, their proprietors seemingly willing to compete in an overcrowded marketplace. As a consequence, the legitimate theatres and minstrel halls lost audiences to the concert saloons, which, by their very nature, offered a more varied entertainment fare. A fight was in the offing.

By December of 1861 the theatrical and minstrel managers issued petitions to suppress the operation of concert saloons. They convinced the New York Grand Jury to call for legislative action. The issue was directed at the questionable "waiter girl system," which was distinctly identifiable with this form of amusement. When, in Albany, the legislature convened in January of 1862, Senator Robertson introduced a bill "to preserve the peace and order in public places of amusement in the city of New York," a bill specifically aimed at curbing the operation of concert saloons. It made it unlawful to conduct any kind of performance—any interlude, tragedy, comedy, opera, ballet, play, farce, minstrel show, or any other entertainment of the stage—until a license had been obtained from the city of New York. No license was to be given for places where wine, beer or strong drinks were sold to audiences of such exhibitions or when female attendants were permitted to furnish refreshments to the audience where such performances were given. Noncompliance was subject to up to six months imprisonment or a fine of as much as $500 or both. The bill dealt exclusively with the city of New York. The new law went into effect on April 24, 1862, and within weeks the Broadway concert saloons were closed and many variety and circus performers were thrown out of work.

But do not despair. Within a year concert saloons will return to Broadway. This time the proprietors will not be theatre men but saloon keepers who will take steps to circumvent the law that had closed the earlier establishments. The "pretty waiter girls" will be back, serving beer, wine, and hard spirits to the patrons but the variety entertainments will be missing. For a while there will be no staged theatricals, only instrumental music and occasional singing. But this will not be the end for variety and circus performers. The halls will soon be back to employing many of these people in the off season, passing another milestone toward the day of full-fledged vaudeville.

A shaky financial status of amusements prevailed into 1862. The high price of paper and other provisions doubled within only a matter of months, a phenomenon caused in part by the expectancy of high profit. Occasionally, a popular military officer lent his name and presence at a performance and a good house was the result. But in Philadelphia theatrical managers were cutting salaries as much as one-half, reflecting a general condition throughout the entertainment world.

Yet, in spite of this, theatres continued to be built. Mr. J. T. Ford leased the former First Baptist Church, Tenth Street between "E" and "F", in Washington, DC, fitted it up as a theatre, and opened on March 19, unaware, of course, of its history-making significance. The initial pieces were *The French Spy* and *The Irish Beauty*, starring Miss Lucille Western. The architect, James Gifford, who had previously made the alterations on the Holliday Street Theatre, Baltimore, fashioned the new playhouse with a parquet, dress circle, gallery, and four private boxes, all in all capable of seating 1,400 people. The new facility filled a long-standing need for a respectable theatre building in the capital, the old one being described as "nothing more than a shed, and a disgrace to the city." Unfortunately, within a few short years, the place would be world famous.

The wagons of the so called Joe Pentland's Great New York Circus arrived in California from the East on March 30 aboard the ship *Radiant* after one hundred and ten days of travel. Under the management of John Wilson, who had just returned to the West Coast from the Orient, the circus opened in San Francisco at the Jackson Street lot on April 6 in a 110 foot round top. The reader may recall that in 1860 Manager Wilson had a circus out under the banner of "Dan Rice," but a Dan Rice circus in name only. Similarly, there is no proof that this 1862 outfit had anything to do with Joe Pentland. Certainly the clown was not advertised in the bills. The problem with writing him out of the California venture with supreme confidence is that he can't be located elsewhere at this time.

As a novel arrangement, the interior of the canvas pavilion was fitted up with a dress circle of some sixteen private boxes, built on a large platform and provided with comfortable chairs. These were intended for families and private parties of those who could afford the extra price. Although Joe Pentland gave credence to the title, the company was composed of George Peoples as clown; Signor Sebastian, bareback rider; and the Orrin family of acrobats.[5] What was considered quite a formidable demonstration occurred on April 25 when the entire circus establishment, consisting of a band of music, performers on horseback and in buggies, followed by luggage and freight wagons, left

MAMMOTH CIRCUS!

AND HIPPODROME.

MR. JOHN WILSON BEGS LEAVE TO inform the public of San Francisco, that having COMBINED ALL THE ARENIC TALENT IN THE STATE, he will have the pleasure of introducing a greater number of

Equestrian and Acrobatic Stars,

(Among whom will be found several new performers, just arrived,) than has ever been presented to the citizens of California. He has also effected an engagement with the celebrated American Clown,

BILL WORRELL,

who will make his first appearance since his return from Australia, after an absence of three years.

The present exhibition combines all the distinguished talent of THREE CIRCUS COMPANIES, including the entire strength of

JOE PENTLAND'S

GREAT WORLD CIRCUS,

which has just completed the most successful season in the interior and Nevada Territory ever known, being received everywhere by crowded and appreciative audiences.

This Mammoth Troupe will perform for a short season only, in the

MAMMOTH PAVILION,

On Jackson street, near Montgomery,

which has been fitted up in elegant style, with every essential to insure the comfort of the visitor,

ON MONDAY EVENING, OCTOBER 20th.

The Manager, in announcing that the new season will excel in novelties even his previous efforts, which won the unqualified approbation of all during his visit in the months of May and June last, pledges himself that the character of the entertainments will prove not only agreeable, instructive, recreative, but will SURPASS ALL AMUSEMENTS ever offered to the San Francisco public.

GRAND SATURDAY AFTERNOON MATINEES,

For the accommodation of families and those living at a distance. Children under five years of age free when accompanied by parents or guardians.

PRICES OF ADMISSION.

Dress Circle.. .... $1 00
Parquette.... ....50 cents
Children Half Price.

Doors open at 7 o'clock. Performance to commence at 8 o'clock.

JOHN WILSON,
Manager and Proprietor.

the amphitheatre in a procession that extended through the streets for two blocks.

The stand terminated on May 19 and the company set out for the mountain regions, following the routing of agent William Pridham, who was well acquainted with moving a circus through California's interior and the Nevada Territory. Their absence lasted until October 20 when they returned for a twenty-two day stand under the designation of Mammoth Circus and Hippodrome and Joe Pentland's Great World Circus. Then, surprisingly, the show was taken as far south as Los Angeles for an appearance on November 29 and 30.

Back at the Old Bowery, Stickney, taking cognizance of the anti-slavery fever, pulled the ten year old *Uncle Tom's Cabin* from his manuscript trunk, although the piece was currently being performed at three other New York theatres. Taking a lesson from Andrew Ducrow of Astley's Amphitheatre, London (now twenty years dead), S. P. mounted Mrs. Stowe's story of slavery "as an equestrian show of magnitude and splendor—real horses, dogs and mules, the whole thing as real as a menagerie" and presented it on February 25.[6]

Stickney took a benefit on March 8, during which he rode his spectacular six-horse act, "The Courier of St. Petersburg," billed as "the first time in 32 years." With this, the circus bowed out, relinquishing the Old Bowery to the throes of low drama. If nothing else, Stickney had proven his managerial ability at the troubled old theatre. He had introduced a series of novelties, produced some clever pantomimes, brought in a number of excellent artists, and, in spite of the whirlwind of public anxiety, hung on well into the month of March. He had given employment to a number of circus people who otherwise might not have found winter work. And he had managed, if nothing more, to remain financially above board.

All was quiet across the Potomac when a new brick amphitheatre was erected in the nation's capital under the direction of Tom King, who opened his 1862 winter season there on January 6 with Dan Rice, his horse Excelsior, and the mules as the two-week star attractions. Little Eliza Gardner, billed as La Petite Eloise, "a half grown Zoyara, a little queen of the circus," impressed audiences as she dashed through balloon after balloon with seeming ease, belying her young age. T. Allston Brown floridly described her as "one of the most delightful miniature, feminine examples of equitation my eyes have ever fallen upon." The little lady, "the butterfly of the ring," had a benefit on

February 26, at which occasion she was given a diamond ring and a gold necklace. The circus continued until March 8, after which the building was refitted for dramatic performances.[7]

Island No. 10, the next barrier interfering with the Union's control of the Mississippi, was undergoing increased fortification. In support, rebel Gen. Johnston moved his troops that had been evacuated from Nashville to Corinth. Gen. Grant pushed his men and gunboats down the Tennessee toward Eastport, MS. Gen. Pope's Union forces approached New Madrid, MO, and troops entered the evacuated city on March 14. Immediately, Flag Officer Foote left Cairo with ten mortar boats and seven gunboats to provide support for the inevitable attack on the island. Heavy fog and rain temporarily delayed any confrontation.

Spalding & Rogers' Ocean Circus, escaping the disheveled conditions within this country, left for South America at the end of March on the clipper *Hannah*. They took with them, in addition to a troupe of equestrians, acrobats, gymnasts, etc., a boatload of new equipment styled for a tropical climate. The cane seat folding chairs and settees were manufactured by E. Chichester on Pearl Street, New York City. The canvas pavilion was made by Henry Dougherty, South Street. Cornelius & Baker of Philadelphia supplied the chandeliers and fixtures. Various decorations and paraphernalia were designed by James C. Foster. Robert Walker was responsible for the extensive wardrobe. The stud of horses were the best the market could offer and included the trained animal Hiram. Rogers accompanied the expedition while Dr. Gilbert Spalding remained behind to look after their other enterprises.

Dan Rice was jeered in Philadelphia during a two-week engagement at the Walnut Street Theatre. The reputation justly or unjustly earned in New Orleans two years previous still followed him like a phantom shadow. Performances for the early part of the week were sparsely attended. The first signs of disturbance began on Thursday evening, March 13. When it became apparent that he was in serious trouble with his audience, the famous jester was unrelenting:

> The house was exceedingly bad, the parquet not being one quarter filled, and the upper part of the house was evidently made up of Rice's deadhead friends. In the course of his numerous harangues on that evening, Mr. McClaren, alias Rice, whether by accident or chance, "let the cat out of the bag." Presuming upon the favor of his audience, he read a speech, couched in very bad English, which he said he had delivered somewhere in Alabama, in which, he remarked, consisted his great offense against the Union. It was made up of adulation of the blessings

of the Union, references to sacred memories, and abuse of northern abolitionists, but no reference whatever was made in it to the old flag. The point to which Rice desired to call attention was the remark contained in said speech, that "the South had been wounded." After reading this sentence, Rice added, emphatically, "I believed so then, and I believe so now." Upon the utterance of this infamous and insulting sentiment a perfect storm of hisses broke forth, intermingled with applause from his deadhead friends. The hissing rather seemed to disconcert him, for it was violent and prolonged, and the signs of disapprobation continued during the rest of the performance whenever Rice appeared.[8]

On Friday, March 14, everything seemed to go smoothly until Rice came into the ring. He was at once showered with missiles of rotten eggs and received with hisses and shouts of derision. Thereafter, whenever he appeared that evening he was subjected to the same boisterous and unfriendly welcome. For the succeeding performances, disturbances were kept under control by an army of police officers assigned to every level of the theatre by Mayor Henry; and Rice took advantage of the security to desperately plead his case. The Philadelphia engagement was profitless and unpleasant for both the clown and his adversaries.

From that time on Rice's popularity diminished; but thereafter he made every effort to show his patriotism. He was active in raising the 83rd Pennsylvania Volunteers from Erie County. After the war, he erected a monument at Girard, PA, to the memory of that unit's dead. Upon receiving $32,000 from the government as compensation for the seizure of his steamboat by Gen. Freeman, he requested the money be given by the President to wounded soldiers and their families.

The path of Dan Rice resembles Greek tragedy with its elements of greatness, frailty, and atonement. A Rice contemporary observed some years later:

> It is impossible for the boys of today to understand the popular enthusiasm that Dan Rice's appearance aroused. It is no exaggeration to say that he was one of the biggest men in the country, and when announcement was made that Dan Rice was coming would set that section of the woods on fire, and every boy in the land would be wild with joy. But that time is past; and yet, perhaps, there is no man living who would be so generally recognized unannounced as Dan Rice.[9]

Abraham Lincoln and Dan Rice were good friends. In all likelihood, their unique relationship began in Lincoln's early days, strengthened by the propensity of each to tell humorous stories. In light

"DR." JAMES L. THAYER.

of Rice's patriotic difficulties, one might find it strange that the friendship continued after Lincoln became president. Nevertheless, according to Robert S. Dingess, whenever Rice visited Washington with his show during the war years, he was invited to the White House after the evening performances, and usually the presidential carriage was waiting for him. After being ushered into Lincoln's private office, the two men would exchange stories and jokes and all in all find great pleasure in each other's company and relaxation from the stresses of the day.[10]

The clash of the blue and the gray at Shiloh was the second great battle of the war and the most bitterly fought engagement of the whole struggle. Grants army of raw troops, encamped about Shiloh church, a site below Pittsburgh Landing on the Tennessee River, were taken by surprise on the morning of April 6 by forces under Gen. Albert S. Johnston. The Confederates burst from covering woods and began driving the bands of Union soldiers from their camps. The battle continued all day with terrific losses on both sides. By nightfall the Union soldiers had retreated almost to the river. However, overnight Gen. D. C. Buell arrived with 25,000 Union troops and Johnston had suffered a fatal wound while leading a charge. The Rebels, under his successor, Gen. Beauregard, were driven from the field the next day. The Union armies of some 70,000 lost about 13,000 killed and wounded. The Confederate loss was 10,000 out of some 40,000 men. By its defeat, the South had missed a chance to break up the Union advance in the west.

While the battle of Shiloh was being fought, Gen. Pope's soldiers and Foote's gunboats seized the important Confederate Island No. 10. The cannon fire from the *USS Carondelet* and *USS Pittsburgh* subdued the shore batteries on April 7, giving Pope's men the advantage they needed to storm ashore. The island was easily taken.

A few weeks later Commander David G. Farragut, from his flagship *USS Hartford*, gave the order to run his fleet past the fort batteries of St. Philips and Jackson at the mouth of the Mississippi. When the moon rose at 3:40 a.m. on the morning of April 24, the forts began bombarding the passing Union armada and fire boats were sent out to ignite the fleet. The air was clouded with smoke and flames from the belching artillery of both shore and river. During the chaos, Farragut had himself tied to a mainsail, from whence he uttered those unforgettable words, "Damn the torpedoes, full speed ahead." Forts St. Philip and Jackson were soon abandoned, paving the way for the occupation of

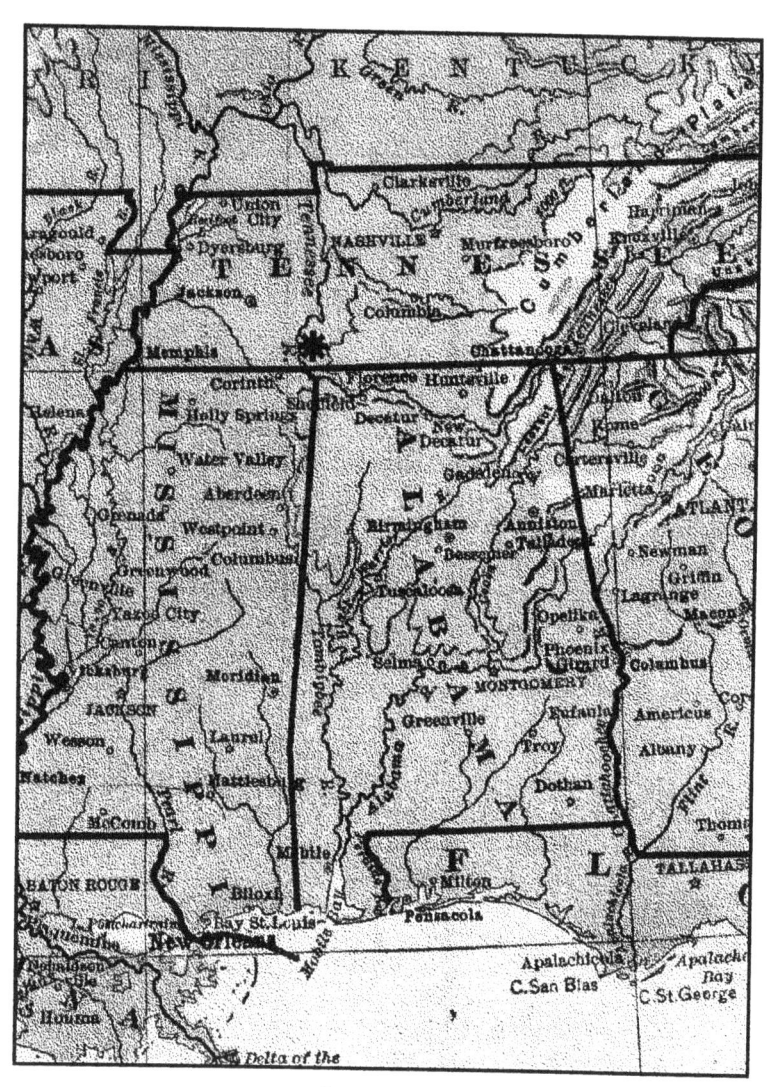

"✻" Shiloh

New Orleans by Union forces. On April 29 the Stars and Stripes were raised over the New Orleans Custom House. The doorway to the Mississippi and the principal Southern port were in Union hands. This does not mean, however, that the river was open and safe to travel. It would be well over a year before the Crescent City was visited by a circus company.

In the spring of 1862, James M. Nixon took a lease on New York's Palace Garden. This place was first opened on July 1, 1858, as a promenade resort during the summer months by DeForrest & Teesdale, where musical concerts and other exhibitions were presented. C. V. DeForrest leased the grounds to Nixon, who proposed converting and enlarging it into a place of Elysian beauty similar to the Cremorne Gardens of London. Added to the property were a stretch of canvas under which equestrian performances were given, a building devoted to the display of trees, flowers and shrubbery called Floral Hall, and a concert pagoda designated as the Palace of Music—in all an intermingling of natural beauty, ballet, opera, and circus. Our old friend Col. T. Allston Brown was business manager for the concern.

The American-style Cremorne Gardens opened its doors to the public on June 9, 1862. With the recent ruckus over the concert saloon issue in the state legislature, the management clearly announced that "no vinous, malt or spirituous liquors will be furnished or tolerated." The usual evening began at 7:30 with an hour and a half musical—ballet, concert, opera (a change of program weekly). Patrons could stroll about the grounds while listening to such artists as Carlotta Patti, Sig. Sbriglia, Mme. Strakosch, or an orchestra led by Harvey Dodsworth.

After the music was terminated, equestrian exhibitions of another hour and a half duration were performed. Nixon's circus artists included the French equestrienne, Madame Louise Tourniaire; the Conrad Brothers, Charles and William, clowns and gymnasts; the clown Julian Kent; and Horace F. Nichols, the veteran rider, equestrian director, and ringmaster.

The usual summer garden food fare was available to patrons—ices, creams, jellies, confectionery, cakes, fruits, etc. As an extra feature, the little men, Commodore Foote and Colonel Small, appeared "in their beautiful chariot, drawn by Lilliputian ponies," a pint-size welcoming committee. Some Iroquois Indians gave exhibitions of tribal dancing. Thomas Baker, of Laura Keene's Theatre, led the promenade orchestra. The pantomimes *Spirit of the Flood*, *The Golden Egg*, and *The Wizard*

Skiff were presented in turn. Fireworks displays were frequently given at the close of the evening. Admission for all was 25¢; reserved armchairs in the Palace of Music, 25¢ extra; orchestra armchairs, 25¢ extra.

One of the features at Cremorne Gardens, "the chief joy of the Cremorne," was the beautiful Spanish pantomimist and *danseuse*, Isabel Cubas. Cubas was born in Valencia del Cid, Spain, in 1837 and came to America in 1861. In September of that year she appeared at New York's Winter Garden, where she attracted public notice as a fascinating and voluptuous dancer. She was under Nixon's management and had, it was said, been recently married to him (this was not true, since he was still married to his wife, Caroline, at this time). For her benefit on October 6, she performed in J. T. Haines' time-worn piece, *The French Spy*.

The garden was shut down at the approach of cold weather. It had been a noble effort by the tireless proprietor but the outcome was a weak imitation of the English original. The season at the Cremorne did not live up to the flourish of printers' ink advertising the opening. Nixon had assembled a company of artists from the world of music and dance, which were intermixed with the more commonly appealing artists of the arena, a little something for everyone. But the novelties were not of a high order and the artists already too familiar to the New York public. The admission price was reasonable, it is true; but the prices for refreshments were far too high for a broad portion of the promenaders. At the outset, bad weather kept people away; with better weather the business picked up somewhat but in the end the "great expectations" were not realized. The near 3,000 in attendance at the eventful opening tapered off dramatically after the first week. The effort failed to pay and was not repeated another year. The conclusion was that proprietor Nixon had spread himself thin with his various management projects:

> Mr. Nixon has some clever ideas, but he lacks the stamina to carry them out in the same spirit in which they are conceived; he is not steady enough; he has too many irons in the fire at once, and frequently burns his fingers in the vain attempt to haul them out and work them up at one and the same time.[11]

The summer circus season started out with a promise of trouble. The spring weather was hostile to the men under canvas, unleashing cold temperatures and plenty of rain. There seemed to be a pattern of winters lingering longer each year, delaying the dateline for the first seasonal shout of "Here we are, Mr. Marster!" The year was by no means a good one. Some managers made a little money, some held out with nothing to show for it, and still others fell by the wayside. Ohio was overrun with shows—Dan Rice, George F. Bailey & Co., VanAmburgh & Co., Thayer & Noyes, and others, leaving the state "showed out." Dr. Spalding made a little money with the Dan Rice circus, but the VanAmburgh and Lent shows were said to be the ones that came out of the year with the greatest success. The Canadian territory appeared to be one of the most profitable.

The L. B. Lent circus was out under the almost unpronounceable title of "The Hippozoonomadon," with the breath-taking addendum of "Lent's Mammoth National Circus, S. P. Stickney's Great Western Circus, J. G. Shepard's Great Eastern Circus, G. C. Quick's Hippopotamus Co., and Sands, Nathans & Co.'s Four Performing Elephants from Cooke's Amphitheatre, London." Press agent Charles H. Day called Lent a practical publicizer, particularly capable of judging the value of an attraction on its merits of an advertisement.[12] This was certainly confirmed by the 1862 press notices, couriers and small bills. They called special attention to the Quick-Smith-Nathans hippopotamus (Cushing having sold his share to J. J. Nathans) which, under Frank Howes' management, was rented to the rotund proprietor for the tenting season of 1862 and exhibited along with the arenic performances.

> The hippo flourished and grew prodigiously. The "hog show" made sad havoc with rival managers, as hundreds and thousands waited for and flocked to see the "only living hippopotamus."[13]

Advertising cuts show four elephants pulling the hippo cage which carried a twelve piece band atop. The copy promised the "River Horse" would make its entrance at the head of the procession, drawn by the largest elephants in the world—Victoria and Albert and Antony and Cleopatra. The well-read Lent used Classical and Biblical allusions to the beast (referred to in the *Clipper* as the "Hooping Jerusalem") to entice even the most devout into the tented exhibition. The ads read in part:

> From the White Nile, Egypt, the Great Behemoth of which Job says, Chaps. 4, 41, "Upon the earth there is not his like!" He is the only real Amphibious Animal ever exhibited, living in the water or out of it, under the water or on top of it. This is really THE GREATEST WONDER IN THE WORLD and will be exhibited in his IMMENSE AQUARIUM and in the ring at each performance.

A *Clipper* Hartford correspondent, calling himself Reynard, commented on the lavish use of posters weeks in advance of the show's arrival. Such display induced the local circle of piety to request a special showing of the beast *sans* circus performance. Lent acceded by having the hippo and elephants put through their paces at a unique ceremony sandwiched between the matinee and evening performances for those who "couldn't reconcile spangles with Christianity."[14]

During the tour through New York State and into Canada, the hippo and elephants were supported by an able cast of performers, some stars in their own right. A special import from *"La Cirque Imperiale,* Paris, and the Royal Amphitheatre, London," Ariana Felicei, appeared in an act called *"Les Reine Des Fees."* It is unclear what this queen of the fairies did for such billing but the advertised credentials were sufficient to justify it; although elsewhere she was identified as a rival of Zoyara. Mons. Rochelle and William Ducrow, Lent regulars, did their bit on *la perche*, the cloud swing and the leap for life. Vaulter and acrobat, Tom King, was there with his equestrienne wife, Virginia. The Stickney family—S. P., Emma, and young Robert—brought substance to the equestrian part of the program. Adolph Gonzales, the "Chilian Wonder," contributed his leaps and acrobatics. Richard Hernandez and Frank Howard were the scenic riders. The clowns were William Kennedy, Gary DeMott, and L. Nicholas Burke. The band was led by Charles Boswold.[15]

Dr. James L. Thayer and Charles Noyes began a partnership for the first time this year, one that was to last through 1869. The two men went on the road under the title of Thayer & Noyes Great United States Circus, opening in Girard, PA, on May 3.

Charles W. Noyes entered the circus business in the 1840s and was soon working with animals. While at Franconi's Hippodrome, New York City, he conquered the unruly elephant, Jennie; and the following summer, accompanied by her, joined the Crescent City Circus, probably owned by Dan Rice. Rice purchased the animal and renamed it Lalla Rookh. While in Rice's employ Noyes taught Lalla Rookh to walk the rope, broke a number of panthers and tigers, worked the perch and double trapeze with Omar T. Richardson, the bareback rider, appeared in the tournaments, and acted as ringmaster. He broke Rice's trick horse Excelsior, Jr., and presumably Old Putnam, the first rhinoceros trained in America. He continued working for Rice through 1861; then in the

I. A. Van Amburgh

fall of that year married the daughter of Agrippa Martin, once keeper of the famous bull, Hannibal.

The Thayer & Noyes' star attraction was the first-class bareback rider, James Robinson, whom we met when he was riding for the Nixon- Cooke circus at Niblo's Garden. Robinson, whose real name was James Michael Fitzgerald, was apprenticed to clown John Gossin at nine years of age. He remained with Gossin for two years, after which time he was indentured to John Robinson. He spent nine years with Old John and left at the top of his profession. Attractive in physique and personality, as a pad and bareback rider or carrying a boy on horseback he challenged all comers, offering up to $10,000 and his championship belt to anyone who could exceed him.

Alongside Robinson was a number of capable entertainers. Eaton Stone and John Glenroy added their skills of riding; Dr. James L. Thayer was joined by Jimmy Reynolds and Charles Seeley in the clown department; William Hogle and John Keefe performed the gymnastics; and Charles W. Noyes served as equestrian director and ringmaster.[16] In addition, the program was enhanced by some four-legged actors— Thayer's trick mules, Noyes' performing horse, Gen. Winfield Scott, and, as the advertising read, "fourteen of the prettiest, best and most valuable ring horses ever brought before the public."[17]

In his memoirs, John Glenroy left us an observation of public response to the war during his season with Thayer & Noyes:

> At every place we visited at that time excitement was intense, and we everywhere met volunteers going to the front to fight for the Union. Southern sympathizers were scarce in New York State in those days.[18]

The *Clipper* tells us that by the end of September the company left their wagons at the home base of Girard and took to the rails with plans for visiting Cleveland, Columbus, Indianapolis, St. Louis and other large cities.

Goodwin & Wilder's North American Circus went out this year with new wagons, harness, etc.—the wagons hand printed by the gymnastic team of Snow Brothers. Added to the title was "and Mrs. Dan Rice's Great Show." Mrs. Rice, formerly Margaret Ann Curran, had married Rice in Pittsburgh in 1842. Their first child, Elizabeth Margaret Rice, was born on February 11, 1844. Two years later another child was born, Catherine Ann Rice. The girls were affectionately called Libby and Kate. The name of Libby was to create confusion for later chroniclers since Mrs. Rice was also called by that diminutive. All the women became performers within Rice's arena. Margaret, as a star attraction, was billed as "Mrs. Dan Rice," with the attending publicity reading: "With her beautiful Menage Horses, Surry and Arab, in her elegant school of Lady Equestrianism," and as the "Equestrienne, with her racer Daniel Webster and the milk white steed Surry."[19]

Mrs. Rice, whose husband had presented as a model to the ladies of America, divorced him in 1860. She married Charles Warner, former treasurer of the Dan Rice show and a man some years her junior, in the fall of 1861. Charles Warner was a native of Great Barrington, MA. For some years he was assistant bar keeper at Florence's Hotel, corner of Broadway and Walker, New York City. Dan Rice introduced him to the profession as his treasurer in 1856, a job he held until 1860. Warner was well respected for honesty and other personal qualities.

Goodwin & Wilder's North American Circus and Mrs. Dan Rice's Great Show advertised the horse American Eagle, a highly trained animal belonging to Mrs. Jacob Showles (sister of Mrs. Dan Rice), and the white horse, Surry, a blind trick animal, as well as the mules John C. Heenan and Tom Sayers (named after the famous prize fighters), both owned by Mrs. Rice, "Queen of the Arena." The troupe carried two sideshows—Judge Ingalls exhibited snakes and other curiosities and the Whitney Brothers had a minstrel troupe.

Alongside Mrs. Rice were tight-rope artist, Jeanette Ellsler, and her clown husband, Nat Austin; Jacob Showles and his wife; John Barry, somersaulter and trick rider; Charles Shay, Japanese juggler and knife thrower; the gymnastic Snow Brothers; clowns Bobby Williams and J. C. Rivers; Master William Austin, the youthful gymnast; etc. The show traveled around New England. Admission was 25¢ for adults and 15¢ for children.

Yankee Robinson, perhaps one of the most inventive of amusement managers, formed a show he called "The Great Histronis." This was not a circus; rather, it capitalized on the history-making events occurring at the moment. Taking advantage of the patriotic fervor generated by the war, the program was made up of representations of the lives and times of American ancestors and the momentous and evolving contemporary chronicles, enacted by some one hundred women, men and horses. In a piece entitled *The Days of '76*, with comical allusions to the current rebellion, Robinson was able to pleasingly ply his Yankee character as wise-cracking Darius Dutton. The main show, which was performed in a new kind of pavilion, was augmented by a band of negro minstrels. Patriotism was displayed by admitting new army recruits into the performances free of charge. On July 28, the ingenious Yankee made a speech from the top of his ticket wagon, offering a $1.00 bounty for each new enlistee.

Gardner & Hemmings' Great American Circus with nine baggage wagons, a new pole conveyance and a new bandwagon, and twenty-eight newly purchased government horses, came out of the barn on Monday, April 28, at Frankford, PA, the enlargement made possible by the addition of John O'Brien as a silent partner with one-third interest in the organization. He also acted as assistant manager.

The troupe was headed by the talented Gardner family. Dan, still an attraction as a clown, was assisted in the laugh department by John Foster. Richard Hemmings was a standout both on the tight-rope and a wild horse. Miss Eliza Gardner continued to draw applause for her youthful riding, along with Madame Camille and La Petite Camille. Charles W. Parker, the posturer and contortionist, recovered from a severe illness just in time to resume his usual business of turning himself out of shape, and then back again, and then into all sorts of boxes and packages. And there was George Derious, one of the best man-monkeys in the business; Henry Moreste on the horizontal bars; and the Wallace Brothers, general gymnasts and acrobats. The trick horses were great favorites in "The Zouave Halt," in which they laid down, sat up on end, rolled over, changed sides, ran in Indian file, herded together, etc., all at word commands, with or without riders.

After leaving Frankford, the show appeared to be following a route which led them dangerously close to areas occupied by the Confederates. The threatened invasion of the "free states" effected the routing of many shows. On Tuesday, April 29, they were at German town; Wednesday, Chester; and Wilmington, DL, May 1st and 2nd. Later, they arrived in Harrisburg when marshal law was proclaimed due to the advancing rebel forces. Gettysburg, Hagerstown and Wilmington had been billed but since the company was already within eleven miles from the Southerners, it was determined prudent to retreat. To avoid disaster, the show closed the season early on September 8 in Hanover, PA.

The draft order went into effect on the first of August, coming, as it did, on the heels of the seven days of fighting before Richmond. The conscription law, which took many by surprise, effected nearly every class of society. Certainly, it was not received with glee by those

SOMETHING ENTIRELY NEW

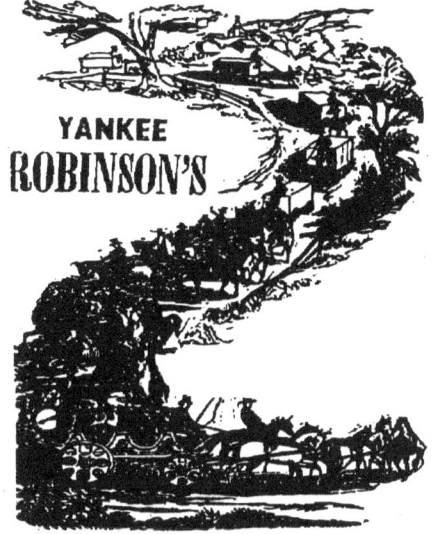

YANKEE ROBINSON'S
GREAT HISTRONIS!
The only establishment of the kind ever organized.
OVER 100 MEN AND HORSES.
FIVE LADY PERFORMERS.
TRIPLE BAND—BRASS—STRING—MILITARY.

The three GREAT EPOCHS in the history of our beloved country:
THE DAYS OF '76,
    UNCLE TOM'S CABIN,
        CIVIL WAR OF '61 AND '62.

It is too true that but very few of the large traveling establishments are suitable for ladies and families to visit. This one, being an exception, is justly termed the

GREAT MORAL EXHIBITION,

suited to the era we live in.
No old fogyism, but everything on the progressive plan and suited to the tastes of a promiscuous assemblage.

NEW STYLE PAVILION,
    NEW AND IMPROVED PORTABLE BOX SEATS,
        LARGE ELEVATED STAGE,
            APPROPRIATE SCENERY,
                COMPLICATED MACHINERY,
                    &C., &C., &C.

This is YANKEE ROBINSON'S 18th Annual Campaign. From his extensive knowledge of the South, he is enabled to give true representations of our "Southern Cousins." Remember YANKEE ROBINSON is the only individual who has ever successfully

"DONE THE DRAMA UP IN A BAG."

Midday matinee at 2. Evening performance at 8. Admission 25 cents. No half price. No extra charge for reserved seats.

AT UTICA,
(*Opposite Mr. George Hopper's Lot.*)
Wednesday, October 8th, 1862.
oct3—dtd

RICHARD HEMMINGS, Circus Proprietor and Manager.

who were eligible. "Actors and actresses gagged at it on the stage and audiences gagged at it off." It was unpalatable to most, yet most admitted that something had to be done to strengthen the armed forces, since able bodied men were becoming scarce. The occurrence sent men of draft age looking for physicians to give out certificates of disability; and, not surprisingly, there was an abundance of doctors willing to do just that.

The Confederate Congress had passed a similar act in April. All white males of ages 18 to 35 were required to serve; but, as in the North, a draftee could buy a substitute for himself. At this time there were Southern outcries about civil liberty infringement, a ridiculous irony from a Confederacy bent on protecting the right to own slaves.

Bull Run was in the news again when on August 29 and 30 Pope's army, which was drawn up along the Rappahannock to defend Washington, faced off with Lee's two corps under Jackson and Longstreet. When Pope advanced on Jackson, who held his ground until reinforcements by Lee and Longstreet arrived, the entire Confederate Army attacked the Union forces and compelled another retreat to Washington. The clouds over the capital grew darker.

A little over two weeks later, Gen. Lee crossed the Potomac and carried the war into the North, thereby striking terror into the hearts of the people of Maryland and Pennsylvania. Then, on September 17, his troops met the numerically superior forces of Gen. McClellan at the little creek of Antietam in Maryland. The all day battle resulted in the loss of about 11,000 men on each side. The next day Lee withdrew from the field. He had expected aid from the people of Maryland, which had not occurred; so he re-crossed the Potomac into Virginia. The Union victory, such as it was, was a psychological lift to the people of the North. Within a week, on September 22, President Lincoln issued the Emancipation Proclamation.

Hardly had the gates closed on the Cremorne Gardens, when James Nixon sent a company to Washington under the management of T. Allston Brown with plans for opening on Thursday, October 16. At this time, Washington was relatively free from military threat. McClellan, with his Army of the Potomac, was implanted on the Union side of the river, albeit under continual urging from the President to engage the Confederates and force them south.

A semi-permanent wooden and canvas building was erected at Pennsylvania Avenue and Seventh Street, said to be the same structure

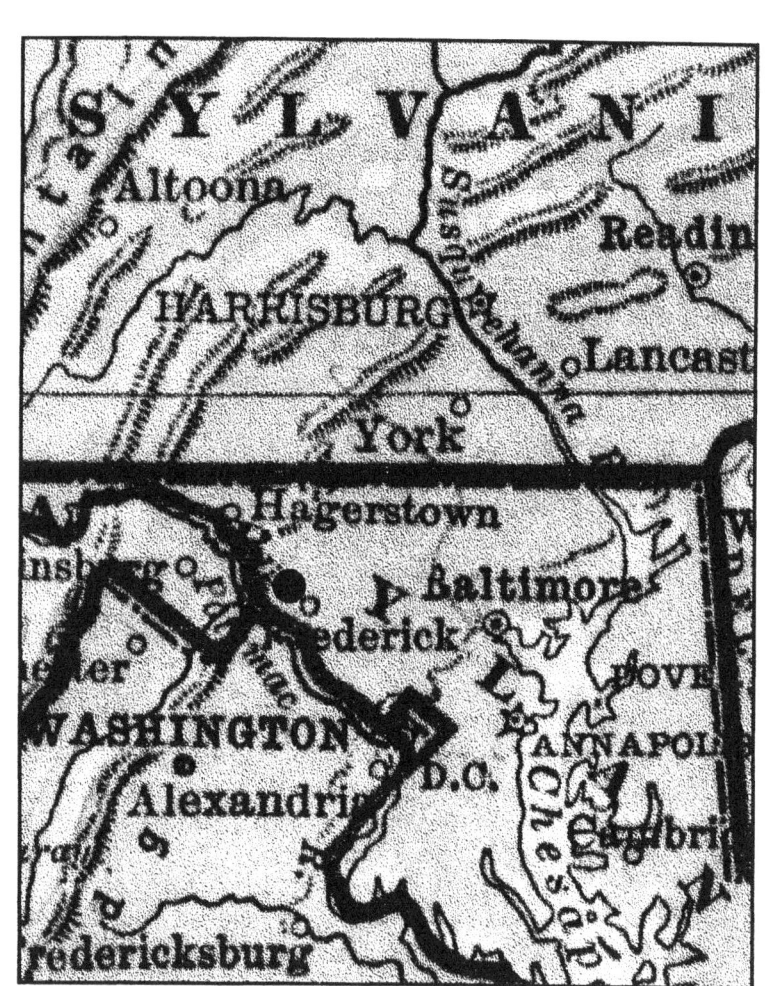

"●" Antietam

used at the Cremorne Gardens, New York, "the interior being high and dry, the seats so arranged that all can get a good view of the arena." The advertisement revealed that some 500 arm chairs were taken from Cremorne Gardens for use in Washington; and that a circus marquee was attached at a cost of $3,000, over which was a balcony for promenade concerts to be given every noon and evening. But a notice abruptly appeared in the papers, announcing a postponement of the opening until Saturday, October 18. Apparently the building had not been readied for occupancy in time.

> On Saturday night the new and beautiful Exhibition Temple was formally opened to the public. The rush of patrons was extensive, and, long before the time designed for the commencement of the entertainments, the auditorium was densely packed. Hundreds were compelled to undergo disappointment, the management refusing to sell more tickets than there was capacity for accommodating the purchasers.[20]

Nixon's advertisements were generous in their use of space and vociferous in descriptive phrasing. "Look out for the striped canopy!" "Behold the mammoth bill boards!" They identified the establishment as being "Nixon's Cremorne Garden Circus, From the Cremorne Gardens, the Palace of Music, and Equestrian School, New York, with a Full Equestrian Company and the Popular Spanish Ballet Troupe." Here Nixon continues to intermix art and entertainment. The initial ads made a particular point in suggesting that the interior of the building was "entirely different from the objectionable tents under which the ordinary strolling showmen are forced to give their entertainments," a statement which might suggest the presence of a tented competitor within the locality. And there was.

The Gardner & Hemmings circus was already set up on the city market lot. In his reminiscences, Richard Hemmings recalled that he and his partners decided to take a show to Washington to get money ahead for the 1863 season. As has been already recounted, they had closed the summer tour early at Hanover, PA.

> We opened negotiations with a man by the name of Grover, who managed a theatre there. He came on to Philadelphia to talk over our proposition, and before he left we had arranged with him to bring on our show and work on percentage basis. We had great difficulty in moving our show there, either by rail or boat, as every conveyance was occupied in transporting the soldiers, ammunition and supplies; but at last we

managed to get there, and opened under a 120-foot round top where the market is now located, and we did a big business.[21]

Presumably, both parties vied for the large number of daily visitors to the city, as well as the thousands of soldiers billeted in and around there. The Nixon camp was well fortified, featuring the exciting *danseuse*, Isabel Cubas, as well as Dr. James L. Thayer and his comic mules, the Conrad Brothers, Barney Carroll and daughter, Charles Madigan, Charles Devere, William Naylor, Thomas Armstrong, Sidney Webb, Mlle. Augusta (her first appearance in America), and the little men, Colonel Small and Commodore Foote. Also Harry Whitby, the successful horse-breaker, was there with his young apprentices, Willie, Johnny, and Elvira. The latter, ironically, would in a short time become Mrs. Richard Hemmings.

According to Hemmings' account, in order to adequately compete with the Nixon troupe, an a.rangement was made with P. T. Barnum for the services of the Albino Family, General Tom Thumb and Commodore Nutt. In retaliation, Nixon debased Barnum in his newspaper advertisements. Hearing of this, Barnum went to Washington "with fire in his eye," got hold of the best newspaper man in town, and sent him forth to do, what the *Clipper* later labeled, "the battle of the dwarfs." With the master of publicity as a foe, Hemmings suggested, Nixon's camp soon retreated to Baltimore.

Further investigation tends to challenge the accuracy of such recollections. In examining the Washington, DC, *Daily National Intelligencer* from September 20 through December 31, 1862, we find no reference to a Gardner & Hemmings circus. Perhaps they were too impoverished as a relatively new organization to utilize newspaper advertising. But after Nixon's initial announcement on October 15, an opposition ad appeared the following day. It was for Barnum's Museum, Circus and Mammoth Amphitheatre at Louisiana Avenue and Tenth Street, which was exhibiting the Albino Family, Commodore Nutt, General Tom Thumb, Old Adams' California Bears, the famous grizzly Samson, and all the members of the Great American Circus, which included Richard Hemmings and Dan Gardner in the list of performers. The same day an item appeared on page one:

> Barnum, of world-wide reputation, is now daily and nightly affording our citizens an opportunity of witnessing his famous museum and circus. Thousands are rushing to see the wonderful sights which he unfolds for the amusement of young and old.[22]

A few days later, in an advertisement of October 20, Nixon, with unabashed bravado, dropped the glove for a so-called "battle of the dwarfs":[23]

A WAY TO TEST RELATIVE MERITS, and add to the fund of the Soldiers' Aid Association, the undersigned seeing a card signed P. T. Barnum, manager of Barnum's Bear Show, &c., in which he states that he has THE SMALLEST DWARF IN THE WORLD, begs leave to issue the following conditions of a challenge, to wit:

1. To place Commodore NUTT and Commordore FOOT together on a platform in some respectable building in this city, and let the public determine which is the *smaller* of the two.

2. To allow a committee chosen by Mr. Barnum and myself, and an umpire appointed by the committee, to enter into conversations with the Dwarfs on ordinary subjects—politics, geography, military matters, works of art, foreign languages, &c., and then determine the comparative mental powers of each.

3. To allow both Dwarfs to give specimens of their performances, to show the extent of their artistic acquisitions.

4. To allow the proceeds of the exhibition to go to the fund of the Soldiers' Aid Association.

5. To show the authenticated family records of both, so that their ages can be unmistakably determined.

The above stipulation I have drawn from a letter previously sent by me to Mr. Barnum, but which he has not answered. Perhaps it did not reach him; so I offer the above in order that he and the public shall see them, and in the hopes that he will accept my proposition.

JAMES M. NIXON
Proprietor of Cremorne Garden Circus

It is not surprising that Barnum, in his own defense, responded with a card in the newspaper the following day:

☞ The only reply Mr. Barnum thinks necessary to make to the challenge contained in this morning's paper is that he will not aid in a newspaper warfare for the purpose of giving notoriety to an itinerant adventurer, whose only features are the "armed chairs" and a party of bogus *figurantes*, palmed upon the public as "Spanish," but whose faces have never been outside of the United States, not withstanding their pompous foreign announcement.

With regard to the proposed donation to the Soldiers' Aid Association, Mr. Barnum has already paid thousands of dollars to aid the war for the Union; and he agrees that the services of Commodore Nutt, General Tom Thumb, or any other attraction which he has control of, are at the FREE disposal of the Soldiers' Aid Association whenever they hold a fair or exhibition where they may be of use to them. And Mr. B. will also present one thousand dollars to this Association whenever the showman alluded to will give five hundred dollars, after having paid up his unfortunate employees.

The ladies and gentlemen who daily and nightly throng Mr. Barnum's establishment declare that never within their memory has been seen any "man in miniature" worthy of being named or thought of, or who will in the slightest degree compare with these symmetrical, intelligent, and talented little gentlemen—Commodore Nutt and General Tom Thumb; and, furthermore, that they never before witnessed in any one establishment such a vast and amusing concentration of talent and novelty as are to be seen at Barnum's Museum, Circus and Menagerie.

With this reply to the notoriety seeking sojourner, it is respectfully recommended that the gentleman move along to some locality where his genius will be better appreciated.

Barnum's reply was quite unnecessary, for on the 25th a display ad announced the last two days of the Barnum's Museum, Circus and Menagerie. Coincidentally, on the 26th McClellan moved his Army of the Potomac for the first time in two months across the river and into Virginia. The Nixon adversaries—Thumb, Nutt & Co., along with Gardner & Hemmings—left leave their field of battle on the 28th. Nixon had Washington to himself.

Unrivaled, the Nixon Cremorne Garden Circus seemingly prospered. Eaton Stone, the celebrated equestrian, styled the "Wizard Horseman," began an engagement on October 27, in which he impersonated the "Comanche on the War Path." Dr. James L. Thayer was still on hand with his black and white mules, as were the original company of circus performers and, for a short time longer, the enchanting Isabel Cubas. William Conrad, the Teutonic clown, took a benefit on November 8. On the 11th, *The Field of the Cloth of Gold* was unveiled, a piece that Nixon had previously staged at Franconi's Hippodrome to great success. On the 12th, Prof. Heller, "adept in the mysterious arts of chemistry and rapid manipulations" appeared. The English magician and pianist had arrived in America in the fall of 1852 and made his debut at the Museum in Albany, NY; after which, he spent some years performing throughout the country.

There were more November arrivals and additions. The clown Jimmy Reynolds was introduced into to the program on the 17th. Pony races were advertised for the 22nd, along with the Sherwood family, and with them, of course, the original "Pete Jenkins." More new faces were gradually supplemented, among which were Luke and Charles Rivers, the clown Frank Phelps, and a cornet band.

Gardner & Hemmings opened a new amphitheatre in Philadelphia on Monday, November 24, just a month after leaving Washington. The building, formerly known as National Hall, was located on the south side of Market Street above Twelfth. The large room on the second floor of the structure, formerly used for meetings, was fitted up "neatly but not gorgeously." This upper-story circus exhibition was only the second such on record. There was a balcony in the south end of the room—admission 50¢. Under the balcony were the dressing rooms, etc. On the north end of the ring, rising step by step, was the parquet or pit—at 25¢. The gallery above this could be entered for 15¢. A critic suggested that more flash was needed outside the house since the locale had not been used for public exhibitions in the past. The performances were executed by Richard Hemmings, little Eliza Gardner, the Delevanti Brothers, the Kincades, and Frank and Marie Whittaker. Dan Gardner and John Foster were the clowns of the arena.

It was during this stand when James E. Cooper entered the circus business. Cooper had started professional life at age fifteen by opening a line of omnibuses from Philadelphia on the old Second Street Pike to Fox Chase. He sold this line after three years and purchased the Germantown Road Omnibus Line. Shortly afterward, he sold out and moved to Washington, DC, where he started another omnibus line and in no time controlled every line in the city. He remained there until the present winter season, when he returned to Philadelpia and entered the circus business with Dan Gardner, Richard Hemmings and John O'Brien at National Hall.

On December 3 it was revealed that James M. Nixon planned to establish a theatre in Alexandria where spectacles would be produced, replete with scenery, machinery, horsemanship and dramatic effects. It was noted on the 5th that he was at present in Washington and would personally superintend the direction of his affairs. The double company was divided and a portion moved over to Alexandria for opening on Monday, December 8.

With Nixon's departure to Alexandria, the building was turned over to Tom King, the champion leaper. Still operating under the banner of Nixon's Cremorne Garden Circus, King opened on the 8th with Barney Carroll and daughter, the Conrad Brothers, William F. Smith, Mons. Rochelle and others for a week's engagement. This has all the appearance of Nixon's divided company. The lateness of the season seemed to present no problem. The weather remained pleasant and, we were informed, the amphitheatre was now being heated by patent furnaces, making it the most comfortable arena ever erected in the city. The Washington public exhibited sufficient interest to allow the engagement to be extended through Saturday, December 20.

During this stand, some fifty miles removed the battle for Fredericksburg occurred. The Army of the Potomac, a force of 120,000 men led by Gen. Ambrose E. Burnside, who had replaced McClellan, held the north bank of the river at Falmouth. With his 78,000 men, General Lee established himself on the high bluffs of the Rappahannock River near Fredericksburg. On December 13, Burnside transported his men across the river by pontoon bridges to attack Lee's strongly entrenched troops. Six assaults and two nights later, under the cover of a storm, the remainder of the Union army was brought back to Falmouth, with a loss of 12,653 men. Business in the New York theatres fell off by half once the disastrous news was received.

On Monday the 22nd the circus troupe returned from Alexandria where, the advertisements boasted in typical Nixon style, "for a period of two weeks they appeared before 21,000 people." The double company apparently remained until Friday, the 26th, when Dr. Richard P. Jones, the affable circus writer, took a benefit. With that, the Nixon Washington adventure ended for the year.

The gloom brought about from the Fredericksburg disaster was turned into rejoicing only a few weeks later. At the battle of Murfreesboro, or Stones River, TN, fought from December 31 to January 2, the Confederate forces under Gen. Braxton Bragg were repulsed by the Union army under Gen. William S. Rosecrans. The victory opened the way for the Union advance to Chattanooga and finally to "Atlanta and the sea."

"✦" Battle of Fredericksburg

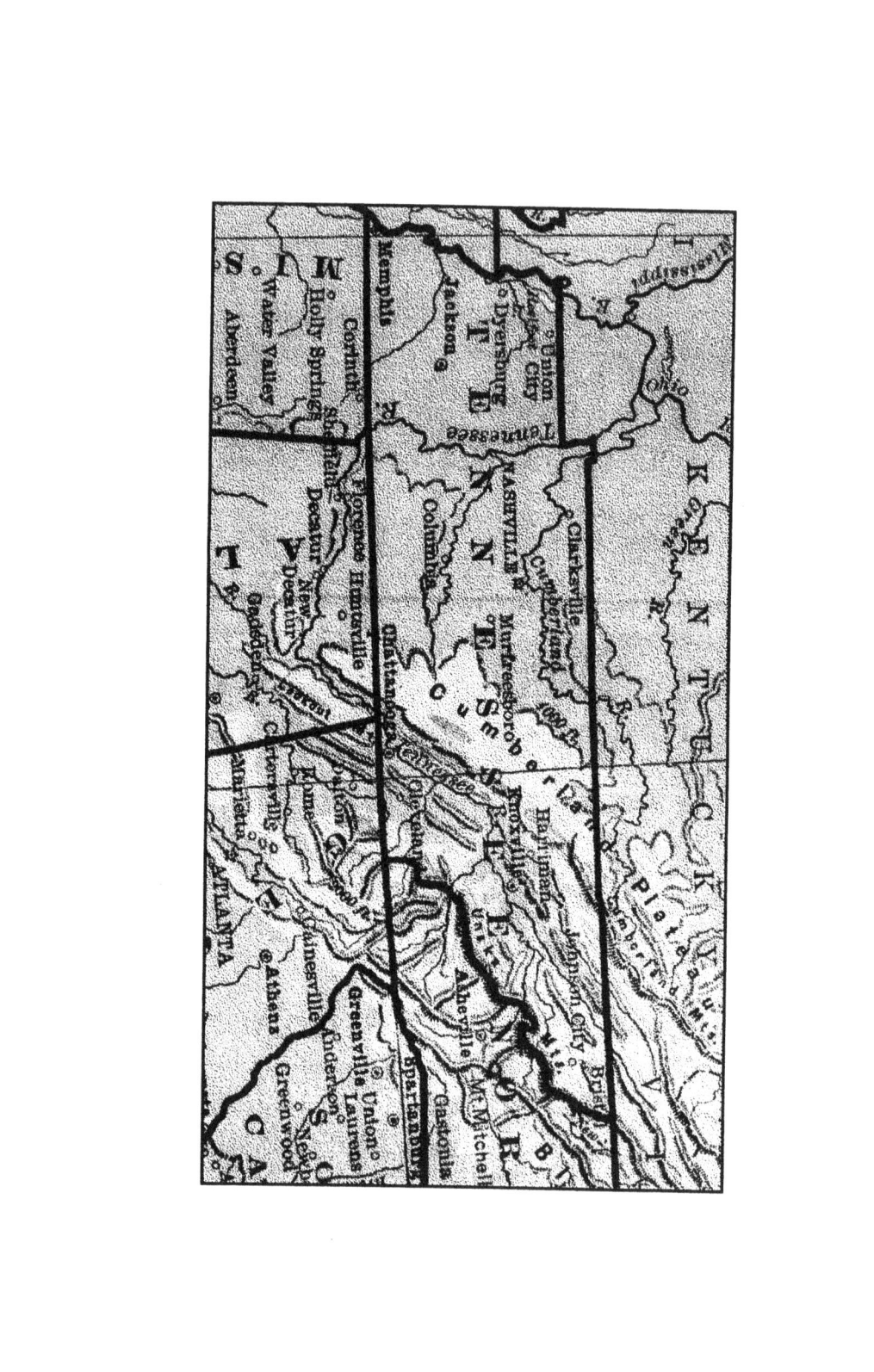

CIRCUSES AND MENAGERIES, 1862: Antonio Bros.; George F. Bailey & Co.; Bartholomew (California); George W. DeHaven; Gardner & Hemmings; Goodwin & Wilder with Mrs. Dan Rice; Tom King (Washington, DC); L. B. Lent; E. F. & J. Mabie; Madigan & Carroll; Nagle & Kincaid; Nixon's Cremorne Garden (New York); Old Cary; Dan Rice; Alexander Robinson; Robinson & Lake; Robinson & Toole (Canada); R. Sands & Co.; Yankee Robinson (quasi-circus); Spalding & Rogers; (South America, West Indies); S. Q. Stokes (later Zoyara); Thayer & Noyes; VanAmburgh & Co.; John Wilson.

NOTES

[1] Information on river boats comes from notes submitted by Stuart Thayer and from his *Bandwagon* column, "One Sheet," for November/December, 1974, p. 21.

[2] On November 25, 1873, Keeler left for Cuba as a special correspondent for the New York *Tribune*. He served the newspaper in Santiago during the excitement over the *Virginius* massacre—the execution of 53 men aboard a U. S. ship by the Spanish in 1873 because the vessel was carrying arms to Cuba. On the night of December 17, 1873, while en route from Santiago to Havana on his return to New York, he either fell or was thrown overboard and disappeared into the sea—dead at but thirty-three years of age.

[3] Conklin, "Showing Under Two Flags," p. 113.

[4] Webster, p. 2.

[5] Others included J. S. K. Nellis, William Franklin, Daniel Long and wife, etc.

[6] Odell, VII, p. 402.

[7] Letter to the *Clipper* dated January 11, 1862, under the name "Young Rapid," New York *Clipper*, January 18, 1862, p. 318.

[8] Taken from the Philadelphia *Sunday Dispatch* of March 16, reproduced in the New York *Clipper*, March 22, 1862, p. 391.

[9] Dingess Manuscript, p. 345.

[10] *Ibid.*, p. 344.

[11] New York *Clipper*, August 30, 1862, 158.

[12] Day, *Ink from a Circus Press Agent*, p. 67.

[13] Day, "History of American Circus and Tented Exhibitions," p. 32.

[14] New York *Clipper*, May 31, 1862, p. 51.

[15] Others on the bills were Mary Phelps, R. C. Rochford, Mlle. Irene Blanche, John Burnside, J. Benshaw, George W. Hall, Charles Jennings, James Glenroy, Maurice Sands, Hubert Forrest, James Spalding, Mlle. Ella Burke.

[16] Others listed were Mlle. Elizabeth, J. W. Thompson, Johnny Clark, and Mme. Duval.

[17] Rochester (NY) *Daily Union and Advertiser*, May 9, 1862; from Chang Reynolds' collection.
[18] Glenroy, p. 127.
[19] MacAllister, *People of the Early Circus*, p. 57.
[20] Washington (DC) *Daily National Intelligencer*, October 20, 1862, p. 1.
[21] Fostell, p. 45.
[22] Washington (DC) *Daily National Intelligencer*, October 16, 1862, p. 1.
[23] Washington (DC) *Daily National Intelligencer*, October 20, 1862, p. 3.

DEATHS IN 1862: Wire walker **Mons. DeBach**, in Havana, Cuba, of yellow fever, March; **Charles Reed**, with the Madigan circus, fell from the top of a center pole at Greenpoint, Long Island, May 17; **Charles Watson**, a member of the Watson family, in Plymouth, England, July 13; **Henry P. Madigan**, patriarch of the Madigan family, of consumption in Kingston, Jamaica, December 15, age 48; **Charles H. "Doc" Bassett**, California circus proprietor, of fever in Equador; **James M. June**, brother of John J. and Stebbins, and nephew of Lewis June; **Charles Wright**, who may have been the first "lion keeper" in America; **Alexander McCord**, known in the profession as Signor Tilghman, acrobat and contortionist, killed in one of the Battles of Bull Run; **Madame Farini**, in Havana, November 30 (or December 11), after falling from being carried on a tight-rope; **Sarah Batchelder**, equestrienne, in Callao, Peru, early August; **Mme. Shepherd**, equestrienne, in London, England, June 22.

"✿" Chambersburg, "✳" Carlisle, "✦" Gettysburg

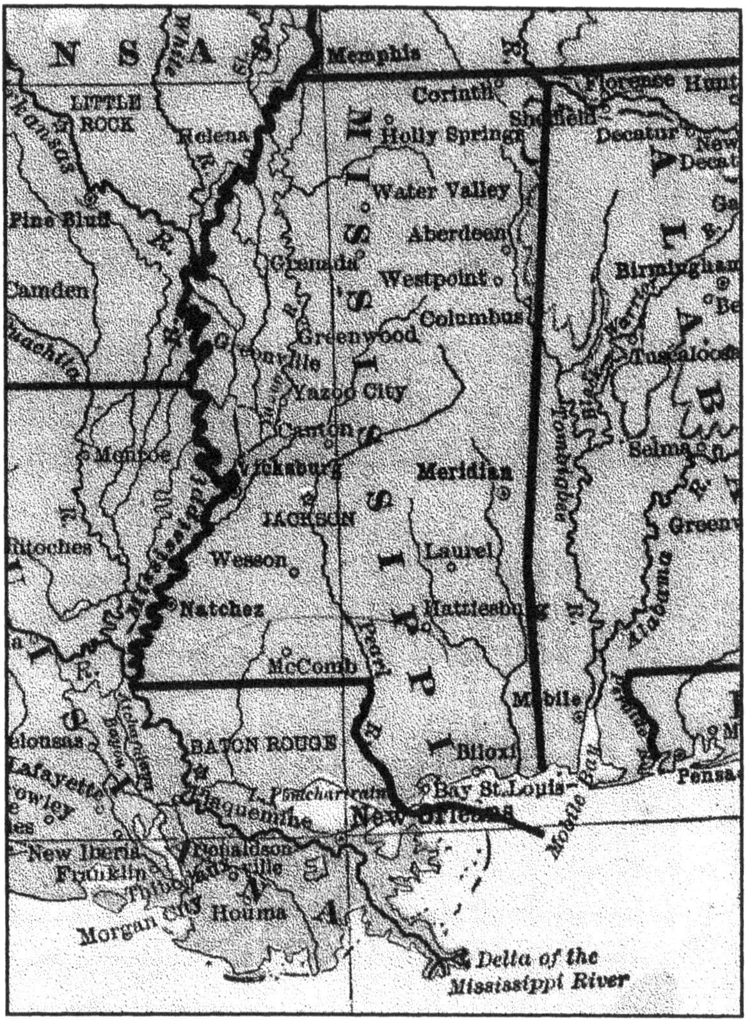

Memphis
LITTLE ROCK
Helena
Pine Bluff
Camden
Corinth
Holly Springs
Water Valley
Aberdeen
Westpoint
Columbus
Grenada
Greenwood
Yazoo City
Canton
Monroe
Vicksburg
JACKSON
Meridian
Wesson
Laurel
Natchez
Hattiesburg
McComb
Mobile
Biloxi
BATON ROUGE
Bay St. Louis
New Orleans
Mobile Bay
New Iberia
Franklin
Houma
Morgan City
Delta of the
Mississippi River
Birmingham
Decatur
Selma
Pearl R.
Mississippi
Tombigbee
Alabama

1863

The North won three of the most important battles of the Civil War this year. Two of these victories occurred in early July at Gettysburg and, after a long siege, at Vicksburg. In the fall, the third crucial engagement was staged in the area around Chattanooga. On January 29, Gen. Grant was put in command of the Army of the West with orders to capture Vicksburg. The location of the city, sitting on the east side of the Mississippi, overlooking a hairpin bend in the river from a high bluff, made such a campaign difficult. All earlier attacks against it had failed. But what transpired in the spring is something from the pages of a theatrical piece. Grant put his men to work with pick and shovel in an attempt to dig a canal across the neck of land opposite the city and thus bypass Vicksburg by turning the Mississippi from its old bed. Alas! this back-breaking effort failed to change the course of the mighty river.

Then it became clear to Grant that Vicksburg could be approached only from the south and east. To accomplish this the Union fleet would have to face the Confederate batteries while the gunboats went down the stream as the foot soldiers marched along the west and opposite shore. The plans completed, the troops set out in the dark of night; but, lo! the Confederates learned of the operation and sent a party across the river to set fire to houses along the shore so that their gunners might have light to see the enemy movement. In the turmoil that followed, all but one of the Union vessels ran by the batteries in safety and, once past the city, Grant's soldiers were transported to the eastern bank. This was accomplished by the end of April.

Before the Union finally took over Vicksburg, the South won one of its greatest victories of the Civil War at Chancellorsville, a town located in eastern Virginia, adjacent to the Rappahannock, about half the distance between the two capitals. At the start of the battle, Lee had about 60,000 men in a region east of Chancellorsville and south of Fredericksburg. The Union army consisted of an overwhelming force of 130,000. Hooker sent his forces across the river to attack the Confederate positions on April 27; but, out-maneuvered and out-fought, the Northerners were sent reeling back across the Rappahannock on May 5 with losses in killed, wounded, and missing amounting to 17,000, or

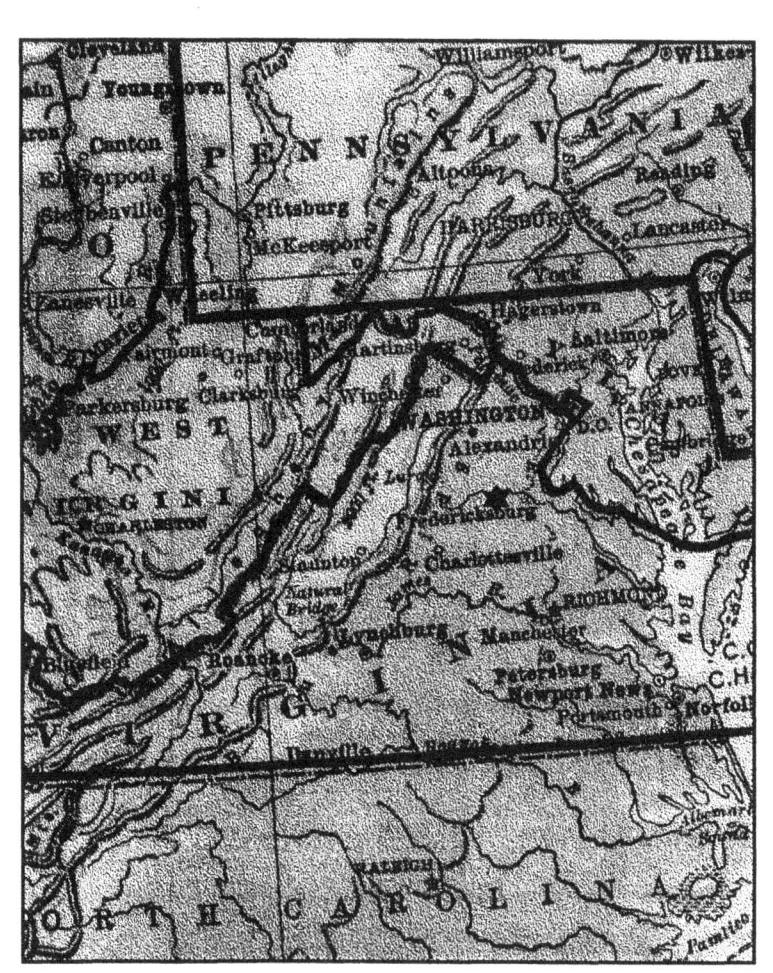

"★" Chancellorsville

about 13 percent of the total force. The Confederates lost 13,000 or more than 21 percent of the Army of Northern Virginia; and with the death of Stonewall Jackson, they lost an irreplaceable leader. The South paid dearly for its victory.

South-central Pennsylvania suddenly became off-limits for circuses by June 23 when Gen. Richard S. Ewell's rebel forces crossed the Potomac and approached Chambersburg.` Carlisle and York were taken by them on the 27th and 28th as they advanced within ten miles of Harrisburg. Then, on the 1st of July, the historic battle of Gettysburg began. With the Union victory, southern Pennsylvania was no longer a battlefield. There is nothing to indicate, however, that during those days of Confederate incursion any circuses were within the danger zone.[1]

Directly following the battle at Gettysburg, Gen. Grant ended a six weeks' siege of Vicksburg. On the 4th of July, Gen. Pemberton, no longer willing to withstand the bombardment, surrendered the city. Four days later, Gen. Banks captured Port Hudson, LA. The entire Mississippi river was now under Union control.

Because of a drop in enrollment of volunteers and a high rate of desertion, the first compulsory draft occurred in July, momentarily turning the public mind away from amusements. By executive order, citizens were compelled to report for military duty. Until the Civil War there had been no general military draft in America; consequently, the compulsory service embittered the public. Like in all wars, there were those who wanted no part of soldering and did what they could to avoid it. Enrolling officers roamed about, taking names and ages, making many draftable men fearful of induction. In the backwoods of the Ohio Valley and other such places, men "hid out" to avoid serving. There were instances of conscription officers being murdered. Draft riots occurred in cities and towns from Massachusetts to Wisconsin. Mandatory drafting was made even more unpopular by provisions that allowed a draftee to procure a substitute to serve in his place or to avoid induction by paying a fee of $300 to the federal government.

> The public are on the "anxious bench"; hot weather is at hand, and the idea of shouldering a musket, toting along a heavy knapsack, etc., with the thermometer at 90 degrees, has induced many people to hurry off to the country, and this, with the fast approaching close of the season, is thinning out the attendance of our theatres, halls and saloons.[2]

In mid-July a bloody draft riot erupted in New York City. "It's a rich man's war, a poor man's fight," was the cry. Racial and class hatreds surfaced into lynchings and arson. Tensions mounted on Monday, July 13, when about 4,000 men, mostly poor Irish laborers, marched to the draft drawing. When the first names were read, the crowd surged forward, causing the police to open fire. In the following two days, as many as 70,000 people may have been caught up in the "carnival of violence," as one observer called it. Order was restored on the 16th when five regiments from Gettysburg moved in with cannons and Gatling guns.

The prospect of success looked more promising for amusement enterprises than it had in the past two years. Despite unrest created by the draft, New York and other large cities were filled with partying troops. There were soldiers in the theatres, in the music and minstrel halls, in the underground "free and easies" on Broadway, in stages, cars and lunchrooms—soldiers everywhere. Then, too, the general public was beginning to take the war in stride and now had the money to spend on diversions.

Still, the start of the summer season did not project this for circuses. Early on, nasty weather set in, disrupting operations and discouraging attendance. VanAmburgh & Co., touring in Indiana in June, found business to be unusually bad, exacerbated by various local conditions. "The present is the worst season this company has ever experienced—high board, poor towns, bad roads, and fearfully high licenses eating up the receipts."[3] Added to this was the discombobulation caused by the battle along the Rappahannock.

But shortly the circus situation, mirroring the military successes of the North, gave reason for managers to sing a more joyous anthem, with some shows doubling their receipts from the 1862 season. "The country people are said to have plenty of money, and they turn out *en masse* at every show that comes along," was the report.

Peter Conklin claimed that after the fall of Vicksburg, a circus he was with entered the area and performed to $10,000 a day, "all soldiers, blue coats and brass buttons, not a female in the crowd."[4] Although the gross income suggested here may be an exaggeration, it is indicative of the financial opportunities for shows following close on the heels of the battling forces or spreading their canvases where troops were congregated, awaiting consignment and with little entertainment. Because of the restricted territory, routing through the Confederacy being out of the question, many companies were paying more attention to the larger cities, taking advantage of soldiers home on leave as well as an urban society eager for escape from daily news of the fighting. The adult admission price for the eastern states held generally at 25¢. Beyond the Ohio River to the west, audiences paid double that amount.

The successful season may have been due in part to circuses placing greater emphasis on sideshows, which were potentially big money-makers, with receipts reaching over $150 a day or more. There was a recent instance of one such establishment which, at season's end, had more money in the till than the circus itself.[5]

These auxiliary entertainments, generally exhibited in a small tent or tents alongside the main canvas, were usually run by men who had secured and paid handsomely for the privilege to accompany the circuses and take advantage of the crowds enticed thither by them. Some circus proprietors, however, managed their own sideshows, thereby enjoying the full monetary rewards.

Generally, the sideshow manager of one of these concerns started out early in the morning in a two-horse wagon so as to be up and prepared to "bally" as soon as there was a visible stir of bodies to work on or when the circus parade, like the pied piper, assembled a following of people at the show lot to watch the pitching of the big top. At this time, the "blower," in stentorian tones, would inveigle the locals to part with anywhere from 10¢ to 25¢ for the privilege of entering the little tent to observe a five-legged cow, a sword swallower, a fat woman, an Ethiopian band, or a myriad of other curiosities. When it was time for the circus performance to begin, the sideshow closed its doors and remained "not open for business" until the main show was over and the spill of bodies flowed from under the white canvas pavilion onto the open grounds. Then, with no holds barred, the "blower" would go at it again, working his verbal magic to fill his little curiosity shop before the townspeople disappeared homeward.

This year VanAmburgh & Co. built two "splendid curiosity wagons" to house wax figures and views of the war's battlegrounds. For L. B. Lent's circus, Joseph Cushing, the American showman from London, purchased a 50-foot sideshow canvas and covered every available space with full length paintings—numbering forty-two—of the various performers. This was considered to be a new idea. The interest in such exhibitions sent Avery Smith and Gerard Quick to Europe for the purpose of collecting animals and curiosities in that part of the world.

D. W. STONE.

Political sensitivity at this time had a profound effect on the selection of circus titles. Words such as "National," "Union," "Monitor," and the like, implied a loyalty to the Northern cause in way of condescension to local patriotism. After the partnership between Robinson & Lake was dissolved in Cincinnati on January 12, John Robinson went out under the designation of Robinson & Bros. for the 1863 season. Richard E. Conover speculated that because the Robinson name was so identified with being a Southern circus, "Southern horses, Southern riders and Southern enterprises against the world," when the show was confined to the North, discretion necessitated the elimination of the well known showman's identity by obscuring it through another title.[6] Later, with a flash of patriotism, the show toured as the Great Union Combination. Then, in 1866, with the war over and Southern territory being invaded by any number of shows, the flag of John Robinson's Great Combination Circus was boldly unfurled. But, ironically, Robinson's circus was not among the shows that rushed into the South.

After having parted with John Robinson and the enterprise of Robinson & Lake, William Lake took out Lake & Co.'s Great Western Circus, managed by Levi J. North, the Edwin Forrest of circusdom, who also had an interest in the show. Starting from Springfield, the troupe moved through Illinois, Iowa, and Indiana during their regular season. Then, perhaps taking advantage of army concentrations, the managers became the first circus to enter Nashville since the start of the war. They set up at the corner of College and Jackson Streets on a Tuesday, November 3, and remained through Saturday, November 28. North disposed of his interest before the show opened for a week at Cairo on December 8. Prominent among the performers were William, Agnes and little Alice Lake; the riding family of Eben W. Perry and his children Jennie and Master Thomas; Hiram Marks, "Byronic clown" and scenic rider; the contortionist William Lester; gymnast George Cutler; and the Lazelle Brothers, groupings and trapeze work. There was the performing horse, Don Juan, and a spotted trick mule, three and a half hands high, that leaped over three large horses standing erect. All this could be seen for 50¢, "servants," 25¢.

On the 27th a number of soldiers of the 5th Kentucky Cavalry charged the front door of the circus. Entrance was blocked by the guards stationed there and a general fight ensued. There were several shots fired which resulted in the death of a corporal of the Provost Guard and the wounding of one of the cavalrymen and death of another. The miscreants were placed under arrest and supposedly given their just rewards.[7]

Nearly every year we see new men entering into circus management. Some last but a short time, while others remain in the hunt and become stalwarts in the profession. New entries for 1863 were John O'Brien, S. O. Wheeler, and Ben Maginley. Of the three, John O'Brien was the most successful and would become a prominent figure in circusdom for the next twenty years.

John V. "Pogey" O'Brien was born in Frankford, now a part of Philadelphia, the son of a stone mason. At the age of 13, he started his professional life as a stage driver and worked at that occupation until he bought out his employer in 1857. He entered the circus business in 1861, when he leased harness and horses to Gardner & Hemmings and acted as boss hostler. In 1862 he purchased a one-third interest in the show and performed the duties of assistant manager.

Disposing of his share of the property to James E. Cooper five weeks into the 1863 summer season, he organized "Bryan's (sometimes referred to as Brian's) National Circus with Mrs. Dan Rice" for touring in Pennsylvania and New York State. Mrs. Rice, now Mrs. Warner, performed her blind, white horse, Surry, and her charger, Champion. Husband Charles Warner was the treasurer, Dr. Richard P. Jones handled the press, and Charles Castle did the contracting. The bills featured the likes of the Whitby family, George Derious, Frank Whittaker, William Kennedy, Charles King (a pupil of Harry Whitby), the Conrad Brothers, and Nosher's Keystone Cornet Band (later referred to as Britner's Keystone Cornet Band). The admission was 25¢ with no half-price tickets and no reserved seats.

The description of "Show" or "Great Show," so familiarly connected with Dan Rice's circus advertising, which was exploited by Mrs. Rice the previous year, is missing here. The Supreme Court of New York State granted an injunction against her and others using the words in advertising when associated with the Rice name; however some ads did include the phrase, "managed by Mrs. C. Warner, formerly Mrs. Dan Rice."

Silas O. Wheeler newly appeared on the circus scene with Wheeler's International Circus out of Boston. Little seems to be known of his previous activity. Circus historian Copeland MacAllister has speculated that Wheeler may have been associated with George K. Goodwin in a menagerie venture at 98 Hanover Street, Boston, advertised for the winter of 1859-60 and which toured New England the following summer. He may also have been connected with Goodwin & Wilder's North American Circus in 1862.[8] Whatever his past, S. O. Wheeler's circus opened on April 20 at Cambridgeport, MA, just across the Charles River from Bean Town with equestrienne Louise Tourniaire as the featured attraction.

Louise Tourniaire, often referred to as Madame Tourniaire, was born in Germany of a family of acrobats by the name of Ciseck (or Zhieskick). She apprenticed to the Tourniaires in Europe as a child rider at the age of 5 and later married a member of that family, François Tourniaire. At the *Cirque Napoleon* in Paris she became the first female to successfully ride a four-horse act. In the early 1840s, Londoners were astonished by the nerve, daring and grace displayed in her equestrienne feats and by her outstanding *manège* act. The Tourniaires came to America in 1846—Louise, François and Louise's three equestrian brothers, Benoit, Theodore and Ferdinand, who had also been pupils of François and who all took the name of Tourniaire professionally.

The "Wild Men of Borneo" were a feature in Wheeler's sideshow. They were in fact Hiram and Barney Davis, sons of a Weston, Massachusetts farmer, both mentally retarded and small of stature. Silas Wheeler had connections in Weston, MA, and may well have been the first to exhibit this famous team. The boys' agent was Hanaford A. Warner of Waltham, MA, with whom they lived when not on the road.

Wheeler moved into Canada but, finding it not to his liking, did a turn-about for New Hampshire and other New England states where he met with a more prosperous reception. The season closed on the Boston Fairgrounds at Harrison Avenue and Newton Street.

Maginley's Cosmopolitan Circus, a new show, was launched in July by roly-poly Ben R. Maginley. This colorful gentleman, who was born of well-to-do Philadelphia parents, left home at age seventeen to join a dramatic stock company. During his stage career he performed in many of the major dramas of his time and developed into an experienced character actor. At the start of the war he was stage manager and low comedian in the New Memphis Theatre company at Memphis, TN. An unsuccessful investment in an arenic venture forced his entry into the circus business. He employed Oliver Bell to break horses for the establishment, who, within the short span of ten days, succeeded in making ring stock out of them. Maginley, a robust, hearty man of some two hundred and forty pounds, entered the ring as clown for the first time on August 17, 1863.

Dan Castello was another who ventured into circus proprietorship for the first time this year. With Matt VanVleck he put together a wagon show out of Fairplay, WI, Castello & VanVleck's Mammoth Circus, and opened in Dubuque, IA. Among the company were William Smith, two-horse rider; John Glenroy, somersault rider; Joseph Tinkham, hurdle rider; Charles Burrows, Richard Hammon, John Burns, and George M. Kelley, acrobats; Natt McCollum, banjoist and Ethiopian entertainer; and Frances Castello (probably Mrs. Dan Castello), rider. Castello and Tom Burgess were the clowns. M. VanVolkenburg was the manager; Tom Poland, master of the arena; and J. R. Murphy and L. VanVleck were ahead of the show. The trick horse, Monitor, and the educated bull, Don Juan, were featured. The successful summer tour took the circus through towns in Iowa, Wisconsin, Illinois and Minnesota. In the fall, VanVleck consolidated with Maginley's Cosmopolitan Circus for a winter season in a wooden amphitheatre in Memphis, where Ben Maginley was so popular, with the intention of producing horse dramas. Castello left the organization to break horses for a summer tour.

L. B. Lent's Equescurriculum, which had reported good business in New York State in June—"never has the show business been so good as now; the country people are said to have plenty of money, and they turn out *en masse* to every show that comes along"[9]—nonetheless, moved into Canada by July and was very successful there.

A *Clipper* correspondent was on hand for a performance in Brooklyn when Lent's company returned to home pasture near season's end. The program, as recounted by him, began with Wallace's trained bears, followed by an impressive cavalcade, with the riders and horses uniformly costumed and decorated. Next, Robert Stickney performed a principal act of horsemanship, throwing backward and forward somersaults with rapidity and precision. Tom King and William Smith cooperated in *la perche*. In turn, Charles Shay's trick dog, Fanny, romped around the ring doing whatever the trick dog was trained to do. Charles Madigan spelled the dog with his equestrian act called "The Changes." The *battoute* leaps of brother James Madigan was an outstanding follow up, as the performer went over eight horses with great ease. He was relieved by a group of educated dogs and monkeys, a trained bull and buffalo, and then returned for a double act of horsemanship with Tom King. Charles Madigan and C. Donavan were outstanding in their

Emma Stickney

JOHN O'BRIEN

portrayal of the Motley Brothers. James Madigan reappeared in another act of horsemanship, proving he was one of the best pad riders in the business as he leaped banners, sailed through balloons, and threw forward and backward somersaults. William Smith in his *l'échelle* act and a pair of comic mules finished the program. Admission 25¢, no half-price.

Thayer & Noyes' United States Circus organized in Girard and opened there on May 2. Concentrating on the larger cities, the show moved in Pennsylvania, Ohio, Illinois, Indiana, Iowa, Wisconsin and closed with a week in Chicago. Their parade feature was a new band chariot drawn by sixteen cream colored horses. On the rear panel was painted a circus ring with Thayer and Noyes introducing their star, James Robinson. On the front panel was a full length portrait of the band leader, Thomas Canham.

The success of Thayer & Noyes, described in the Cincinnati *Commercial* when the show made an appearance at that city in late June, exemplifies the newly found prosperity of circuses generally:

> The capacity of our street railways is tested twice a day, but the Company, by "massing" their cars, are succeeding very well in accommodating the immense numbers making a pilgrimage to the corner of Eighth and Freeman. The circus has created a genuine *furor*, and their very new pavilion is likely to be christened by a week's tremendous business.[10]

The receipts under their spanking new 120-foot canvas averaged $1,100 a day for the first four days. This was considered an excellent box-office gross. Still, there were occasions during the season when companies took in over $2,500 on the day.

G. F. Bailey & Co.'s Grand Circus organized in Danbury, CT, and then cut a wide swath through a greater part of the Union—traveling in New Jersey, Pennsylvania, New York State, Maine, Michigan, Ohio, Wisconsin, Iowa, and Illinois. The company had the famed hippopotamus this year, as well as Sands, Nathans & Co.'s four performing elephants and Herr Driesbach's menagerie. The hippo was touted as being the only such beast in the United States—"Any other animal advertised by unprincipled showmen as a hippopotamus is a deception and a humbug."

Report has it that when the circus moved from Buffalo to Detroit for a June 23 opening, the performing elephants and the hippo, in the care of the keeper, Ali, were sent by boat, the hippo's special cage being transported overland with the regular equipment. As the steamer came within three miles of its destination, the huge beast broke its chains and plunged into the river. A row boat was at once lowered and Ali set forth to entice his charge shoreward. But exhilarated at the aquatic experience, the animal proceeded to play hide and seek, diving out of sight and then surfacing some distance from its frantic rescuers, while a large, black mastiff on board the steamer barked incessantly. The dog had been trained as a companion to the hippo and the two had become almost inseparable. At some point, the dog was unfettered and allowed to leap into the river to join its oversized pal. After a period of affectionate greeting, the canine swam ashore with the hippo in pursuit and the situation was normalized to everyone's relief. What a behemoth story. Did Barnum have a hand in this?

The company was composed of Sam Burt, the hurdle and bareback rider; Philo Nathans, principal rider; Charles Rivers, two and four-horse rider; the Denzer Brothers, acrobats and *la perche*; James DeMott, rider; James Ward, clown; etc.[11] Robert Ellingham was the equestrian director and ringmaster; C. H. Farnsworth, the agent; A. D. Atwood, band leader. Admission was set at 50¢, with half-price for children.

The circus appeared in St. Louis for a stand on November 2-21; then, after concluding the date, moved down the river to New Orleans. As they left shore, James DeMott recalled proprietor Avery Smith saying, "You are as safe as if floating on the placid waters of the peaceful Hudson." Fifteen minutes later Federal gunboats detained their craft to warn of Confederate artillery using a kind of shoot and move maneuver to harass the government. At one point a gunboat stopped the circus to instruct them to blow their whistle upon meeting another government vessel and be escorted past a point of danger. The circus followed their instructions and upon moving down river Confederate artillery opened fire and placed forty shells into the hull of their boat.

The suddenness of the attack caught the company by surprise. The table was being set for supper as one bullet struck a stack of plates in the hands of a waiter. The equestrian Sam Burt was putting on his boots when a bullet whizzed under his leg. Manager Quick was seen fleeing to the other side of the boat and taking refuge under a pile of mattresses. After the original fusillade, the Federal vessel fell behind and silenced the battery emplacement. As luck would have it, none of the circus complement were harmed and the show opened on schedule in New Orleans on December 3, 1863.

The S. Q. Stokes' Circus peregrinating around New York State was reportedly enjoying fair business until internal difficulties arose, then grew into a bit of open unpleasantness on the 4th of August at Cambridge, a small town on the eastern edge of the state. Traveling with the show was a "jewelry case runner," a kind of gambling concern. A young countryman, investing money in the game of chance and getting nothing to show in return, expressed his disdain by upsetting the establishment, causing a fracas of some short duration. Later, at the hotel, he confronted members of the company, threw caution to the wind, and proceeded to complain loudly about the affair. This brought a response from a Mr. Russell, the sideshow and "jewelry case" operator, and a quarrel ensued. A number of the show folks joined in, beat the Ruben unmercifully, and then variously stabbed him, one knife being buried to the hilt and left in place.

In the evening, when the time came for the circus doors to be opened for the performance, the local authorities closed the place down. Convinced that there was no point in remaining, the equipment was loaded up and the company prepared to move out; but before they could leave, a crowd of disgruntled locals arrived and set fire to the canvas wagon. The constabulary appeared before more damage was done and arrested several members of the company. James R. Hankins, somersault rider, and young Sam Stickney, the clown, were singled out; but both managed to evade the law and get out of town. An attempt to arrest Russell went awry when he escaped to the roof of a house and for two hours threatened his would-be captors by wielding a large, ugly knife in each hand. Then, when darkness fell, he made good his escape and fled to Canada.

This little unpleasantness must have contributed to open friction within the troupe. A few days later, manager Stokes gave his former riding prodigy, Ella Zoyara, a beautiful blackened eye and then duplicated the fistic art work on H. L. Stebbins, the advertiser. This being deftly accomplished, Stokes left the show in disgust and joined Dan Rice's circus at Williamsburg.

The newly named Zoyara Circus struggled on for a few more weeks before it collapsed. Gil Eaton, the agent, was at Stamford, CT, on August 17, awaiting paper to advertise the place. When it became apparent that the show print company was unwilling to extend more credit, he organized a crew of boys and "chalked" the town. On the 25th the company pitched their canvas in Jersey City but failed to pay for the lot. The

THE MODEL EXHIBITION OF THE WORLD.
DAN RICE'S GREAT SHOW.

Will Exhibit in Salem, SATURDAY, September 19, 1863,
AFTERNOON, AT 2.   EVENING, AT 7.
DAN RICE'S GREAT SHOW!
NEWLY ORGANIZED AND EQUIPPED FOR THE SEASON OF 1863.

Combining in one Exhibition a Mammoth Collection of

Trained Animals, Acting Dogs, Monkies and Ponies, Performing Horses, Educated Mules.

The Wonderful BLIND TALKING HORSE,

EXCELSIOR, Jr.

Together with the Best Troupe of

Equestrians,   Acrobats, Gymnasts and Athletes

Ever brought before the Public. The whole in conjunction with the

CELEBRATEDGAMESOFTHECURRICULUM!

DAN RICE

will positively appear at every performance of the Great Show.

The Great Show will exhibit as follows:

AT LYNN, TUESDAY, SEPT. 15.   AT AMESBURY, FRIDAY, SEPT. 18
AT NEWBURYPORT, WEDNESDAY, SEPT. 16.   AT SALEM, SATURDAY, SEPT. 19.
AT PORTSMOUTH, THURSDAY, SEPT. 17.

Admission to Box, 25 cts.   Reserved Seats, 50 cts.   Children to all parts of the House, 25 cts.
For particulars see Large Bills, Lithographs, &c.

C. L. PHELPS, Director of Publications.   J. B. WARNER, General Agent chief of police dropped in on the show and made a collection. After the evening performance, as the wagons started for Brooklyn, they were met at the ferry by a constable with a writ of attachment for debt. The bill was settled and the circus was allowed a final gasp in Brooklyn. But on the 29th the sheriff took possession, bringing the unfortunate season to an end. The show stock and equipment were disposed of at public auction on October 20.

It was announced in May that James M. Nixon and Thaddeus Barton had leased the circus lot in Baltimore on Calvert Street, known as the "City Spring" lot, for the purpose of erecting a summer garden, similar to what Nixon had done in New York. Within short order the report came out that the Baltimore city council had rejected the plan, explaining that the lot was to be closed and fixed up for what it was intended—a city spring.

Undaunted by this defeat, James Nixon returned to Washington and opened under canvas May 26 on the lot at the corner of New York Avenue and Fourteenth Street near Willard's Hotel. Billed in the local newspapers as Madame Macarte's Grand European Circus Combined with Nixon's Great Cremorne Troupe from New York, with twenty-five star performers, the company included the Syro-Arabic Troupe of male and female gymnasts; the clowning of James Cooke, Sam Lathrop, and Jimmy Reynolds; Barney Carroll and his adopted daughter in a double riding act; Eaton Stone in his Indian personation on his "wild prairie steed"; and the incomparable Herr Cline on the tight-rope. The sideshow was operated by Lafe Nixon (J. M.'s brother) and Cady Howes.

It was with this company that James Cooke, clown and all-around performer, made his American debut. The Dublin born Cooke, whose real name was Patrick Hoey, began his career as an actor in Mrs. Ellen Burke's traveling theatre, exhibiting chiefly at fairs. After learning acrobatics and feats of contortion on his own, he entered into circus performing. Subsequently, he turned to clowning, taking the great English jester, William F. Wallett, as his model, and for some time filled an engagement at Astley's Amphitheatre.

He left Liverpool on April 20 of this year on the ship *Anglo-Saxon* bound for Quebec, but en route his ship was wrecked. Through good fortune he escaped "together with six shillings, a broken-bladed penknife, and a canary bird in a cage" which he had rescued from the sinking vessel. After struggling to New York City and presenting himself to Nixon, he was placed under contract and first appeared in the tented pavilion at the Washington opening.

Eaton Stone was the recipient of an honorary saddle, bridle, holster, spurs, etc., given to him during a performance at the circus pavilion on May 30 by the officers of the 1st Michigan Cavalry. Stone graciously responded:

> Gentlemen. With feelings of gratitude, I receive this token of respect from the officers of the First Michigan Cavalry; and although I have been the recipient of valuable presents before, in this country and in Europe, there is none I prize more highly than this beautiful saddle and equipments; for whenever I may be seated in it, it will bring to my memory those who gave it, and the many happy hours passed with them. My wish, gentlemen, is that you may all safely return to your native homes with pride and honor, and there enjoy peace, happiness, and long lives of prosperity.[12]

Still, it was Mme. Marie Macarte, with her beautiful stud of trained horses and Shetland ponies, who was the center piece of the circus program. Her personation act of the "Venetian Carnival" was billed at the beginning of the run. On June 1, the equestrian spectacle of *Dick Turpin, the Bold Highwayman* was first introduced, including "Turpin's Ride to York" and "The Death of Black Bess," with Macarte enacting the role of Turpin. On June 6, the closing day, she took her benefit. To promote the event, a free attraction was announced to precede the matinee, with Mlle. Josephine Devinier making an ascent on a tight-rope "across New York Avenue and completely over the Pavilion tent."

The Nixon company then went to Baltimore. The first advertisement began on May 26, which announced the opening for June 1, the tent to be located on the corner of Charles and Camden Streets. But on the 1st the *American and Commercial Advertiser* carried a postponement notice. "Now performing with immense success in Washington," the ad read, "will commence a series of entertainments in this city on Monday, June 8th, 1863." General admission 25¢, reserved seats 50¢, children in reserved seats half-price. Still listed in the advertising as "upwards of twenty stars" were riders Madame Macarte, Eaton Stone, Barney and Marie Carroll, clowns Sam Lathrop and Jimmy Reynolds, rope dancer Herr Cline, contortionist Charles Parker, and a Syro-Arabic Troupe of male and female acrobats.

An elated member of the Baltimore press lauded Nixon for producing "something new to our citizens in the shape of an equestrian performance, as everything appeared in fine condition, and the entertainment gave most excellent satisfaction." On June 10 a number of new acts were introduced. "Mlle. Zara has become the talk of the town," it was observed, "and many yet doubt if in reality the person represented is a female."[13] Here we go again. The last two days were advertised—TAKE NOTICE! POSITIVELY LAST TWO DAYS—for June 12 and 13. Madame Macarte was featured in *Dick Turpin, the Bold Highwayman*, with Tom King as Turpin's pal and supported by Horace Nichols and "the entire dramatic and equestrian troupe."

Then the company took to the road, opening at Annapolis on June 15. Plans to go to Frederick were abandoned because of a rebel raid through the valley. The show returned to Baltimore on the 22nd for three days at Gay Street alongside the Bel Air Market. The new location was intended to give the inhabitants of Old Town and vicinity a better opportunity for attending than during the previous stand. This was followed by two days in Wilmington, DE, June 25 and 26, and one in Havre de Grace, MD, on Saturday, the 27th, before jumping to Philadelphia at Broad and Locust Streets for the Fourth of July week. After this there was a series of dates throughout Pennsylvania and New Jersey. A week in Harrisburg proved particularly profitable, since the show arrived just as the contingent of soldiers stationed there received their pay. At Allentown, July 23, the clown, Jimmy Reynolds, was married to Frankie Christie, a member of the company. Along the way, rope-walker Josephine Webb—quite likely the Josephine Devinier previously advertised on the bills—was badly injured. Finally, by mid-September, Madame Marie Macarte was posting an "at liberty" notice in the *Clipper*.

John Hunt Morgan is remembered as the notorious leader of the cavalry regiment known as Morgan's Raiders. His movements into Northern territory brought panic to the centers of population situated in his path. James A. Bailey was in advance of Robinson & Bros.' Circus and Menagerie when Morgan made his fourth raid behind Union lines. For some inexplicable motive, Morgan crossed the Ohio River at Brandenburg, KY, into Indiana, then moved northeast into Ohio. We learn from Bailey's diary that he was billing Madison, IN, on July 10, a town located about half the distance between Brandenburg and Cincinnati:

> The first place that the people commenced to make preparations to received the Rebels was at Madison, the day before Versailles. The town was full of drinking soldiers. We left there Saturday and went to Versailles. When we got there the Rebels were at Osgood. We got away from Versailles at 7 a.m. and the Rebels came in at 10 o'clock.[14]

Versailles was approximately thirty miles north of Madison and Osgood another four miles to the northwest. The proximity to the fighting serves as another example of the precarious nature of trouping during the war years.

Gardner & Hemmings started the season with John O'Brien and James E. Cooper as partners. Five weeks after opening, Cooper bought out O'Brien and the firm continued under the aegis of Gardner, Hemmings & Cooper. After moving about in Maryland, Delaware, and Pennsylvania early in the season, the company went into Ohio beginning with a June 29 date in Conneaut. While visiting Zanesville on the 25th of July, they found themselves inadvertently close to Morgan's rebel unit. He had gone through the suburbs of Cincinnati and was making his way toward Columbus. This is as close as the rebels got to Zanesville, some fifty miles away, but it was close enough. The raiders, who were in the habit of changing their tired mounts for fresh ones confiscated along the way, would have stripped the circus of its ring stock had the opportunity arisen. This possibility sent Gardner & Hemmings' circus troupe scurrying. As it happened, down to 364 officers and men, Morgan surrendered to the Federals the following day.

E. F. & J. Mabie's concern was dissolved with Jerry Mabie going it alone. Edmund F. and Jeremiah Mabie grew up on a farm near Patterson, Putnam County, NY. They were in partnership with Seth B. Howes from 1843 to 1846. In the fall of the latter year, Howes left the company and Jeremiah acquired Howes' share. The following year they moved their quarters from Brewster, NY, to Delavan, WI, being the first circus to quarter in Wisconsin and pave the way for the 90 odd circuses later organized there. The company title then became E. F. & J. Mabie's Grand Olympic Arena and United States Circus.

This year, with animals only, Mabie's Grand Menagerie started from Delavan on May 1, unveiling a fine specimen of the ostrich family recently purchased from the VanAmburgh organization. Prof. Sears was featured as "The Lion King." The elephants Romeo and Juliet were also an attraction. From the Wisconsin quarters the troupe moved into Illinois and Indiana. Admission 50¢, children half-price.

Dan Rice's Great Show, under the proprietorship of Dr. Spalding, opened in Albany, NY, on May 4, then followed along the Erie Railroad in New York State in June—Portage, Hornellsville, Addison, Corning, Bath, Wayland, LeRoy, etc. The company continued with dates in New Jersey, Connecticut, Rhode Island, and Pennsylvania. One of the features was "Dan Rice's Dream of Chivalry, the Rebel Raid on a Union Picket." Admissions 50¢, 25¢, children 25¢. Rice had signed a three year contract with Spalding, but reneged before the first season was finished. The show broke up after a disastrous tour and was sold for debt.

Yankee Robinson's Triad, starting with a forty-horse show and a new set of scenery, opened in Syracuse, NY, on May 9. The program consisted of dramatic performances in conjunction with gymnastics and other variety acts. The military spectacle of *The Days of '76; or, The Struggle for the Union* was presented with four grand tableaux vivants—"Washington in Realms of Bliss," "Outbreak of the Rebellion," "Battlefield at the Antietam," and "The Traitors' Doom." Admission 50¢, children under ten half-price. After touring in New York State and then working into Ohio, Michigan, Indiana, Illinois, and Iowa, the profitable season closed in Peoria on October 23.

R. Sands & Co., with James W. Foshay as manager, opened in Danbury, CT, on April 20. James Melville and family were along. Sam Long was the clown. The show set up in Boston on the Agricultural Fair Grounds in mid-June for a week of turn-away business. Later, the company made one of the longest jumps within the shortest time that had previously been accomplished. Following the performance on Friday July 31 at Auburn, ME, the train of cars traveled that night and throughout the weekend, moving across Canada, until they arrived at Port Huron, MI, on Monday morning—nine hundred miles in a matter of sixty hours.

California and the West Coast, far removed from the fighting, was not profitable for showmen, there being no money in the country to spend on exhibitions. John Wilson's Mammoth Circus, with the same program as the previous November, returned to the Metropolitan Theatre, San Francisco, for a stand from January 16 to January 20. The theatre was occupied for a spring season by Lee, Worrell & Sebastian's Great Circus from May 1 to 14. By fall, Wilson and H. C. Lee had combined their shows as the Mammoth Circus and Roman Hippodrome and descended upon the Jackson Street lot for a stay under canvas from October 23 to November 26, advertised as consisting of "46 Ladies and Gentlemen," with Signor Sebastian and family making their farewell appearance.

James M. Nixon erected an arena in New York City, at Fourteenth Street and Irving Place, opposite the Academy of Music, which was opened as the Alhambra—a name justified by its pseudo-Moorish design—on August 31. This was a new 85 by 90-foot round top of canvas enclosed with the old sidewall that had been used for the traveling circus. The ring was a standard size of 42 feet in diameter, with wooden curbing 2 feet high and 2 feet in width. The house was divided into two parts—the pit and dress circle. Admission to the former was 25¢ and to the latter, called reserved seats, 50¢. The regular seating consisted of hard planks, similar to what was used by all traveling companies (although some circuses used a carpet covering on them). The boards, no wider than 8 inches, were placed on uprights, simply laid on, being neither nailed nor tied. There was space between the ring curbing and the tiered boards where camp stools could be added when the regular seating was filled; so on a good night the lucky late-comers might find softer sitting than those who had arrived earlier.

We are again indebted to a *Clipper* correspondent for a description of the opening night program. The *entree* consisted of three ladies and nine gentlemen—including Louisa Wells, Jennie Sylvester (Mrs. William Aymar), Mrs. Barney Carroll, Horace Nichols, Barney Carroll, Jimmy Reynolds, Eaton Stone, and William Odell. There followed a double globe act by two unnamed performers. Barney Carroll then did a two-horse act, during which he carried William Odell. James Cooke, the English clown, dressed in the cap and bells style of the old court fools, played to this act and made a less than sensational debut to a New York audience:

> At times a person is disposed to like him for his wit, but then again he says something very stale and flat, and at once removes the favorable impression already made. He has fallen into the same error that Dan Rice has, that the audience are only present to hear him talk, and he keeps his tongue going incessantly.... His jokes are all old, worn out, and stale ones that have been peddled around the country for twenty years by every jester.[15]

James Nicolo and his boy were introduced next for air and ground exercises, with the youngster receiving generous applause. Nicolo came to America from England, bringing three boys—Thomas, George, and John Ridgeway—in 1853 and appeared with them at Franconi's Hippodrome in acts of posturing and acrobatics. After several seasons, the troupe returned home, where the boys became prominent as the Ridgeway Brothers. This year Nicolo was back with another boy, Bobby Nicolo, known as "The Flying Boy" (later combining with William Rodney and Thomas Tolliday as the Talleen Brothers).

Charles Parker followed on the program with a contortion and chair trick act and was accused of dragging out his performance for too great a length. The veteran, Eaton Stone, succeeded with a graceful turn of bareback riding. Then came the gymnast who was considered the wonder of the 19th century—Mons. Verrecke—a man who had astonished Europe with his feats upon the trapeze. At this time, he performed on a single trapeze suspended by a rope from the center pole:

> After being up there about ten minutes, and executing feats such as every gymnast in this country, who makes any pretension to trapeze performances, could perform, he pulls a snare drum up to him, which he straps over his shoulders, and then while sitting on the trapeze bar plays on the drum for several minutes. He then places the back of his head, or what is called the nape of the neck, on the bar and in that position

strikes three taps on the drum, and—his "wonderful, exciting, and daring" performance is at an end.[16]

In all fairness to the newly arrived Parisian, performing under the canvas roof of the Alhambra did not allow his regular gymnastic gear to be properly installed. As a consequence, the first appearance was a failure. Not wanting to continue under such circumstances, Verrecke cut off his engagement after only a few performances.

Almost immediately, theatre manager Lingard placed him under contracted for the New Bowery, where three weeks later, on September 21, he proved he was all he was represented to be:

> He is, in his peculiar exercise, unapproachable. He attempts feats from which the most daring, skillful, and carefully trained athletes have shrunk, feats which the public would consider simply impossible did they not behold them.

After a week at the New Bowery, Mons. Verrecke signed a one-year contract with manager Lea of Baltimore at a very liberal salary, making his first appearance at the Front Street Theatre on October 19.[17]

Following Verrecke on the Alhambra program were two unnamed importations from Europe who performed the Brothers Act, consisting of ground gymnastics, an exhibition which our reporter found very ordinary. He was enlivened, however, with the principal riding of Marie Carroll: "Her graceful bearing and pleasing presence cannot fail in adding greatly to the attraction of this establishment." The eleven Bedouin Arabs who replaced her in the ring executed a four-high posturing act and a series of somersaults that did not impress the *Clipper* representative, who expressed his disdain by labeling them "hash eaters who have just got their fill, and are laying down for a quiet snooze." The show closed with the performance of a trick pony, the property of George Metcalfe of the Bull's Head Hotel.[18]

On September 21, young Nicolo made an impressive appearance in the Zampillaerostation Act:

> He is quite a youth, but in this act excels every artist that has ever yet attempted it in this country. He is without doubt the most regularly and beautifully formed as well as fully developed young gymnast we ever saw stripped. He performs his act with the greatest precision and coolness, and, in this act, takes the rank of first and foremost. In fact, he is about the only real artist Nixon offers to his patrons.[19]

James W. Wilder

Throughout the stand at the Alhambra, Nixon continued to augment his regular equestrian company with visiting "stars." Mme. Marie Macarte came on October 12, still riding with "ease, daring and certainty." Gymnast H. W. Penny, late of Miles' Circus Royale of Canada, seemed to please with his *l'échelle périlleuse*. A young lady, Sophie Sagrino, billed as the most "daring and fearless rider in the world," made a debut that was anything but memorable on 14th of September: "It seemed just as difficult for her to keep her balance on the pad of a horse as it is for a good rider to fall off."

November and cold weather arrived, hand in hand. The flimsiness of the Alhambra structure, in the face of this, made it necessary to close up on the 2nd. In assessing this latest project, the *Clipper* pointed out what appears to be a recurring weakness in the Nixon management style:

> He opens with a great flourish of trumpets, engages a good company, promises much (performs very little of it, however), and in a week or so discharges all his best people and fills their places with inferior artists.[20]

For all practical purposes, the Chattanooga campaign began when Gen. Rosecrans' Army of the Cumberland occupied the city of Chattanooga on the 9th of September after Confederate Gen. Bragg evacuated it without a fight, knowing he was severely outnumbered. But although Rosecrans' forces held the city, they were precariously surrounded by mountains and the Tennessee River. The Confederate Gen. Joseph Wheeler's cavalry made continuous assaults on the Union lines of communication, seizing supply wagons and destroying a critical railroad bridge near Murfreesboro, some hundred miles north, cutting off provisions to the Union troops.

On October 16, Gen. Grant, currently at Vicksburg, was put in command of the Departments of the Cumberland, the Ohio, and the Tennessee—the new Military Division of the Mississippi. Grant and his generals began their operations against the Southern entrenchment on Lookout Mountain on November 23. The race up the ridge turned into a rout, sending the Confederates in a retreat toward Chickamauga, in northern Georgia, thus ending the battles of Chattanooga and Missionary Ridge. The South was driven from Tennessee. The North claimed a major victory and took control of the railroads centered in Chattanooga. Grant was promoted to lieutenant general. Circuses were one battle nearer to extending their movements southward.

The old Wallack's Theatre in New York City was converted to circus performances and opened for the 1863-64 winter season by L. B. Lent on November 18 as the Broadway Amphitheatre. Dress Circle and Parquet, 50¢; children under ten, 25¢; Family Circle, 25¢ without distinction of age. The doors opened at 7:00 p.m. and the performance began at 7:45. Saturday matinees were at 2:00 p.m.

Lent had grown into the profession. His father was a dealer in animals and for a short time had a traveling menagerie. By the age of twenty-one Lent was an agent for June, Titus & Angevine's menagerie. In August of that year he purchased an interest in J. R. and W. Howes' menagerie and from that time to the present year was involved in management, through partnership or on his own. In 1843 he took Sands & Lent's Circus to England, and upon returning to America, the Sands & Lent partnership continued for some ten years until Lent withdrew. Starting in 1857, he had L. B. Lent's National Circus on the road; and for the next twenty odd years was connected with circuses as an agent or business associate. Lent was an all-round circus man, considered to be the best general agent and router of his day.

A performance at the Broadway Amphitheatre was favorably reported by the *Clipper* editor. The first act to impress him was the feats on the horizontal bars by the three Spanola Brothers, who were said to have equaled anything of the kind that had been tried in America. The posturing of the Melville family—James and his sons George, Frank and Samuel—was also lauded. He found Robert Stickney to be "a chip of the old block," throwing back and forward somersaults off the pad with great precision while his horse was traveling at a rapid gate. Signor Gibbonoise impressed with his contortion exhibition. James Melville's bareback act was also worthy of mention. Sallie Stickney was her usual vision of grace and elegance. And the clowns, Joe Pentland and Jimmy Reynolds successfully filled out the comic interludes.

By mid-December, Louise Tourniaire, the bright star of Lent's circus galaxy, had taken to saddle; William Ducrow was exhibiting feats on the slack rope and performing a hurdle act on a trained buffalo; there were genuine Bedouin Arabs leaping and tumbling about the ring; and Wallace's troupe of performing bears was creating the appropriate "oh's" and "ah's" from circus-goers. Then, the winter season at an end, the lights dimmed and went out on the 9th of April and the house was cleaned and re-decorated and re-named the Broadway Theatre.

On November 19 the battlefield at Getttysburg was dedicated as a national cemetery. The speaker chosen for the occasion was Edward Everett, a noted orator. In addition, President Lincoln was invited to make a few appropriate remarks. The crowd listened for two hours to Everett's extravagant discourse. When Lincoln's turn came, the tall, lean man addressed the crowd with his usual high-pitched delivery and in a little less than three minutes finished his Gettysburg Address. Everett wrote to him later: "I should be glad if I could flatter myself that I came as near the central idea of the occasion in two hours as you did in two minutes."

Ten days earlier the President had attended the theater to view a presentation of *The Marble Heart*. The actor starring in the piece was John Wilkes Booth.

CIRCUSES AND MENAGERIES, 1863: George F. Bailey & Co.; John O'Brien with Mrs. Dan Rice; Brooklyn Arena (winter); Castello & VanVleck; Gardner & Hemmings; Cady Howes (New York, winter); Lake & Co.; Lee, Worrell & Sebastian (California); L. B. Lent; J. Mabie's Menagerie; Maginley & VanVleck; Melville, Cooke & Sands; Miles' Circus Royale (Canada); Mrs. Charles Warner (Philadelphia, winter); Nixon's Alhambra; Nixon-Macarte; Old Cary; Dan Rice; Robinson & Deery; Robinson & Howes (Chicago, winter); John Robinson; Yankee Robinson; Sands, Nathan & Co.; Shay & Aymar; Spalding & Rogers; S. Q. Stokes; Stow & Co.; Thayer & Noyes; VanAmburgh & Co.; S. O. Wheeler; Whittaker's Amphitheatre (Philadelphia, winter); John Wilson (California).

NOTES

[1] A sixteen year old sutler's clerk, selling provisions to the soldiers, Master James A. Bailey, destined to become one of the greatest showmen of all time, wrote in his diary for Sunday, July 26: "The first place that the people commenced to make preparations to receive the Rebels was at Madison. The town was full of drinking. Soldiers left there Saturday, and went to Versailles. When we got there the Rebels were at Osgood. We got away from Versailles at 7 o'clock a.m. and the Rebels came in at 10 o'clock."

[2] City Summary, Monday, June 1, New York *Clipper*, June 6, 1863, p. 59.

[3] New York *Clipper*, August 5, 1911, P. 9.

[4] Conklin, "Adventures of 'Pete' Conklin," p. 153.

[5] The performers for Cushing included Julia Morgan, jig dancer; Millie Francis, *danseuse*; Mlle. Louise, vocalist; Billy Holmes; Abijah Course, comic singer; Johnny Wilcox; Master Frank Morgan, Ethiopian performer; etc. Judge

Ingalls, with a large kangaroo and a curiosity show, had the concession with Brian's Circus. E. Quick and J. Townsend with George F. Bailey & Co. were exhibiting Barnum's "What Is It?" along with a minstrel band. Frank Thompson managed a variety and curiosity show with O. S. Wheeler's Great International Circus. Harry Buckley and William Coup had the Albino Family with Jerry Mabie's concern. Shaley's fat woman and a batch of monkeys were with Gardner & Hemmings. Frank Howes had a variety show and the "wild hairless mare" with Thayer & Noyes. R. Sands' sideshow was run by George Burnell, with performers Billy Drew, Frank Lum, J. H. Taylor, and Billy Hart. The sideshow for Melville, Maginley & Co.'s Great Eastern Circus was operated by Ned and Charley Straight, featuring performers Johnny Cole, Joe Childs, George P. Madden, Al Royce, and Lizzie Walker. Sallie Thayer, *danseuse*, and La Petite Flora joined later.

[6] Conover, p. 20-21.
[7] Nashville *Dispatch*, November 29, 1863, p. 2.
[8] MacAllister, *Uncle Gus*, p. 9.
[9] New York *Clipper*, August 5, 1911, p. 9.
[10] New York *Clipper*, July 4, 1863, p. 94.
[11] Others included Le Sieur Tremaine, James Benton, Henri Clarence Clermont, Gustave Ducrow, Joseph J. Jones.
[12] New York *Clipper*, June 13, 1863, p. 70.
[13] Baltimore *American and Commercial Advertiser*, June 9, 11, 1863, p. 1.
[14] Bailey's diary is part of the McCaddon Collection at Princeton University library. The excerpt included was submitted to me by Stuart Thayer.
[15] New York *Clipper*, September 19, 1863, 171.
[16] *Ibid*.
[17] New York *Clipper*, November 7, 1863, p. 233.
[18] New York *Clipper*, September 19, 1863, 171.
[19] New York *Clipper*, October 1, 1863, p. 195.
[20] *Ibid*.

DEATHS IN 1863: The *manège* horse owned by Levi J. North, **Tammany**, on John Robinson's farm in Attica, NY, age 26; **"Big Sam" Long**, negro minstrel (not the clown), of pneumonia in Paducah, KY, January 29; **William C. Preston**, old circus agent, at Memphis, February 9; **Thomas Jefferson Shelley**, fat man, in New York City, February 27; **Garry DeMott**, in New York City, March 27, age 53; **Tom Swann**, clown, in Scarborough, England, October 5; **Jacob Denzer**, one of the Denzer Brothers, at Lowell, OH, October 25; **Joe Cowell**, manager for Simpson & Price, in London, England, November 14; **Madame Margaret Frances Ormond**, equestrienne, of yellow fever, in St. Jago, West Indies, December 4; **Augustus Lehman**, clown, of yellow fever, in St. Jago, West Indies, December.

1864

As the fourth year of the war began, Northerners were realizing the cost of the fighting in both dollars and human life. "When and how will it all end?" was the question people were asking themselves. On the other hand, the Union was experiencing a time of prosperity. Business was flourishing and the country people were finding a ready market for their produce. Labor was commanding higher wages, with more people working at steady employment. Farm prices had soared. Manufacturing was at peak level. "The city of New York is like a vast beehive," a correspondent observed; "everybody is busy making money out of each other and the government."[1]

The amusement industry was running on high; never before had activity shown such sweet rewards. After the first shock of secession tapered off, the public sought to drown out the unpleasantness by attending the entertainment establishments and soldiers on leave or ready to leave were a new-found audience for amusement managers. The tenting season of 1863 had most likely been the best in circus history and proprietors were correctly anticipating another banner year ahead. With money in their pockets, managers willingly put it into refurbishing and expanding their outfits.

But the economic news was clouded when in June a floor amendment in Congress increased the federal income tax. With a national debt over $1.5 billion, the government raised the annual levy to 10 percent for income over $10,000 a year, to accompany an existing tax of 5 percent of income between $600 and $10,000. A new law this year required circuses and other entertainments to pay an annual license of $100 and 2% of the gross receipts, causing the leading theatres in New York to raise their prices for the winter season beginning in September. On the road, the prices of hotels and everything else were excessive.

On February 1, President Lincoln gave orders for an additional 500,000 men to be conscripted for a three-year service of duty. "It takes more soldiers to enforce it than we get from its enforcement," Gen. Henry Halleck remarked. Evasion and desertion were becoming more frequent and open meetings were held to protest the draft. In an attempt to ease tensions, the government acted to reduce exemptions.

Recruiting Station in City Hall Park, NYC, 1864

In March, Grant became commander in chief of all Federal armies and moved his headquarters to Virginia. Seeing that the long fighting had severely weakened Lee's forces, he began a relentless campaign of increased attrition, forcing bloody but inconclusive battles at the Wilderness, Spotsylvania, and Cold Harbor. He then encircled Richmond and laid siege to the important railroad junction of Petersburg.

In New York City a permanent building of corrugated iron was erected on the site of the former Alhamba. Modeled after the *Champs Élysées* in Paris, it was heated with steam and carefully designed to house winter entertainments. Described as "the new and superb equestrian temple," the place was designated the Hippotheatron. The architect was Lawrence V. Volk; W. G. Lord was the contractor. The main part of the structure was 110 feet in diameter and supported a dome rising to the height of 75 feet and topped with a cupola.

The auditory was divided into orchestra, dress circle, and pit. Orchestra seats were "armed sofas," the admission to which cost 75¢. Behind this was a dress circle capable of seating some 500 people. The pit could accommodate another 600. These seating areas were surrounded by a hallway or promenade where standing room could be arranged. When the occasion merited, some 2,000 spectators could be sorted and packed into the place. The ring was said to be the largest ever used for indoor performances in this country, 43 feet 6 inches, a foot and a half larger than Astley's of London. An interesting feature was the use of two ring entrances stationed opposite each other, which allowed utility and flexibility for *battoute* leaping and the staging of spectacles.

The place was opened on February 8 by James Cooke. He presented a company of such familiars as the Sherwoods, Dan Gardner and family, Marie Macarte, Richard Hemmings, William Kincade, and Horace F. Nichols as master of horse. The clown department was filled by Sam Lathrop, Nat Austin, and Charles W. Parker (Parker began his career as a contortionist but became a performing clown, famous for his "Whoa, January!" entrance greeting). Later arrivals included Eaton Stone, Sam Long, and Henry Cooke's performing dogs and monkeys. This combination lasted until a new management took over in April.

When Thayer and Noyes disbanded for the 1863 season in Chicago, James Robinson, who was the feature rider, and Frank Howes, who had the sideshow privilege, went into partnership and erected a building there on a Washington Street lot opposite the Court House, owned by Alexander White. The amphitheatre, built by the firm of

Tobbin & Tavier, had an interior 100 feet in diameter, arranged to accommodate around 2,000 people.

The managers encountered an obstacle prior to the completion of the building. The good brethren of the First Baptist Church, an immediate neighbor to the new construction, were appalled at the prospect of having the likes of Sodom and Gomorrah on their very doorstep. In consequence, the church officials applied for an injunction to block further development of the amphitheatre on the grounds that an ordinance relating to the erection of wooden buildings had been violated. The circus proprietors had anticipated the problem by applying for and receiving a variance prior to the start of construction.

Not to be denied, another injunction was sought by the Baptists on the grounds that the temple of amusement would have an immoral effect on its parishioners, be a nuisance during their devotionals, and cause insult to the ladies as they wended to and from their place of worship. The case was argued before the Honorable J. M. Wilson of the Superior Court, who in his wisdom found that the circus, far from being as above described, was an entertainment deemed respectable and countenanced in all communities and one that "developed the power of man as well as the strength of the horse." Ergo, the Robinson & Howes' National Circus opened on November 23, 1863, and lasted through April 15 of this year. Business was said to have been excellent. No record is available of church attendance.

The arrival of G. F. Bailey & Co.'s Circus was food for celebration to the people of New Orleans, who had not seen one for nearly three years. The move South at this time was fortuitous, for the opening at the Academy of Music on December 3, 1863, was well received by both public and press.

On January 9, Professor Nicolo and his son, Robert, who had only recently arrived on the steamer *Morning Star* from New York City, introduced their startling feats on the trapeze to wide-eyed locals. Their act continued for about a month before having to leave for other commitments. On their final performance of February 5 they were presented with a gold medal by Union officers, who had made up a good part of the audience.

The circus played to full houses throughout the stay, which lasted until February 16, when the company started back northward. In less than three weeks after the departure of the circus, citizens of

Louisiana restored the state's Union government and elected Michael Hahn as governor.

The Hippotheatron came under new management with the return of Spalding & Rogers' Ocean Circus from a two-year tour of South America and the West Indies where they had been playing out the war. Their occupancy of the New York amphitheatre was probably the result of a misfortune during the company's voyage home.

After leaving Nassau on March 23, the circus troupe encountered a gale on the night of April 2, which forced their brig *Hannah* onto a bar some ten miles south of Barnegat, NJ, a small community north of Atlantic City. At the first sign of daylight the members of the company and stock were evacuated, all reaching shore safely save for two horses; but the canvas, seats and all the fixtures belonging to the company were lost and the ship, which was also the property of Spalding & Rogers, valued at $25,000, was unsalvageable and uninsured. Nevertheless, the show must go on, and with all necessary tenting equipment at the bottom of the ocean, the Hippotheatron was the best alternative.

Their company was composed of Kate Ormond, Charles Fish, William Pastor, William Duverney, Ferdinand and Theodore Tourniaire, acrobat Henry W. Ruggles, William and Henry Rolland, Mrs. Jerry Worland and her daughter "La Petite" Annie, Thomas Stuart, Señor Carlos do Carno, and Señor Don Antonio Marquez. The Worlands, along with most of the other performers, had been with Spalding & Rogers in South American. During the tour, Jerry Worland met with an accident and was sent back to New York City, where he died on the 24th of April, a day before the company opened at the Hippotheatron.

The four-week engagement was closed on May 21; after which, the Hippotheatron remained quiet for five months, until Mr. James M. Nixon's well-worn name became connected with the establishment. Spalding & Rogers began their touring season at Albany, NY, on June 6 and then moved into Canada, Michigan, and Wisconsin, closing with a Chicago stand on October 6-8 and, soon after, departed for Havana.

Generally, circuses were tending to open their seasons later in the spring, perhaps confirming what advance agent Charles H. Castle once said, "Managers ought to chop off the season at both ends; twenty-six weeks on the road is enough for any tent trick."[2]

New organizations starting out this year included Robinson & Howes, Slaymaker & Nichols, and Melville's Australian Circus. Robinson & Howes' Railroad Circus opened at Kenosha, WI, on the 19th of

April. The proprietors made use of flat car transportation to reach major cities—St. Louis, Cincinnati, Rochester, Albany, Brooklyn, etc.—before returning to Chicago. A visitor for the *Clipper* during a stand at Williamsburg, LI, July 29-30, found the company to be "one of the most solid organizations" he had ever seen:

> It is in every respect complete. The ring stock, for style and condition, cannot be excelled. The company is a first-class one, there not being a dead fakir among them.

In addition to Frank Howes as ringmaster and the riding of James Robinson, he admired trapeze performers Burrows and Kelley; was impressed with Sam Rinehart, his somersaulting being only equaled by James Madigan; Lester was outstanding as a contortionist; Burdeau & Pepper were comical in their tumbling; Blake's *l'échelle* was nimbly performed; young Gonzales, a Lent pupil, was a tumbling standout; and the clowning of J. L. Davenport and Walter Aymar adequately fulfilled the funny men department.[3]

Slaymaker & Nichols' Circus, under the management of Goodwin & Wilder, had trouble getting out of the barn but opened on May 17 at New Rochelle, NY. Not a big show, two box wagons carried the main canvas, the center poles and side poles. Several more wagons took care of the seats and ring curbs. There were a few others for miscellaneous properties, a wardrobe wagon, and some carry-alls for staff, performers and band. The show used no menagerie and had no elephants.

In the company were W. W. Nichols, George Derious, and James M. Cooke, the principal riders; the gymnast Snow Brothers (Benjamin, William, Henry), and their educated dogs, monkeys and ponies, and learned trick horse, Pegassus; talking clowns John Allen and Jim Burt; Simmons, the conjurer; Caroline (Mrs. James M.) Nixon and daughter, Frank, and the trained horse, General Scott; an Ethiopian troupe, etc. Prof. Silloway led the band; Flint Peasley was the agent. On July 20, Caroline Nixon, who was the niece of W. W. Nichols, died at Bangor, ME, at only 35 years of age.

Their year was spent in the northeastern states and Canada. The show closed September 29, after which the entire stock was offered for sale. The list included forty-five horses, a pair of black Shetland ponies, two sets of entry dresses, eight baggage wagons, six light wagons for performers, a new buggy, fifty sets of harness, saddles, and bridles, 100-foot round top, seats, chairs, poles, etc.

The Sheet-Metal Hippotheatron, 14th Street, NYC

T. Allston Brown

The new concern of Melville's Australian Circus, under the banner of James Melville, opened in Nashville at the corners of College and Jackson Streets on March 24 for matinees. The military authorities disallowed evening performances except on Saturdays. Melville and the Conrad Brothers were the main attractions. The company included James and Madame Louise Melville, Jeanette Ellsler, Nat Austin, James Cameron, C. W. Parker, etc. F. A. Keeler was the manager and Robert F. Dingess the agent. Admissions were 75¢ and 50¢. On Saturday night of the 26th the evening's proceeds were donated to the Refugees Asylum of the city. After closing on Saturday, April 2, the circus went on to Cairo and Galena, IL, and as far west as Leavenworth, KS—virgin territory—where on the 4th of July the gross was nearly $5,000 for three performances.

Thoughout the hostilities, Kansas was off-limits to traveling amusements, who considered the state too dangerous because of the "hazards of brawling armies and piratical bushwhackers." James Melville's Australian Circus, however, was one of two to risk entering the state. The company was in Leavenworth for three days, beginning Monday, July 4. Three performances were given on the 4th of July, the first at 10 a. m. for the other two days the regular performances occurred at 2:00 and 7:30 p.m. Admission was 50¢, reserved seats 75¢, and children to reserved seats 50¢. The Melville company followed with Atchison, June 30; Weston, MO, July 1, and Kansas City on the 2nd.[4]

Although a menagerie only, the other tented attraction to visit Kansas in 1864 was Mabie's Grand Menagerie and Moral Exhibition, billed to exhibit in Oskaloosa on Tuesday, September 6. Admission was 50¢ for those over 10 years of age; under 10 years 25¢. The business agent was F. L. Couldock. Prof. Sears entered the dens of performing lion, leopards, panthers, and cougars. The educated elephant Romeo performed a variety of feats, such as posturing, balancing, dancing, and standing on his head. There were also trick kangaroos, trained ponies and monkeys, and comic mules. A parade was promised: "a Grand Moving Panorama, over a mile in length, which will pass through the principal streets, affording the public a gratuitous view of the splendid Caravans, Horses, Trappings, Paraphernalia, &ct." A band chariot drawn by a team of elephants and camels lead the procession. Other stands in Kansas included Troy, September 3; Grasshopper Falls

(Present day Valley Falls), the 5th; Oskaloosa, 6th; Topeka, 7th; Clinton, 8th; Baldwin City, 9th; Leavenworth, 12th, 13th; Atchison, 14th.[5]

At the end of April, Gen. William T. Sherman began stripping his troops of what he considered "excess baggage." Company tents were eliminated along with many other camp comforts. The regiments were reduced to one supply wagon. Then, on May 7, the Battle for Atlanta began at Dalton, GA, where Joseph E. Johnston's Army of Tennessee, 60,000 men, held their winter camp. The Confederates had prepared strong defensive lines, but Sherman sent his men at them anyway. The march to the sea had begun.

When the *Great Eastern* steamed into the Hudson River to its mooring on the New York City docks, it carried with it Seth B. Howes. He was returning from England where, during his seven years abroad, he had toured with the Howes & Cushing's United States Circus. Howes, often designated as the first master showman produced in America, was another of those circus people from Brewster, Putnam County, NY. Getting an early start into show business when only eleven years of age, he accompanied his brother, Nathan A. Howes, in exhibiting Hachaliah Bailey's elephant, Betty, through New England.

Young Seth first performed in the ring as a rider with the Howes (Nathan A.) & Turner circus in 1826. He went on to become a scenic rider and equestrian manager before entering into management with Enoch Yale and John Miller in Miller, Yale & Howes' Circus of 1837. As manager, he has sometimes been given credit for being the first to have a billboard made and to paste up paper out of doors, previous advertising having been posted by the use of tacks. Always ready to try something new, he joined with P. T. Barnum in the importation of the first herd of elephants to this country, which proved to be quite an attraction. He also imported the first drove of camels trained to work in harness. In 1848, with brothers Nathan and Jacob, he launch the Great United States Circus, supposedly the largest such organization yet seen in America. Then, with Barnum, Sherwood Stratton, and Lewis B. Lent, he organized P. T. Barnum's Great Asiatic Caravan, Museum and Menagerie. The show opened on June 1, 1851, and toured for four years. He was in part responsible for establishing Henri Franconi's Hippodrome in New York City. Fashioned after the original in Paris, it opened on May 2, 1853. In 1856, in partnership with Joseph Cushing, he took the Great United States Circus to England and gave the British entrepreneurs schooling in the American style of circus management.

James Robinson

Pete Conklin, Shakespearean Clown

On the return to America, Howes took Smith, Quick, and Nathans as partners and the show went out as S. B. Howes' Great European Circus. Considered to be one of the largest and finest aggregations on the road, it carried impressive parade flash, particularly the elegant display of numerous English pageant wagons. One was an allegorical tableau car, three tiers high; another, the Chariot of India, was pulled by a team of elephants; the Car of Jerusalem was drawn by spotted donkeys; and the Fairy Chariot of Titania was powered by fourteen Shetland ponies; the whole of which was followed by a mounted drove of performers in full armor.

James Crockett and Sanger's den of six performing lions, an act that had been contracted in England and had accompanied Howes to America, was a featured attraction. Crockett, born in Preston, England, the son of a circus musician, was following his father's calling as a member of Sanger's band before he was forced to abandon the sharps and flats of the profession because of weakened lungs. As it happened, Sanger had bought five lions at that time but had no one to perform them until Crockett volunteered, his only attributes being an imposing stature and youthful impulse. But he proved himself to be a man of great nerve and unwavering courage and was soon performing the feats of VanAmburgh and Carter and traveling around Great Britain and the Continent, winning plaudits and receiving gifts from royalty.

Managed by Avery Smith, Howes' Great European opened in Detroit on May 9. Following the Michigan stands, the wagon show toured in Indiana, Illinois, Wisconsin, and Iowa. A successful two weeks in St. Louis, starting October 24 was said to have brought in receipts averaging $2,300 a day. However, the reader should be cautious about literally accepting income figures. The alleged dollars received is given to indicate the highs and lows of circus conditions. Some years ago when the Midwest showman, Robert L. Sherman, was asked by a colleague to guess the house gross of such-and-such a town, he answered, "Just half as much as you're going to tell me."

Peter Conklin, who had joined the show at Springfield, IL, came into his own as a circus clown on this engagement. Conklin entered show business with Clarke's American Troupe of Ethiopian Minstrels but, as was the fate of many such organization, within a few weeks the company fell flat financially. In 1856 he entered the circus business, joining Major Brown's Mammoth Coliseum, under the proprietorship of S. E. Brown. While with Mabie's Grand Consolidated Menagerie and

Circus, 1857-1859, William H. Stout, the equestrian manager with the company, was instrumental in introducing Peter to the clowning trade.

While with the European this year, Conklin acquired the title of the "Great Western Clown." His deep voice was described as a "delicate avalanche of thunder." His badge of identity was an enormous diamond pin. At Vicksburg, in admiration for his work, he was presented with a horse and trappings by General Morgan L. Smith. In New Orleans he won kudos from the press:

> Peter Conklin, the clown, during his brief stay amongst us has won golden opinions from all men, and proved himself one of the mainstays of the great show. His jokes and joking oddities have nightly been received with delight, until at last his appearance in the ring was attended with a universal grin from the audience, on the *qui vive* as they were for the rich things to come. His local hits were to the point, but the point was tipped with gold, kindly but sarcastic. He always commanded the attention of his audience; is one of the most promising clowns we have ever seen; and we sincerely hope to see him soon again.[6]

The Howes' circus re-organized in St. Louis under the management of J. J. Nathans. It then worked south, performing in Memphis, where James Robinson joined; and Vicksburg, where Dan Castello and Robert Johnson were added; and on to New Orleans for a winter engagement.

Yankee Robinson was out again with his unique combination, moving around in Illinois, Indiana, Iowa, Wisconsin, and Minnesota. The ingenious Yankee, in producing an assortment of dramatic, gymnastic, and equestrian performances, found a format suitable to the times, an entertainment made up of such variety as to be pleasing to everyone. An issue of the Chatfield (MN) *Democrat* had high praise for the troupe:

> To say that the big show is a success is but to reiterate the expression of all who visited the exhibit while here. The perfect delineations and superior acting of Yankee Robinson were received with great applause—he is a whole show within himself.... In fact, the acting of the whole company is good, and well worthy the patronage of the public.[7]

The proof of Robinson's success was exhibited at season's end by his purchase of the Melville circus, as well as a four hundred acre farm in Rice County, MN.

Dan Castello's Great American Circus started at St. Paul, MN, with a May 9-11 stand. Traveling on the steamboat *Jeanette Roberts*, the show carried twelve horses and "enough good performers to make out the company." Levi J. North was listed as manager and may have had an interest in the proprietorship. After going down the Mississippi, stopping at such places as Hastings, MN; LaCrosse, WI; McGregor, Dubuque, Davenport, Keokuk, IA; and Cairo, IL; Castello moved up the Ohio River to Shawneetown, IL; New Albany, Louisville, KY; then up the Wabash to Vincennes and Terre Haute, IN; ending at Chicago in early September. The following month the show was back down the Mississippi into the White and Arkansas Rivers before connecting with the 17th Corps at Little Rock, under the command of Gen. Steele. It then went back down the Mississippi to Vicksburg and elsewhere, still following the troops. The itinerary confirms the openness of river travel at this time.

It was, however, not without danger. The performers had a scare while at Commerce, MO. After playing to a good house in the afternoon, there came rumors of rebel guerrillas in the area. With the evening house well filled, the rumors were confirmed by the sight of three rockets being fired into the air from different locations around the town, which created a panic within the company. The circus program was conducted with a dispatch heretofore unmatched, the tent was taken down in record time, and the entire troupe boarded onto their boat, which steamed up the river as fast as the old boilers would allow.[8]

The Robinson & Deery Metropolitan Circus had a near meeting with rebel forces as well. The show began the season on April 25 at Attica, NY, with an all new outfit costing $20,000. It toured primarily in New York State and Pennsylvania until it closed the season at Lancaster, NY, October 14.

The narrow escape from a rebel incursion occurred during meanderings in southern Pennsylvania, a stone's throw from the Maryland border. While the company was showing at Connellsville on July 27, halfway through the program word came that an enemy raiding party was only a short distance from town. The management cut the performance off, packed up and left in quick order. The next stand was Mercersburg but word had arrived that that place was already occupied by the rebels. Robinson telegraphed ahead to see if the report was true. The Confederates answered the wire that everything was clear; but the circus manager, smelling a rat, refused to be duped and made tracks away from the danger, passing up Greencastle and Chambersburg, which was billed for the 29th and 30th. Instead, the company joined a seven-mile-long line of refugees headed for Harrisburg, then halted at Carlisle, where they had advertised for August 2.

Old Cary, who had managed of every kind of a show, "from the five legged dog sideshow to a menagerie," was on the road this year with Old Cary's Great World Circus. He started in Little Rock and toured through Illinois, Indiana, Ohio, and Michigan, traveling by railroad and boat. He went into Wisconson and then rejoined the Mississippi and floated back down to Little Rock. The roster included Barney Carroll, Joe Tinkham, William Sparks, the Bliss family, V. Cary, Yankee Miller, Mme. Carroll, Miss Carrie Cary. Ned Straight was orchestra leader; Charley Straight, ringmaster.

While in Cairo in April, some four or five hundred soldiers marched past the doorkeeper and entered the tent. Not content with giving a complimentary entrance to such a number, the manager announced there would be no show. In response, the brave defenders of the Union threatened to slash the canvas and kill the horses. With a threat of such severity, Old Cary had no alternative but to comply. The performance was given; after which, wisely, the company packed up everything and quickly left town.[9]

When Bryan's (or Brien's) Great Show and Tom King's Excelsior Circus left the barns in the spring of 1864—with Tom King the featured performer and John O'Brien the proprietor and manager—there was no indication that this year would mark one of the great milestones in arenic history—the introduction of Adam Forepaugh, Sr., into the circus business.

Adam Forepaugh, whose real name was Forbach, an indication a German ancestry, was another Philadelphian. He, like many youths of his day, left school early to learn a trade; in this case, working for four dollars a month as a butcher. This job selection was seemingly too tame for a man as shrewd and energetic as Forepaugh, who soon gravitated to the occupation of buying and selling horses and cattle. The expanding use of horse drawn trolley lines lured our young entrepreneur to New York City where he became one of Gotham's largest horse dealers and supplier for several of the horse railway companies and to the Union army.

To the good fortune of the circus world, Providence brought about the transaction of forty-four of Forepaugh's horses to John O'Brien, at a cost to the circus proprietor of $9,000. Not surprisingly, when payment came due, Forepaugh was forced to accept a share of the

Tom King Excelsior Circus as settlement and to "join on" to protect the investment.

Although King enjoyed title recognition, he was surrounded by many with names familiar to the circus-going public. There were Mme. Louise Tourniaire and Virginia King, equestriennes; Louis Zanfretta, Mons. Rochelle, and William Smith, acrobats and gymnasts; Jimmy Reynolds and James Ward, clowns; William Naylor, hurdle act; John Naylor, tumbler and leaper; George Wambold, contortionist; William H. Green, six-horse rider; J. C. Clark, rope performer; etc.

The show moved about in Pennsylvania, Ohio, and Michigan until August 20 when Tom King left at Port Huron over a disagreement with O'Brien. A card appeared in September within the advertising columns of the *Clipper*:

> Having withdrawn from the associate management of O'Brien & King's Excelsior Circus, I take this method of requesting Mr. O'Brien to remove my name from the top of the bills.... I will give him twenty days from this date to do this. There are several honorable men in the Company, but I am sorry I ever associated myself with an omnibus driver. Tom King.[10]

This simple ad would turn out to be a suitable epitaph for the headstone of John V. "Pogey" O'Brien.

Dr. Spalding made another attempt at putting out a show under the Dan Rice name—Dan Rice's Great Show. The circus traveled in New York State, Ohio, Illinois, Michigan, and some of the larger cities, such as St. Louis, Baltimore, Washington, etc. The company was comprised of Dan Rice, Kate Ormond and Ferdinand Tourniaire (who were married on May 15, at the close of Spalding & Rogers' Ocean Circus at the Hippotheatron), S. Q. and Emma Stokes, Fred Barclay, Henry Cooke's performing dogs and monkeys, etc. Admission 25¢, no half-price.

VanAmburgh & Co.'s Mammoth Menagerie, Moral Exhibition and Egyptian Caravan, with its assortment of rare animals, opened their season on April 20 at New Rochelle, NY, under a new variegated canvas, which was said to be "a show in itself" (a second reference to the use of colored canvas, the first being in 1861 when E. F. & J. Mabie's Menagerie and J. J. Nathans' American Circus carried a tent of red, white, and blue). The menagerie went into Connecticut, Maine, Vermont and New York State with a giraffe as a drawing card. The company played the Chittenden County Fair at Burlington, VT, on

S. O. WHEELER'S
RENOWNED
INTERNATIONAL CIRCUS
In alliance with
HATCH & HITCHCOCK'S
ROYAL HIPPODROME,

Organized in one Colossal Exhibition, for the travelling season of 1864.

Introduction of the recently invented

Self-Propelling Road Carriage,

Exhibiting the tremendous novelty never seen before, of an ordinary road carriage DRIVEN OVER THE COMMON HIGHWAYS WITHOUT THE AID OF HORSES OR OTHER DRAUGHT ANIMALS! Being, beyond doubt, the most simple, useful and ingenious piece of mechanism ever put into practical use.

The Mechanical Carriage will precede the combined Companies' Procession in town on the day of Exhibition, and be exhibited to the Circus audience, with an explanation of the machinery, gratis.

September 27 and 28, and other fairs at Middlebury on the 29th and Brandon on the 30th. The season was brought to a close at Newark, NJ, on November 2, ending one of the most prosperous summer tours in the history of VanAmburgh & Co., and leaving proprietor Hyatt Frost with a smile on his face.

Silas O. Wheeler opened his second season on the road at Cambridgeport, MA, this year in alliance with J. A. Hatch and Lyman A. Hitchcock. The notable feature of the show was the newly invented Self-Propelling Road Carriage. The bills described the vehicle as "an ordinary road carriage driven over the common highways without the aid of horses or other draught animals." The cut included in the advertising shows it to be just that, a carriage propelled by steam. The oddity was used to precede the procession into town, followed by a free exhibition on the circus grounds along with a lecture on how the thing worked.

Although this mechanical toy headed the bill, there were human performers as well. The Sherwood family made their presence felt, including Charley Sherwood's "Pete Jenkins," and the riding of Madame Sherwood, youthful Ida, and Master Charley. Jacob Showles was the Indian rubber man; his wife performed her trained horse, American Eagle. Sam Wellsler and Bobby Williams were the clowns. Along, too, was a Master Thompson, described as a youthful gymnast, and the necessary pair of comic mules, this time disrespectfully called Jeff Davis and Beauregard. The show toured in the northeastern states with a short dip into Canada. Adult admission 35¢, children 20¢.

There was an announcement in December that Wheeler and Hatch & Hitchcock had leased the National Theatre on the corner of Portland and Traverse Streets in Boston and were engaged in arranging it for equestrian entertainments. In later ads the names of Hatch & Hitchcock disappeared, indicating that Wheeler continued the project on his own. The place was said to hold about 2,000 people, with seats sloping from rear to front and with galleries on three sides, a natural arrangement for a converted theatre. Wheeler's circus opened on the 26th with performers Eaton Stone, Sam Stickney, the Showles family, Frank Whittaker, Joe Pentland, the Denzer Brothers, etc.

This year Thayer & Noyes leased VanAmburgh & Co.'s animals and the VanAmburgh name for two seasons. The organization left winter quarters with nine new cages—including a tapir, polar bear, an African ostrich and the elephant Hannibal—all from the VanAmburgh collection. Other advertising features included Dr. Thayer's comic mules; the Colossal Golden Chariot or Mythological Car of the Muses; George Batcheller, the "great *voltigeur,*" jumping over ten horses and an elephant; the lion tamer Mons. Davis, billed as the "only successful rival of the Great VanAmburgh"; and a fine stock of ring horses. The show, behind the routing of Andy Springer, traveled in Pennsylvania, Ohio, and western Virginia. Admission, 50¢ and 25¢.

On July 13, Gen. Sherman and his cavalry began a rampage around the city of Atlanta, destroying railroads and anything else they encountered in preparation for the siege. By August 2, extensive wharves, warehouses, and ammunition dumps had been established to service the troops and an intricate railway system developed to bring in other supplies. All of the reinforcements were in close proximity of the city. The Confederates were greatly outnumbered and, once Sherman began his move, put up little resistance. Finally, on September 2, Sherman wired President Lincoln "Atlanta is ours, and fairly won!" In less than a year, circuses, too, would take Atlanta in force.

In California, John Wilson filed suit against William Hendrickson for dissolution of their partnership. Trouble between the two occurred first in 1859 when Wilson had a unit of their circus company in South America and Hendrickson was managing another on the West Coast. The two had a successful season the prior year and some money was laid aside for real estate investment. When Wilson returned he was informed that Hendrickson's company had a losing season and the reserve funds were used up in an attempt to keep the show running; but, sorry, this could not be verified because "the books had been lost." Later, Wilson learned that certain real estate had indeed been purchased by Hendrickson using partnership money. Finding this to be irregular, Wilson sued for a deed to one-half of the property so purchased, as well as for the dissolution of the partnership.

The seats were dusted off and the Hippotheatron re-opened for the 1864-65 winter season on October 3 under the interminable proprietorship of James M. Nixon. The skilled and sizable company was comprised of François Siegrist and Marietta Zanfretta; the Sherwoods (Charles, Virginia, Ida, and Charles, Jr.); Young Nicolo; monkey-man Mons. William Olma (William Smith); Talleen Brothers; William Odell; and James V. Cameron, equestrian director and ringmaster. The clowns were Nat Austin and James Cooke. On October 10, Eaton Stone appeared with Mons. Baptiste, the monkey-man, in *L'Homme du Bois.* James Melville and family (Samuel, Francis, and George) came on

October 24. New faces for the month of November included the performing dogs and monkeys of Henry Cooke and young Bob Stickney and his father. Louise Tourniaire was on the bill in December along with the gymnast Verrecke. The Christmas pantomime, *Harlequin Bluebeard*, was replaced in February with another pantomime, *Harlequin Mother Goose*, which ran to the end of March, when the aerial vaulter George Barthelon and the Conrad Brothers were added to the bill. Another pantomime was put up, *The Fairy Prince O'Donohue*, which was succeeded on May 15, 1865, by *The Elixir of Life, or, the Birth of Harlequin*.

At the end of the season for Robinson & Howes' Railroad Circus, Horace Norton replaced Robinson in management. On November 14, the Howes & Norton's Circus opened in Nashville on the lot at the corner of College and Jackson Streets. The Lake family was there, still popular from their visit almost exactly a year earlier. They shared the bills with Charles and James Madigan, Charles Fish, gymnasts Kelley and Burrows, clowns Albert Aymar, John Lowlow and John Davenport, and contortionist William Lester. J. E. Lechler and J. J. Justice were the agents.[11] On Monday, November 21, the tent was moved to Market Street near the Louisville and Nashville depot, which was considered a much better location.[12]

With Gen. Thomas' Union soldiers encamped around the city waiting to attack Hood's Confederate forces, money was plentiful. Prices were 75¢ and 50¢ for admission, 25¢ for an orange and the same for a glass of pink lemonade. The tent being pitched in "the very heart of the city" supported the expectation that the show would escape the shelling from the rebel forces nearby. This proved to be wrong; for, according to John Glenroy, who was with the troupe, during the six-week stay the company experienced numerous cannonades, with shells sometimes landing within twenty yards of the canvas. If that wasn't enough, during a sweep for horses, a Union army officer expropriated eighteen of the circus' animals, paying the sum of $1,800. This left the company with two mules and a single, lame ring horse. An item appeared in the Nashville *Union* on December 8 to the effect that, "notwithstanding the impressment by the military authorities of nearly all the horses of the circus, this operation was still open and going ahead."[13]

The maintaining of horses for the armies was a major problem. General Henry Wagner Halleck had reported earlier that they were being used up so rapidly that a remount for the whole service was required every two months. Compounding this dilemma, the trading of broken

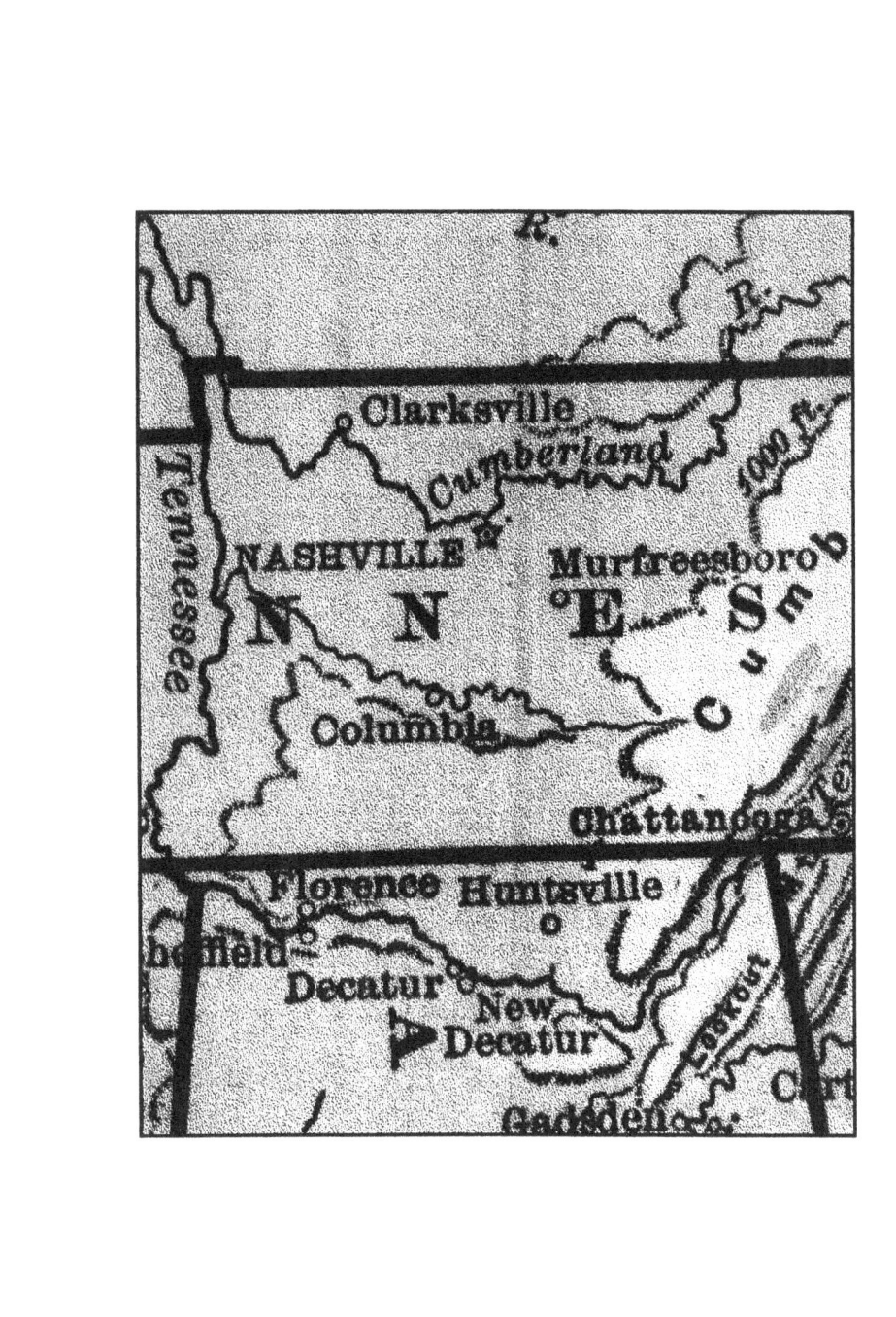

down animals to the army was scandalous at this time. Of the 315 horses received from the vicinity of Cincinnati at the start of the war, 211 were rejected as being unfit for service. Unscrupulous contractors and careless government examiners were the cause. "The tricks of the jockey are transferred from the low race course and the horse market to the supply of our army in its now most important arm." Difficulty in obtaining decent mounts created a huge problem in developing new cavalry units. The poor caliber of horses being sold to the government can be exemplified by one regiment at Nashville which required three fresh supplies in less than six months. It was estimated that all other cavalry units were in a similar condition.

On the other hand, the Confederate cavalrymen were required to supply their own mounts. If a horse was killed, or otherwise lost, the soldier was given a thirty-day furlough to return home and obtain a new one. This led to the practice among soldiers of selling their horses whenever they wanted to go home, or of stealing horses whenever they needed a replacement.

The Union army could be indiscriminate in its procurement of mounts as well. Thomas telegraphed Grant on the morning of December 6 that his aides, under the direction of Gen. Wilson, were out pressing horses into service and as soon as he had sufficient mounts he would attack Hood. The aim was to have between six and eight thousand troops astride within three days. Forthwith, they commandeered horses off the streets of Nashville—dray horses, saddle horses and farm stock. By necessity, every available horse was subject to confiscation.

Frank Howes complained to Gen. Thomas about his loss of horses. Thomas replied he could do nothing. But by good fortune, the following day Vice-President Johnson arrived in Nashville. The persistent Howes arranged a meeting with him, explained the dilemma, and pleaded for help. Somehow he convinced Johnson to seek advice from the President and, after an exchange of telegraph messages, Lincoln suggested that the animals be released on the condition that substitutes were found by the circus management. It took Howes nearly a week to meet the terms of the agreement, but finally Howes & Norton had their horses back.[14] Under date of December 11, the *Union* published a notice advising of their return, and on the 14th an advertisement revealed that the circus would positively be in Nashville for only one week longer.

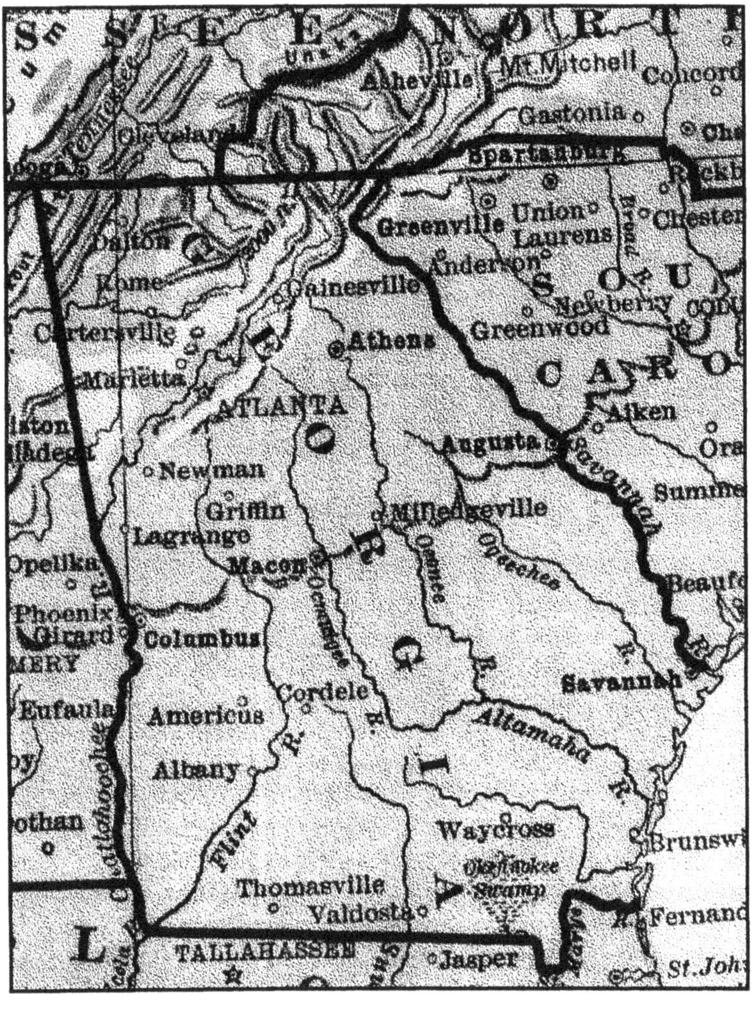

Asheville
Mt Mitchell
Gastonia
Spartanburg
Greenville
Union
Laurens
Chester
Dalton
Rome
Gainesville
Anderson
Newberry
Greenwood
Cartersville
Athens
Marietta
ATLANTA
Aiken
Augusta
Savannah
Newman
Griffin
Milledgeville
Lagrange
Macon
Opelika
Ocmulgee
Oconee
Ogeechee
Phoenix
Girard
Columbus
Savannah
Cordele
Eufaula
Americus
Altamaha
Albany
Waycross
Flint
Swamp
Thomasville
Valdosta
TALLAHASSEE
Jasper

On the 15th the forces of Gen. Thomas and Gen. Hood collided. The well-traveled Southern clown, John Lowlow, recalled the scene occurring within the canvas pavilion:

> That night, while the city was full of wounded men and prisoners, and while the guns were booming like thunder, our show was jammed. Whether the people came to meet each other and to hear the news or whether they wanted the fun in the ring to relax their tensely strung heart-strings, I can't say, but it is certain that on Thursday and Friday nights, while the battle was in progress in easy hearing—there, almost on the battlefield—the people and strangers in Nashville came to the circus in great crowds, and laughed like children.[15]

A benefit was given for the poor of the city on the 16th. The receipts were reported to have been $526.50, over expenses of $471.77, leaving the proceeds for charity at $54.73.[16] The hapless poor suffered from the misfortune of inclement weather.

On November 15, Gen. William T. Sherman, after having destroyed all that was left of value in Atlanta, continued his raid through Georgia, cutting supply lines and living off the land until, on December 21, following days of pressure, William J. Hardee and his few remaining Confederate troops evacuated Savannah, making way for Union soldiers to occupy the city. In their wake they had left over 100 million dollars worth of damaged and destroyed property. The occupation of Savannah completed Sherman's march to the sea.

CIRCUSES AND MENAGERIES, 1864: George F. Bailey & Co.; Dan Castello; Davis & McClean; Gardner & Hemmings; Great Union (John Robinson); Hippotheatron, 14th Street, NYC (winter); Howes & Norton (formerly Robinson & Howe); S. B. Howes European; Tom King (John O'Brien); Lake & Co.; Lee & Ryland (California); L. B. Lent; Maginley & Bell; Maginley, Black & Co.; James Melville & Co.; Metropolitan (Robinson & Deery); National (Cincinnati, winter); Nixon's Hippotheatron (New York); Old Cary; Orton Bros.; Dan Rice (Aymar, California; Rivers & Derious; Robinson & Deery; Yankee Robinson; Sands, Nathan & Co.; Slaymaker & Nichols (Goodwin & Wilder, proprietors); Spalding & Rogers; Stone, Rosston & Co.; Thayer & Noyes; VanAmburgh & Co.; Mrs. Charles Warner (Philadelphia, winter); Wheeler, Hatch & Hitchcock; Wilson, Zoyara & Carlos (California).

NOTES

[1] City Summary, New York *Clipper*, January 30, 1864, p. 331.
[2] "Great Fortunes," *Billboard*, December 7, 1901, p.11.
[3] New York *Clipper*, July 30, 1864, p. 134.
[4] King, pp. 68-69.
[5] *Ibid*, pp. 69-70.
[6] Excerpt from the New Orleans *Times*, February 2, 1865, in a portrait of Peter Conklin, New York *Clipper*, June 2, 1866, p. 60.
[7] New York *Clipper*, October 15, 1864, p. 214.
[8] New York *Clipper*, July 16, 1864, p. 111.
[9] New York *Clipper*, May 7, 1864, p. 31.
[10] Advertisement column, New York *Clipper*, September 3, 1864, p. 167.
[11] Also on the roster were John Glenroy, John Clark, W. Kirkwood, David Henderson, Sam Baldwin, William Donovan.
[12] Nashville *Dispatch*, November 20, 1864, p. 2.
[13] Letter from Campbell H. Brown, Tennessee State Library and Archives, Nashville, TN, to Thomas P. Parkinson, dated August 9, 1967.
[14] Glenroy, pp. 137-38. There is another account of this incident printed in a Cincinnati special to the New York *Sun*, related by the great clown John Lowlow in an unidentified clipping, "The Circus in the War," from the files of Stuart Thayer. Lowlow's explanation of the solution is probably apocryphal. He states that after struggling through four days of matinee and evening performances, little Alice Lake called at the headquarters of Gen. Wilson and begged for the return of the horses. She told the general how heartsick she was for them and that she was certain they missed her. She cried and worked her youthful charms and won her case. Every one of the horses was returned to them.
[15] Cincinnati special to the New York *Sun*, by John Lowlow, unidentified clipping, "The Circus in the War," from the files of Stuart Thayer.
[16] Nashville *Dispatch*, December 20, 1864, p. 2.

> **DEATHS IN 1864**: gymnast and general performer, **James Carlisle**, February 16 in Chicago; **Jerry Worland**, tumbler and leaper, in New York City, April 24; **Isabel Cubas**, dancer and pantomimist, in New York City, June 20, age 27; **Caroline Nixon**, equestrienne and former wife of James M. Nixon, at Bangor, ME, July 20, age 35; **Charles Johnson**, 40-horse driver, of pleuritis, in Philadelphia, December 18, age 33; **David D. Ayres**, fell from the trapeze bar, Truxillo, Peru, December 18; **Ebenetiz Howes**, showman, on December 25; **William Hunt**, broke his neck on a vaulting board; **James McFarland**, vaulter and general performer, killed by a hotel landlord at Liberty, MO.

1865

On the 1st of February Sherman's army of some 60,000 advanced northward out of Savannah to sweep through the Carolinas and to join up with Grant's forces. The movement went forward almost unopposed. On March 27, Generals Sherman and Grant conferred with Lincoln on the steamer *River Queen* to work out a strategy for boxing in Lee as a final push to terminate the conflict. The President is remembered to have repeatedly asked: "Must more blood be shed? Cannot this last bloody battle be avoided?" But, in the end, the pincer movement proved unnecessary. A Federal victory at Five Forks, VA, on April 1 forced Lee to abandon both Petersburg and Richmond and flee westward. Finally, with his army depleted and his supplies exhausted, he surrendered to Grant at Appomattox Court House on April 9. Two days later, the Stars and Stripes of the United States was raised over Fort Sumter, where it all had begun.

The war was over but the enmity continued under the wraps of white robes and hoods as the Ku Klux Klan was organized to uphold white supremacy and to combat the "carpetbaggers" arriving from the North. And pockets of marauders and returned soldiers, still with guns in their hands and hatred in their hearts, bullied the local populus and created havoc for touring circuses.

On Good Friday, April 14, Washington, DC, was enjoying sunny spring weather. The city had taken on an aura of gaiety as the American flag could be seen flying from every building of importance and the realization of peace was cause for general merriment. Laura Keene, performing the role of Laura Trenchard in *Our American Cousin*, was taking her benefit at Ford's Theatre that night. It had been previously announced that the President, Gen. Grant and other dignitaries would be attending. Grant was required to be out of town but the President was there along with half of Washington, who were enjoying the occasion until the third act when suddenly the sound of a pistol was heard from the direction of the President's box. Immediately, a man dashed to the front of it and leaped upon the stage. In his frenzy, he brandished a dagger, shouted *"Sic semper tyrannus!"* and fled to the

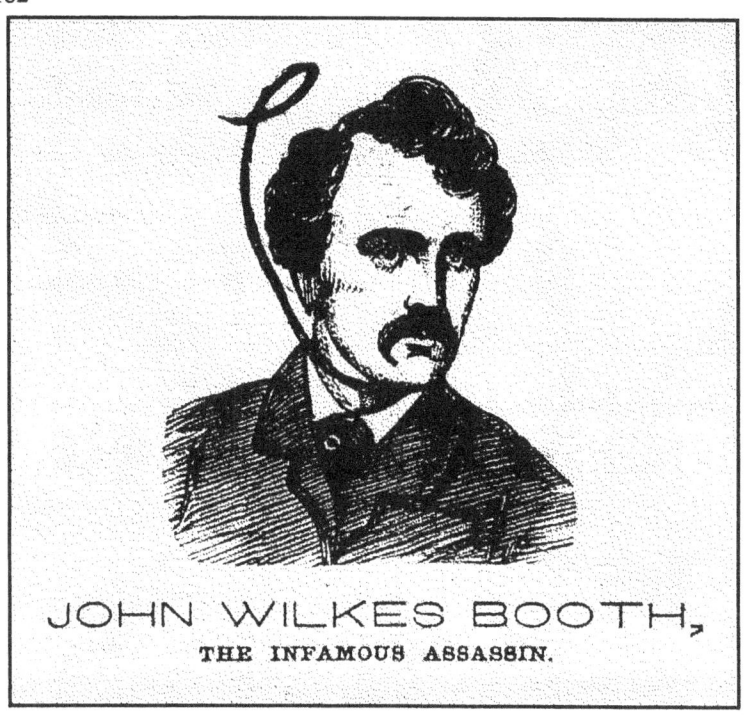

JOHN WILKES BOOTH,
THE INFAMOUS ASSASSIN.

rear of the theatre where his horse was in readiness for escape. Lincoln had been shot in the head. On 7:22 a.m. of the following morning the President of the United States was dead.

The tragedy was witnessed by a young Eliza Logan, who had accompanied her actor parents to the theatre and, because they were friends of Laura Keene, went with them back stage on that fateful night:

> I stood in the wings beside the prompter. The curtain was called and Laura Keene was going on the stage, when a shot ran out. Booth had just shot Abraham Lincoln. I saw Booth jump over the balcony and make for the stage exit, where the people at the door let him out. I sensed the terror in the faces about me and clung to mother's skirts as she and Laura Keene rushed up to Lincoln's box. Laura knelt down and took the head of Abraham Lincoln in her lap. She looked up at mother and shook her head, then she lifted the folds of her full skirt and tenderly wiped the blood from his face. Lincoln's wife was just crazy—I wondered why she screamed so. Afterwards, down in the dressing-room, mother helped Laura remove her bloodstained dress. She handed the

dress to mother and said, "Here, Agnes, take this, I don't want to see it again, ever."[1]

Equestrian John Glenroy, who was residing in Chicago at that time, recalled the contrast between the elation when the news came of the fall of Richmond and the report of the Lincoln's assassination. "On the fifteenth of April Chicago was draped in honor of the dead President," he wrote, "and that was a sorrowful community that day."[2]

Throughout the conflict, amusements had benefited when a noted military personage attended a performance, particularly when the visitation was announced in advance. Audiences enjoyed the opportunity to release their patriotic energy in a show of approbation. In June, Niblo's Theatre was honored by a visit from Gen. Sherman. As he entered a private box with his staff between the first and second acts, the band struck up "Hail, Columbia!" At the moment the General was recognized, the audience arose and paid their respect and appreciation by a healthy demonstration of applause. After staying for two acts, the Sherman party retired from the theatre, perhaps finding the drama too tame an amusement after years of bloody war.

As one might expect, when the last cannon sounded the national economy was starkly contrasted between North and South. In the North the war had stimulated enormous growth and expansion. Because of high tariffs and an influx of paper money, manufacturing establishments, of which there were some 140,000 in 1860, had increased by almost seventy-five percent. Oil was becoming a booming industry with derricks spreading over a wide area of northwestern Pennsylvania. Railroad mileage had almost doubled. Telegraph construction had been expanded to meet battlefield needs. The United States, with its great asset in technological skills, was fast becoming a world leader in the manufacture of iron and steel, textiles and leather goods, as well as the ingenuity for devising industrial and agricultural machines.

The South, on the other hand, was desolate—gutted towns, neglected fields, ruined plantations, destroyed churches, collapsed bridges, and demolished roadways and railroads. Two-thirds of the livestock had been killed. Confederate capital, depleted in a losing cause, was scarce. One-third of the white male population was dead or maimed. With the emancipation of the slaves, Southerners were deprived of two billion dollars worth of property as well as a labor force necessary for recovery.

In spite of the economic boom, the summer started slowly for Northern circuses, an indication that shows were not doing the business of the previous year. The death of the President spread a pall over the entire nation for weeks in the spring. Money was seemingly scarce, with corn and wheat selling for half of what they had brought in 1864. The *Clipper* dourly predicted:

> There is not a company on the road that is doing barely one-half the business it did last season. Many a sawdust performer will reach New York at the close of the season minus several weeks' salary.[3]

James M. Nixon erected another temporary building in Washington with wooden sides and a canvas top, near Sixth Street and Pennsylvania Avenue, to house his arenic entertainments. The structure was designed on the same plan as he had used there three years before. There was a large wooden dressing area, a spacious archway at the entrance with a ticket office on each side, and a stage that could be inserted at short notice. The management included Nixon, William Nichols, and Richard Platt. Charley Sherwood's "Pete Jenkins" and the educated horse, General Scott, were featured attractions when the place opened on May 29. The equestrian department was made up of the Sherwoods, William Nichols, Delevanti Brothers, Messrs. Rivers, Henderson, Campbell, Conklin, and Smith. But the entertainment was not strictly equestrian, since much of the program was comprised of oleo acts enhanced by a *corps de ballet*. The Ellinger & Foote Moral Exhibition—whatever that entailed—was engaged to perform in conjunction to the regular company; however, the troupe remained but one week, closing on June 10.

Competition appeared in the form of Stone, Rosston & Co. on a lot on the corner of Sixth and York Avenue. They may have been responsible for the tapering off of business at Nixon's amphitheatre; for on the 15th, his company moved out, heading into Maryland, Virginia, and North Carolina. This was the same general area where he had taken his railroad show in 1860, but this time there were concentrations of soldiers to boost attendance. After undergoing a series of railroad mishaps, the company returned north and finished the summer performing around the New York City area.

Across the country in San Francisco, John Wilson's Hippodrome, on the site of the old Mechanics Pavilion, was attracting audiences. The place was arranged with two rings, an inner and outer one. In the larger, all sorts of races were contested—hurdle, chariot, Roman, pony, and even running. The smaller ring was used for Ella Zoyara's

S. P. Stickney

principal act on horseback, for Painter and Durand's *la perche equipoise*, for exhibition of the trained colt, Othello, and for other gymnastic and acrobatic activities.

Several events were featured during the short season. *Mazeppa* was produced on January 30, with Mattie Field in the title role. A number of hose companies vied for the championship of the mile run around the hippodrome track. Pacing and trotting horse races were offered with purses of $100 and $250 respectively. Equestrian director, William T. Aymar, took a benefit on February 6 and the season officially closed on the 11th. But the place was re-opened three days later to give benefits for H. C. Lee and George Ryland. It was announced that as part of the program there would be a race for a silver cup, and Ella Zoyara would ride nine horses (a feat never before attempted in California), followed by a display of fireworks.

The former "Great Southern Circus" kept to the mid-western area during this first post-war year. The Great Union Combination Circus and Menagerie, as the John Robinson show was now being called, started from Ohio but went directly into Indiana and Illinois. Early announcements claimed the outfit numbered no less than 300 men and horses. W. H. Hough was the business manager, assisted by John Robinson, Jr.; G. N. Robinson, the treasurer; Fred H. Bailey, agent; and Mons. Louis DeFabier, ringmaster. Prominent among the performers were the Conrad Brothers, Master Willie Dutton, J. L. Davenport, and Jenny Worland. After being on the road twenty-eight weeks, the show went into winter quarters in Cincinnati on October 28.

Thayer & Noyes United States Circus Combined with VanAmburgh & Co.'s Menagerie started the season with a new tent, wagons and harness, ten cages of animals and Hannibal, the largest elephant in the country. Along with Dr. James L. Thayer and Charles Noyes, the compliment consisted of Charles Reed, Mr. and Mrs. Tom King, Jimmy Reynolds, Charles Burrows, William Kincade, Henry Moreste, Joseph Haslett, John Saunders, etc. Tom Canham was the band leader, Andy Springer the advertiser.

The show was to open in Washington for a week at Sixth Street near Pennsylvania Avenue on March 29, but was forced into delay because the VanAmburgh animals—due to floods and other perils of travels—did not arrive until the 30th. The opening came on April 1, the day the news of the fall of Richmond and Petersburg reached the capital. As the show's parade went past the War Department, it stopped while

Hannibal kneeled down and the band played "Hail, Columbia." The procession then moved on through Pennsylvania Avenue to the tent and opened its doors to the joyous crowd that had assembled. It was reported that in spite of adding extra seats around the ring during the week, the circus was compelled to turn away hundreds of people from their large three center pole tent.[4]

Because of the unfortunate delay, the arrival at the capital coincided with that of Stone, Rosston & Co., who had open their summer season for a two week stand at Norfolk, VA, on March 14. Both circuses played out the week and then met again on the 10th of April in Baltimore. Thayer & Noyes set up at the foot of East Street, near the Bel Air market; Stone & Rosston were nearby on the Bel Air lot at Gay and East.

Thayer & Noyes reported their reception to have surpassed what they had experienced in Washington, that despite disagreeable weather and the competition hundreds were turned away at the door. This is undoubtedly an over-statement; still, in all probability, the show outdrew its rival. Both companies were getting 50¢ and 25¢ admissions but as an attraction Hannibal was proving he was worth his weight in hay. And there were those ten cages of VanAmburgh animals; Stone and Rosston carried none. In addition, Thayer & Noyes' strong company of performers was advantaged with two Baltimoreans—Tom King and William Kincade.

If the opposition could boast of no menagerie, they at least had Cullen's Iroquois Indian troupe—chiefs, braves, warriors and squaws, *et al*. They also had Prof. Hutchinson's celebrated kennel of performing canines; the gymnastics of John Murray and G. P. Hutchinson and the Denzer Brothers (Charles, Rudolph, Valentine); the clowning of Den Stone and Charles Monroe; and the versatile Siegrist family—Auguste and wife, Ferdinand, Little Rosa and Master Auguste. Frank Carpenter was the hurdle rider; Le Jeune Burt, scenic rider; William Young, trapezist; Frank Rosston, ringmaster; W. Drexel, Herculean performer. Signor Ferdinand (probably Ferdinand Sagrino) had been doing the outdoor free act on the trapeze; but El Nino Eddie (Eddie Rivers) was brought to Baltimore for additional support to walk a wire outside the tent each day. Stone & Rosston closed their stand on Friday, the 14th, and headed for Richmond, but returned on Monday, June 12, to have Baltimore to themselves for five days.

THE ELEVENTH
EXHIBITION
OF 1865!
WILL EXHIBIT AT PORTLAND,

Wednesday and Thursday,

SEPTEMBER 20th & 21st,
FOR TWO DAYS ONLY!
AFTERNOON AND EVENING,

COR. OF GREEN AND PORTLAND STREETS.

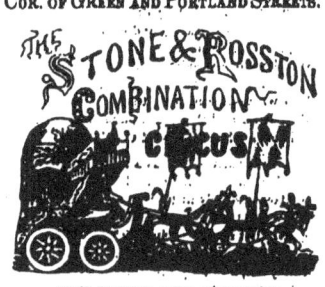

THE STONE AND ROSSTON

CIRCUS COMBINATION,
CULLEN'S TROUPE OF

IROQUOIS INDIANS!
A Brilliant Galaxy of

Equestrian and Gymnastic Celebrities!!!

PROF. HUTCHINSON'S

PERFORMING DOGS,
TRAINED HORSES,
Dancing and Trick Ponies,
DAN STONE'S

COMIC MULES!

Consolidated in ONE EXHIBITION for ONE PRICE of admission for the season of 1865.

The ENTIRE CAVALCADE for this Gigantic Combination on the morning of the Exhibition, will afford the public a GRATUITOUS VIEW of its unparalled magnificence and its unequalled resources.

One of the prominent features of this Collosal Circus, will be the

GRAND FREE EXHIBITION

of the GYMNASTIC MIRACLE of ÆRONANTIC-OSCILLATION, or

FLYING IN THE AIR!

near the immense Pavillion, at one o'clock P. M.

☞ For details, see Mammoth Pictorial and Descriptive Sheets and other advertisements.

Admission 50 cents. - - - Children 25 cents.

Door open at 2 and 7 P. M.

Performance to commence half an hour after.

Thayer & Noyes remained for two days more, leaving on April 17 for Westminster, Frederick City, and other towns in Maryland and Pennsylvania. But, alas! they lost their main attraction at Centerville, MD, on May 7 when the approximately 70 year old Hannibal died, with a loss to the owners estimated at $20,000. He had been with the VanAmburgh concern since coming to this country in 1824. As a reward for his years of service, the VanAmburgh people had him skinned and presented to the commissioners for exhibition at New York's Central Park.[5]

Thayer & Noyes visited Nashville in August, where on Wednesday the 9th the show opened on the College and Jackson Street lot for four days only—"one tent, one single price of admission." The ghost of Hannibal was there but the ads were promoting the mortal version. In death he was still "the largest quadruped in Europe or America." What the patrons saw when they paid their 75¢ and entered the tent is anybody's guess.

S. O. Wheeler was on the road for his third season with his Great International Circus, moving about in New England after opening at the Boston City Fairgrounds on April 26. The show featured John S. Rarey, the famed horse tamer and his equally famous equine student, Cruiser. At each performance Rarey supposedly began with an hour long lecture in which he tamed a vicious horse. Local horse owners were encouraged to bring unruly specimens with which Rarey would demonstrate his ability to subdue fractious animals. It is unclear how long he remained with the show but his engagement extended beyond the Boston date. The circus company consisted of clowns John Foster and Nat Austin, gymnasts H. W. Penny and George Goldie, riders Eaton Stone, William Ashton, and Charles Sherwood and son; Master Frank Ashton did juvenile posturing, Jeanette Ellsler worked the tight-rope.

John O'Brien and Adam Forepaugh began the summer touring with Dan Rice's Menagerie, which was made up of the former Jerry Mabie animals, comprising twenty-two cages. The Mabie property was delivered to Forepaugh at Twelfth and State Streets, Chicago, where the company started the season with a four-day stand on April 24. The menagerie, Dan Rice, his horse, Excelsior, trick mules, and two elephants constituted the exhibition. Rice was engaged for the twenty-five week summer season at a salary of $1,000 a week. The show went into Michigan, Ohio and closed at Dan Rice's winter retreat, Girard, PA.

The circus business picked up as the season progressed and the year turned out exceptionally well; perhaps not as profitable as 1864, but one of the most successful in years. Circuses were reported thick in Ohio in the month of August with the familiar titles of Howes' Great European, Dan Rice's, Gardner & Hemmings, and the New York *Champ Élyées*. Routing in Pennsylvania was particularly solid for business because of the new oil discoveries and the heavy concentration of Union soldiers.

Kansas, which had been avoided by most showmen during the conflict because of its political turbulence, was now opened for travel. Perhaps the first post-war visitor to the state was George W. DeHaven & Co.'s United States Circus when the show's agent, J. H. Owen, billed Leavenworth for a June 21 and 22 stand.

The year marked Andrew Haight's entry into the circus field. Born in Dresden, NY, the son of a merchant and drover, he took over the mercantile operation following his father's death. Upon moving to Beaver Dam, WI, he entered into successful businesses, operating two large stores, speculating in real estate and constructing and keeping a hotel there—the Clark House, complete with a pool room and gambling parlor. He also had a third store and hotel in New London, WI, managed by his brothers. At the age of thirty-four he met George W. DeHaven, who inveigled him into putting up money and entering circus management as a partner.

Under the DeHaven title, the circus started from Beaver Dam, WI, in April and moved down the Rock River on the *Jeanette Roberts*, stopping at towns along the Mississippi, Missouri, and Ohio. Levi J. North was the equestrian director; W. McArthur, ringmaster; and P. H. Seaman, Tom Burgess, and Albert Aymar, clowns. William Naylor did the principal hurdle and somersault act. Mlle. Louise [or Mlle. Castilla] ascended the wire outside the canvas, walking the distance of 300 feet to the top of the pavilion, some 50 feet above the ground. Others on the bill were Mlle, De'Auley, equestrienne; Mme. Annette Seamon, wire performer and *danseuse*; Levi J. North, Jr., two-pony rider; Signor Bliss, ceiling-walker; Henry Burdeau and Louis Carr, gymnasts; Charles Rivers, general performer; Henry Coyle, stilt-walking clown; and the Bliss family contributing their tumbling skills. J. H. Perkins led the brass band and A. T. Britton had charge of the string band. Admission was 75¢, children 50¢.

The DeHaven company steamed up the Missouri and arrived in Leavenworth on the 21st. That the show pleased the entertainment

John S. Rarey

Rarey Exhibiting a Tame Zebra

hungry Kansans can be confirmed by the following passage from the *Daily Conservative* of the 22nd:

> The seats were filled with some of our best citizens yesterday, and all seemed highly pleased. Those who do not attend the circus will miss a first-class performance. The audience filled the canvass to overflowing last night, and as everybody brings away a good report, all would believe those who desire a seat to go early this afternoon and evening. This is their last day here.[6]

The DeHaven outfit was heavily advertised. Ads ran seven days in advance of the performance dates in the Leavenworth *Daily Conservative*. This was repeated in the Atchison *Daily Champion* for the appearance in that city. There, J. H. Owens erected a billboard 80 feet long and 12 feet high on the corner of Commerce and Second Streets and filled the space with circus paper.[7]

It was announced that, after leaving Atchinson, the show would continue up the Missouri, stopping at St. Joseph for June 26 and 27, and then proceed as far north as Council Bluffs, IA, just across the river from Omaha. Returning down river, another stop was made at Leavenworth on July 11, with the *Conservative* expressing satisfaction on the following day equal to that of the earlier stand:

> The mammoth circus of DeHaven & Co. arrived at our levee on their return, on time, yesterday morning, and made a triumphant march through our city to their former place of exhibition. Both the performances in the afternoon and evening were well attended. By urgent request, and to accommodate a large number of soldiers, the circus will give three performances at the Fort to-day—at 9½ a.m., 1½ p.m., and 7½ p.m. We advise all the boys in blue to attend, for it is the best circus ever in this part of the country.[8]

An unexpected and quite astounding episode occurred at the Fort performances. Following Mlle. Louise's outdoor exhibition on the wire, a drum major of the 14th Illinois Regiment stepped forward and announced he could do better. He was immediately challenged by one of the company, who offered to bet him $25 that he could not walk ten feet up the incline. Boldly accepting the wager, the soldier pulled off his boots and mounted the wire in his stocking feet. The disbelieving showman then made the proposal that if he performed the feat successfully his entire regiment would be passed into the tent at no charge. With this, the soldier walked up the wire to the center pole, made an about face in military fashion, and began his descent. In an act of arrogance, about half-way down he stood on one foot, sticking the other out straight, and then sat down on the wire with both legs extended. After arriving again on solid ground, he was greeted by lusty cheers from his comrades.

That evening the wire-walking drum major arrived with a number of his regiment expecting to be ushered into the tent for a complimentary performance. To his surprised, the circus people refused to honor their previous offer. With this, quite a row ensued. Four people were knocked to the ground, the treasurer's box was upset, and the canvas was ripped in places. Further damage was forestalled when the soldiers were finally let in.[9]

There were more frightening encounters with local troublemakers, incidents which occurred with greater frequency than in the past. The thousands of soldiers suddenly idled from their warring existence, still armed for battle, but trying to forget the nightmare memories of the last few years, created a volatile climate in isolated communities, suspicious of the encroachment of strangers. Glenroy recalled that in Missouri nearly everyone carried revolvers and knives, whether on the street or places of business, including waitresses at public dining rooms and barbers in their shops. "It was a common thing to see Negro women walking along the street carrying revolvers in their hands."[10]

George DeHaven & Co. had a jump of 150 miles on board the steamboat *Jeanette Roberts* for an August 7 date at Alton, IL. Because of arriving at their destination shortly before show time, Mlle. Louise's free act was omitted, as well as Signor Bliss' ceiling walking feat, with substitutes inserted in their stead. The next stand, Madison, IN, was over 150 miles from Alton, so a night performance was not given.

Later, when the circus was loading onto their boat, some of the audience came around to express dissatisfaction. Included in this party were a captain and number of soldiers. The demonstration ultimately became a nuisance to the loading process and DeHaven ordered the protesters off the boat. It appeared that the matter was settled; but, when the *Jeanette Roberts* steamed away, the soldiers reappeared and began shooting in her direction. As the boat moved up the Ohio River the soldiers followed at a distance, sporadically sniping at the pilot house. Although there were seventy or eighty shots fired into the moving craft, there were no serious injuries to the passengers.

Frank Howes' Olympian Circus was showing in Warrenton, MO, when the Home Volunteers received full liberty. The soldiers had taken over the town and were making it unpleasant for everyone. Some of them came to the circus lot and demanded free entrance. J. J. Nathans, who was on the door, refused their demands, for which he was knocked to the ground from the butt of a pistol. Nathans gave orders for the audience to be turned out and the canvas torn down, but before that could happen the volunteers broke through the front door of the tent. Inside, they were confronted by a parcel of circus baggage men who managed to beat them off.

After being forced from the lot, the soldiers took to the hills some one hundred yards from the show grounds. There they commenced firing at members of the company, forcing the circus people to form their wagons into a circle to protect themselves and their stock. The firing continued periodically until morning and ceased only when the troop's officer, who had had no part in the disturbance, came to propose a peaceful settlement. The casualties, as Howes Olympian Circus left Warrenton, consisted of wagons filled with bullet holes, J. J. Nathans with a very sore head, and a ring attendant sporting a broken nose.[11]

Robinson & Deery's Metropolitan Circus arrived at Franklin, PA, on June 22. The afternoon performance was completed without incident; but during the evening show, a covey of country yokels, inspirited by liquid encouragement, demolished the oil lamps on the center poles, ripped up the canvas, threw the ticket wagon into a ditch, and created whatever havoc was handy to them. This was another of many examples where a license paid by the circus company received no benefits of protection from the municipality.

When Palmer's Great Western Circus (formerly the John O'Brien and Tom King outfit) performed at Clinton, IA, August 21, a fight occurred between some returned soldiers and members of the show. The final count: six circus personnel and one soldier dead.

The show, managed by H. Palmer, was also performing along the Missouri river route at this time. The troupe featured the equestrian Whitby family—Harry, Elvira, Rosa, and Willie. Alongside were William Kennedy, clown; George Wambold, contortionist; Mons. Rochelle, William Smith, and L. Zanfretta, gymnasts; William Morgan, bar act and hurdle rider; W. H. Green, horse tamer, Hercules, and six-horse rider; J. C. Clark, rope-walker; etc. The agent was billing a route through northern Missouri and Iowa, but the troupe was unable to follow due to heavy rains and bad roads. After exhibiting a week in St. Joseph they turned back south.

The devastation of the routes of transportation in areas where the fighting occurred, coupled with an unusual amount of rainfall in some parts of the South and West, caused problems of movement for several circuses. Occasionally, shows were forced to leave some of the heavy wagons behind and use the railroad. Yankee Robinson, who had purchased Melville's Australian Circus this year, found Missouri roads in horrendous condition, as we learn from a member of the company:

> In twenty years experience I have never seen the like. We have waded, swam, sank, &c., and are all worn out. Our trunk wagon is sixty miles back in the bottom of a river. We undertook to swim it, but the rope broke and away she went. We have not made half the stands, and worse roads, if possible, to come. The country has been raided till the bridges, &c., that were here are all gone, and roads badly washed. The rain is as bad this week as it has been any time this season. The show is working eastward and we expect to get on dry land one of these days.[12]

The Orton Bros.' Great Circus met with similar problems in the same state:

> [We encountered] the wildest rivers and the roughest roads that were ever navigable! We had to swim most of the rivers, for there was 'nary a bridge,' and we frequently did not reach town till two, three, and five o'clock in the afternoon of show days.[13]

With the fighting over, the South provided opportunities for showmen willing to gamble on the outcome. Howes & Castello; Thayer and Noyes; Stone, Rosston & Co.; and George W. DeHaven were quick to seize the opportunity and take the expected risk. They traveled from New Orleans east into Kentucky, Georgia, Alabama, Tennessee and Louisiana, avoiding the devastation of the smaller towns and playing primarily in the major cities.

For the most part, these southern shows moved by rail. This seems almost unbelievable when one observes that, like most of the infrastructure in the South at war's end, the railroads were in deplorable condition. The greatest damage was apparent in Virginia and Mississippi but one cannot exclude the harm created in the five-month raping of the countryside by Sherman's troops in Georgia and the Carolinas. Union forces demonstrated a particular destructive skill, being more mechanically minded than their Southern counterparts. In the summer of 1865, a former Confederate captain confirmed this by the comment: "We could do something in that line, we thought, but we were ashamed of ourselves when we saw how your [Union] men could do it." On the other hand, Southerners did contributed to this ruin as they occasionally tore up their own tracks before retreating.[14]

Well over half of the Southern rail network was destroyed or crippled. "Twisted rails, burned ties, destroyed bridges, gutted depots and shops, and lost or dilapidated rolling stock were the normal heritage of war for most southern lines." Some of the routes were out of service a long time. Operation of the 104 mile rail link between Savannah and Charleston was not resumed until March, 1870. But rehabilitation was helped by the federal government in both the early return of the southern lines and in the sale of government-owned rolling stock and equipment; so that by Christmas, 1865, most roads, ruined though they were, were offering some sort of service.[15]

Early in the year, Dan Castello's Great Show was aboard a boat in New Orleans bound for Matamoros, Mexico, but, the draft being in effect, was unable to procure clearance. Along with Dan, little Dan, and Mrs. Castello, the company included such performers as Charles Parker, James and Josephine DeMott, Horace Nichols, Ferdinand Tourniaire, William Benton, Tom Shields, August Lehman, Joe Randolph, Carlotta DeBerg, and James Cooke. On March 4, there was a bit of difficulty in getting river boats because of the military's monopoly of them, but after prevailing the show succeeded in starting up the Mississippi.

The opening at Natchez on March 13 was marred when a heavy rain set in during the performance. Water dripped through areas of the canvas, damaging many of the heated lamp chimneys and drenching the occupants in the upper tier of seats. The discomfort was repeated on Tuesday, but the weather cleared for the remainder of the week during which the tent was comfortably well filled with dry-footed patrons.

The company was announced to proceed to Vicksburg, thence to Memphis, April 8, and Little Rock, April 9. According to the *Clipper*, the show was working its way to St. Louis to get new wagons and reorganize for the summer tour opening in mid-May.

Shortly, Castello and at least some of his company took on the title of Howes & Castello. It is unclear to me exactly where this occurred. Stuart Thayer places it at Nashville. Confusion is caused by the interchanging of company titles from one stand to the next. The combination advertised at various times under the Castello name, at others under Howes', and still others as Howes and Castello; and the *Clipper* reflected this in its reportage of the show's movements. The rationale for such befuddling behavior might come from the management cutting costs in using up the stock of advertising paper of both shows.

Howes Great European, after opening in New Orleans on December 12, 1864, closed the stand on January 21. The show was in Baton Rouge the week of February 6-11; and then went up the Mississippi, stopping at the river towns along the way. On the 17th a benefit was given in Natchez for the Protestant Orphans Asylum. It was reported that on March 4 they played to crowded houses in Vicksburg.

A stand at Nashville opened April 3 on the College and Jackson lot. Reserved seats, $1.00; ordinary seats, 75¢; children, 50¢. The ads featured the Bedouin Arabs, the elephant Jenny Lind, Australian kangaroos, Crockett and his lions, clowns Pete Conklin and Edwin Crouested, and equestrienne Lucille Watson. By the 8th the show had moved to the more accessible Market Street location. Here, an addition was inserted in the price list—colored persons, 75¢. The run ended on April 15, after which the company went up river to St. Louis where it completed the winter tour.

The show re-organized for summer touring and re-opened in St. Louis on April 24 to such satisfactory business that the stay was extended to a second week. It is at this point that the Howes and Castello managements may have come together. Carlotta DeBerg, James Cooke, and the DeMotts, who had been part of the Castello troupe, were listed in the Howes roster.[16]

Howes band was led by D. W. Reeves, whose aggregation was complimented in the St. Louis *Republican* of April 28:

> Seldom has our city been visited by a finer band of musicians than those connected with Howes' great circus. The band is under the direction of the eminent composer and musician, Prof. Wallis Reeves, and we must confess it to be superb. The bell chimes introduced in some of their popular pieces is alone worth the price of admission. Mr. Howes may congratulate himself in securing the services of such valuable artists.

A circus under the banner of Dan Castello's Great Show opened in Nashville on May 31 with DeBerg, Cooke, and the DeMotts featured in the advertising. It set up on the corner of College and Jefferson Streets for a four day stand, according to the pre-arrival advertising; but on June 1 an advertisement in the Nashville *Dispatch* used the phrase "for a short season." The last ad was carried in the paper of June 7. Presumably that ended the run.

On June 23, the *Dispatch* included a pre-arrival ad for the Howes & Castello Great Circus. It read, "Organization of the New Troupe will open in Nashville for three days only on Market Street, just below the Louisville Depot." Here again we find mention of Madame DeBerg. The stand was for June 26th, 27th, and 28th. The ad stated further routing to be: Gallatin, June 29th; Franklin, June 30th; and Bowling Green, July 1st. By this time the show had stopped railroading and had hired government wagons. A week in Louisville was commenced on July 24.

Nashville had been visited by Castello at the end of May and early June, and by Howes & Castello at the end of June. Were these titles juggled to make the public think they were seeing two different organizations? Or were they using up their old paper? Or were they distinctly different managements? I regret I do not have the answer.

Seth B. Howes sold the Great European to Smith, Quick, and Nathans early in 1865, probably at the St. Louis stand in April, which may explain his combining with Castello there. The two circuses must not be confused. The Castello and Howes organization, under whichever title, followed a southern routing. Howes' Great European, after leaving St. Louis, went to Belleville, IL, for May 8th and then into Illinois, Indiana, Ohio, and New York State.

Along the way, the Great European and the entire circus world suffered a loss with the death of James Crockett on an extremely hot July 6 in Cincinnati. He had ridden in the procession all that morning wearing a tin helmet and having no protection from the sun. With a matinee crowd anxiously expecting his arrival in the ring, the thirty year old lion king fell prostrate and soon died. His replacement in the den of beasts was Alviza Pierce, who had been a Crockett assistant.

Being one of the first to venture into the southern territory, Howes & Castello encountered a public hunger for entertainment. An incident was related by former clown and advance man George P. Knott in an interview for the Masillon *Evening Independent* that illustrates such local sentiment.[17] Now on rails, the show had been billed to appear in Chattanooga, TN, for two days but, meeting with larger houses than had been anticipated, it remained for a third day, scratching the previously set date of Dalton, GA. The disappointed Daltonians could do no better than watch the circus train as it passed through town. Thayer & Noyes, following three days behind, had also billed Chattanooga for two days, but was unable to pass through Dalton as some irate citizens had torn up the tracks.

After closing their summer season on October 14 in Providence, RI, Stone & Rosston shipped the outfit to Charleston, SC, where the winter tour began with the honor of being one of the first, if not the first, to invade the Deep South following the war. The civil and military authorities of Columbus, GA, in anticipation of their arrival, authorized the entertainment starved populous to remain out until 10:30 p.m. so they might witness a performance. The railroad show, coming from Alabama, had contracted with a drayman to haul their equipment at $3 a load. However, when the train got in late, the drayman declared the previous contract void and hiked the fee to $10 for what amounted to some forty loads. Unwilling to accede to such extortion, the circus turned back toward Montgomery, leaving the expectant citizens of Columbus disappointed.

An example of catering to Southern sentiment occurred early in 1866 while the Stone and Rosston show was visiting cities in Mississippi, Alabama, and Louisiana. As one writer put it, "They blew on their Southern feelings." Their advertising suggested that the proprietors had performed in Europe during the war: "These gentleman have, for the past five years, exhibited in England, France, Germany, and Spain, and, upon the cessation of hostilities in America, organized the present excellent troupe for Southern entertainment."[18]

By the time they hit New Orleans, the show had undergone a change to the "Great Southern Circus" in preparation for a tour of Texas. Capt. Thomas U. Tidmarsh, a former lieutenant in the Confederate Army, was engaged as "director," who made use of his reputation to develop a feeling of conciliation between the circus and prospective circus-goers:

> Captain Tidmarsh, having been identified with hundreds of the officers of the Confederate Army during more than four years of the war, feels particularly sensitive upon this point as not being justified in inviting the families of his old companions in arms or other ladies by public placard, in the announcements of which he is the director.... It is necessary for the success in the South of a meritorious show that its manager must have been identified with Confederate officers or Confederate interests. The war is over and this sort of humbug should be stopped. In the North we patronize actors and actresses without inquiring into their proclivities. If they are deserving, Southerners meet with engagements here as rapidly as Northerners do.[19]

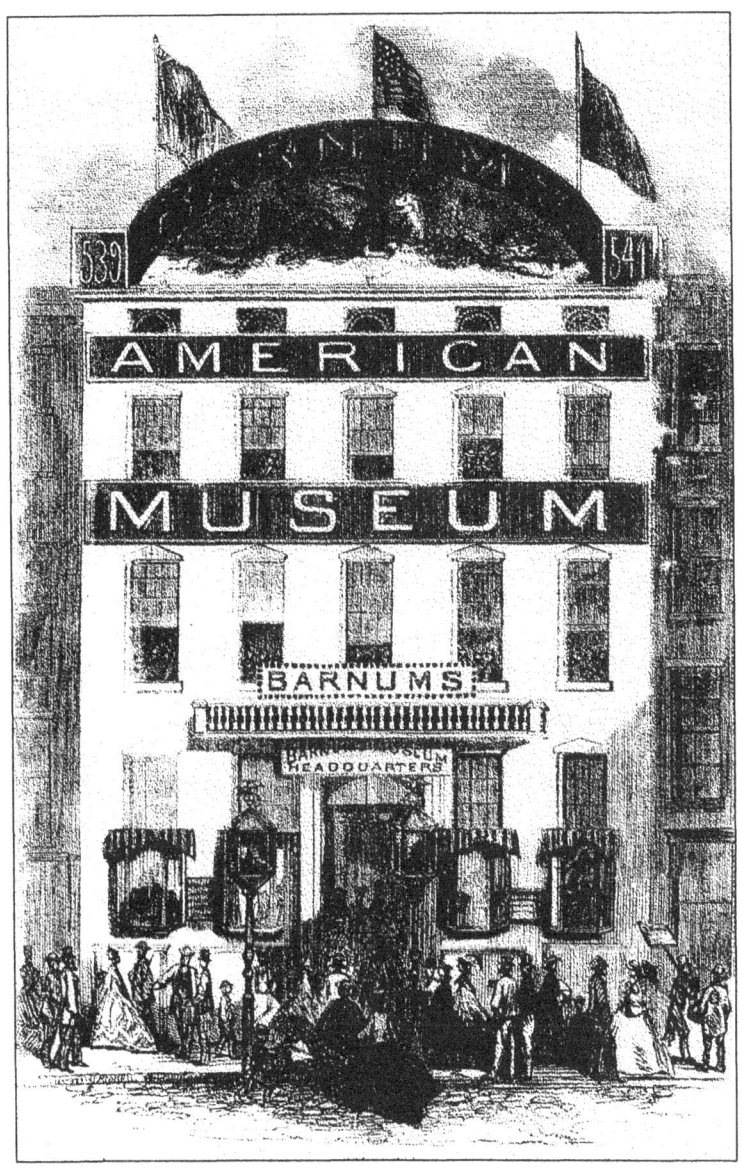

Barnum's New American Museum, 539-541 Broadway
Between Spring and Prince Streets

Conflagration! Barnum's famed museum burned on July 13 while he was addressing the Connecticut Legislature at Hartford. It was surmised that the fire started in the engine room from where fresh air was pumped into the water of the aquaria and where the power emanated to propel the huge fans used to cool the building. There was a loss of most of the live animals and the entire curio collection. The bear and performing seal escaped the flames. Two white whales, which had arrived only a week before, were overly cooked. Barnum described his first view of the charred ruins in his autobiography:

> When I arrived at the scene of the calamity and saw nothing but the smoldering debris of what a few hours before was the American Museum, the sight was sad indeed. Here were destroyed, almost in a breath, the accumulated results of many years of incessant toil, my own and my predecessors, in gathering from every quarter of the globe myriads of curious productions of nature and art—an assemblage of rarities which a half million of dollars could not restore, and a quarter of a century could not collect.

According to Barnum, not a thousand dollars worth of property was saved. The whole was insured for but $40,000; the loss totaled some ten times that.[20] But in spite of the financial tragedy, the great man organized another emporium of curiosities within less than two months.

The new Barnum museum, housed in the converted Chinese Building on Broadway above Spring Street, opened for business on September 6. Part of the edifice was used for dramatic purposes, opening with a piece called *Children of Cypress*. There were five sections for the curiosities. The first contained the lightning calculator, the fat woman, an individual who wrote with his toes, an educated seal, a Circassian woman, a male and female giant, wax figures of Commodore Nutt, Mr. and Mrs. Tom Thumb, etc. The next area contained the aquaria. The Bohemian glass blowers occupied another section. On still another level a space contained the display of shells and other such items, along with a sampling of stuffed animals. Next was a section, directly over the theatre portion of the building, where a large cage exhibited "the happy family," alongside a stereopticon and a shooting gallery.

The museum commenced a circus season on November 20 under the equestrian direction of Eaton Stone. The roster included Stone, Charles and Virginia Sherwood, John Foster, Charles Sherwood, Jr., Prof. Langworthy, etc. In conjunction, dramatic performances were given and the usual oddities displayed. The program commenced with the drama of *The Cross of Gold*. This was followed by an exhibition of the living curiosities and the singing of W. B. Harrison, popular for his song improvisations of current events. All this occurred in front of the curtain while the carpenters were taking up the stage and arranging the ring. The time allowed for this major transformation was just twelve minutes. With the arrival of the holiday season, a new dramatic spectacle was put up—*Dwange, the Arab; or, The Fairy Guardian of the Well*. The Hippotheatron opened on September 25 under the management of Richard Platt and Nathan W. Austin. Austin was a gentlemanly English clown and excellent general performer—an equestrian, a good leaper and still vaulter, a superior juggler on horseback and globe ascensionist (rolling a globe up an incline to the top of the tent and back, after which the globe opened and out popped his trick dog). His first wife was ascensionist and rope dancer Jeanette Ellsler, who was with him at this time. Later the union ended in divorce and he married Madame D'Atalie, the iron-jawed woman and "female Sampson," on May 11, 1876, when both were with Montgomery Queen's Circus.

    The house was packed to overflowing on opening night. The program commenced with the usual introduction of most of the company in a grand entry. Master Frank Ashton appeared in a contortion act. El Nino Eddie performed an equestrian exhibition with Dick Rivers, master of the circle, and Nat Austin. The company then entered into leaps, followed by the Delevanti Brothers on the trapeze. Austin performed his globe on horseback; W. H. Young did *l'échelle*; El Nino Eddie appeared on the tight-rope; Austin re-appeared in a posturing act with the Delevanti Brothers and Harry Bernard; trick ponies and the ballet pantomime of *The Magic Statue* concluded the program. On October 23 the illustrious Louise Tourniaire and James Madigan appeared, along with the pantomime of *The Four Lovers*. In another two weeks the bareback riding of James Robinson headed the bill.

    James M. Nixon left New York on October 19 aboard the *Catherine Whiting*, headed for Galveston with a circus company that included Madame Macarte, Billy Kennedy, the Miaco Brothers, W. W. Nichols, William Odell, Sid Webb, Frank Carpenter, Harry Bernard, Charles Devere, etc. The plan was to visit the principal towns of Texas by rail. If the trip had succeeded, Nixon would have been the first to take a circus into Texas after the war.[21]

    But disaster hit. After leaving New York, the ocean became so rough that the ship had to lay overnight at Sandy Hook. On the 23rd a heavy gale set in and the following day one of the ring horses went overboard. By nightfall, all of the horses had been washed into the sea. William W. Nichols was the owner of most of the ring stock, which he had fortuitously insured. At the height of the storm the ship's engine gave out, exposing the boat and passengers to the mercy of the angry elements for a period of thirty-two hours. Finally, the steamer went ashore five miles south of Carysfort Reef, FL, on October 28. It might be noted in passing that among the company was Charles Devere, who throughout his career received the reputation as a "Jonah," one who brought bad luck to the troupe with whom he was associated. James M. Nixon left the company at Key West, where the *Catherine Whiting* was brought to rest, and went on to New Orleans, presumably with the intention of picking up ring horses and continuing on to Galveston with the remnants of his company.

The circus troupe left Key West bound for New Orleans on November 11. After some eighteen hours, another storm came up. The fury crippled the ship's rudder and unseated the boiler, which was knocked about and punctured so severely that it was impossible to get up steam. After drifting about for five days, another ship came alongside and towed the injured vessel into Pensacola for repairs. Finally the Nixon party went on to New Orleans in a crippled condition. On arrival, rather than destination Texas, members of the company were announced to appeared at the Academy of Music in conjunction with the Thayer & Noyes circus.

Dan Rice made every effort to mend the reputation he had unfortunately attained as a secessionist by having a monument erected in honor of the soldiers from Erie County at Girard, his winter retreat.[22] It was unveiled on November 1, the same day Dan Rice's Great Show closed the season there. A salute of thirteen guns was fired at noon and an hour later an inaugural procession was formed to march through the main part of town, consisting of fifteen veterans of the War of 1812 riding in carriages, a sizable number of marching Union soldiers from Erie County, Masons, Odd Fellows, a fire brigade, the Band Chariot, Monitor Chariot, and War Chariot drawn by richly caparisoned horses, and, impressively, a tableau car of the Daughters of Freedom, mounted with a bevy of young ladies representing the states of the Union, all adorned with sashes of red, white and blue. In the center of this display of pulchritude stood the Goddess of Liberty, draped in white and wreathed with flowers. At about three o'clock the procession reached the public square where the monument stood. The Italian marble memorial, designed and constructed by Chicago sculptor L. W. Volk at a cost of around $5,000, bore the inscription:

> *In memory*
> *of the*
> *officers and soldiers*
> *from*
> *Erie County, Penn.,*
> *who have died*
> *in defense of their country.*

Circuses, which rushed south after Stone, Rosston & Co. had proven there was still money for a good show, performed throughout the winter there for the first time since the start of armed conflict. It has nearly always been the case that following a war people make considerable sacrifices for entertainment to distract them from the hardships incident thereto. Again the most prominent were Haight's United States Circus, Thayer & Noyes United States Circus, and Seth B. Howes' European Circus, Dan Castello's Great Show, and the Castello/Howes combination.

In the fall, Andrew Haight bought out his partner, George W. DeHaven, at Vicksburg and then spent the winter months traveling in the South, operating under the DeHaven name for as long as the printed advertising lasted. Doc Chambers was the agent and Ben Maginley the assistant manager. By October the show was in Algiers, before moving across the river to Tivoli Circle, New Orleans, October 30, where it played to good business until the week of November 20, after which it moved further downtown to continued success.

This organization achieved the distinction of becoming the first to take a circus into Texas after the war. Following a date in Mobile, the former DeHaven's United States Circus shipped out of New Orleans on the *Magnolia* for Galveston, arriving in time to set up their tents for the evening performance on Saturday, November 24. After sending their band out, the patrons who crowded into the tent amounted to a return of $1,600, plus an additional $400 from the minstrel sideshow. From billing the town on Sunday, the Monday take totaled $2,200 and $575; Tuesday, $2,350 and $600.

Andrew Haight

The company then went by rail to Houston for December 1, 2, 4, 5—Friday, Saturday, Monday, Tuesday. On the 2nd, the Houston edition of the Galveston *Daily News* carried this welcoming item:

> The Circus has Come!—Hurrah! All the world, especially the juvenile portion, was in motion yesterday and last night to witness the magnificent performances of the "Great United Circus Company." The unrivaled feats of M'lle Marie, Signor Bliss, etc., commanded universal applause. "Old Sam Lathrop" and his assistants gave their hearers many hearty laughs. Of course "Willie the Pet" met with the approval of all. But go and see by all means and remove the wrinkles from your face.[23]

After turning people away, the circus jumped to Richmond, at which place they hired vehicles to transport them to Austin and San Antonio, playing to crowded houses, including a Sunday performance. "We'll come out of Texas with lots of hard stuff," came word from the company.[24]

Following this, the show bought some horses and hired others and set out into the Texas countryside in the direction of Shreveport. Along the way they encountered audiences who were distinctly primitive when compared to other parts of the country, as revealed by a member of the troupe:

> And of all countries, this beats all. Talk of Hottentots, cannibals, barbarians! Here they are everything but civilized, whooping and hollowing, shooting, and all come to the show with pistols and knives. They shoot through the canvas, call you names that are not very pleasant to hear; and we have to take it all. They shoot all around us as we go to and from the canvas.[25]

With admission of $1 in species and $1.50 in greenbacks—the greenbacks coming primary from Union soldiers—the show was making money and the performers receiving their salaries every Sunday. "Old man Haight pays up good," was the word.

The way back from Texas to Shreveport for Andrew Haight's wearied party—a member of the company bemoaned—was a "long and tedious journey," during which the locals were apt to "put a six-shooter in your mouth and ask you if that was good for a ticket." Half of the trip was sloshing through mud and the other half "quarreling to get something to eat." At last the troupe arrived in Louisiana, happy to go down the Red River to New Orleans again.[26]

The summer season closed for Thayer & Noyes on October 12 at LaPorte, IN. The winter campaign was announced to open at

Louisville on the 23rd. Among the new additions were the Stickneys—Old Sam, Robert, and Emma; Tom and Virginia King, Burrows and Kelley, Jimmy Reynolds, and John Saunders. After leaving the river, they proceeded southward through the interior by rail. It was not long before they were fighting it out with the Howes & Castello circus when both shows entered Georgia and were booked into Macon for November 6th, 7th, and 8th.

A correspondent, who called himself Landry, volunteered a report to the *Clipper* on the meeting of the rival circuses there. He stated that both did fair business but that Thayer & Noyes had the advantage by arriving at the date a day in advance of their rivals, the latter failing to make proper railway arrangements. Defiantly displaying themselves as the United States Circus, they appeared in sharp contrast to Howes & Castello who, flying no national flag, designated their show "European." Because of this, the secessionists gave stronger support to the latter organization, even though Thayer & Noyes carried the better entertainment. This illustrates the dilemma for northern circuses traveling in the new South as they faced the conflict between political sensitivity and financial reward.

The problem was apparently exacerbated, Landry continued, when the occupying military got into the fray. The post commander, a Col. Dawson, telegraphed to Columbus, GA, where both shows were advertised to appear, that the Howes-Castello outfit should not exhibit unless under the "old stars and stripes." "So much were the secesh opposed to the words U.S. that when Thayer & Noyes gave a benefit to the poor of Macon (donating the gross receipts) the canvas held no more than 100 persons at most."[27] In response, the managers of Howes & Castello, feeling that the performance of their troupe in Macon at the same time was the cause for the failed benefit, donated their gross receipts in the amount of $300.

Thayer & Noyes responded to reports of the competition in a lengthy card to Frank Queen, publisher of the *Clipper*, datelined "Academy of Music, Dec. 16th, 1865," and signed "Thayer & Noyes." It began:

> Two successive issues of the *Clipper* gave what purported to be an account of the competition (since decisively determined) between Thayer & Noyes' United States Circus and S. B. Howes' European Circus, so similar in style and the repetition of errors, that we are constrained to believe they were written by the same person, and that the writer was

connected with the latter establishment. Knowing your aversion to a controversy in your paper, and that even if you were not, the presence of the members of both troupes, and all cognizant of the real facts of the case, would prevent the false statements doing any harm amongst our profession, we did not contemplate making any public correction of these errors until it has occurred to us that justice to the citizens of Macon and Columbus required at our hands a refutation of the malicious charge that the pretended result was attributed to the Southern prejudice against Union managers and against the title of our circus (the United States Circus).[28]

The card went on to explain that although all advertising carried the title of "United States Circus" the show had experienced "only the most marked courtesies" from the Southern people on their tour through Tennessee, Georgia, Alabama, and Louisiana, during the months of October, November, and December. It revealed that the organization had a contract to play an engagement at the New Orleans Academy of Music in December; so the outfit was shipped inland by rail to cover the principal cities en route. They were advertised to appear in Macon on the same days that Howes & Castello were booked. The Howes' show did not arrive in time to exhibit the first night, but Thayer & Noyes' receipts amounted to $1,800 from admission prices of $1 for Whites and 75¢ for Blacks. On the 7th and 8th, with the two companies playing day and date, the crafty Howes management lowered the general admission to 50¢, with a faint allusion to 25¢ for reserved seats, and thereby besting their adversary.

> As we did not reduce prices, and our Exhibition having been seen by most of the citizens the first day, naturally the rush was for the fresher and cheaper show, especially as they made an imposing street procession. Neither our politics nor our United States flag had anything to do with it, as was demonstrated in the next city As, however, we took about as much money the first day as Mr. Howes in the two, and being young and inexperienced showmen, we were glad to learn the valuable lesson of reducing prices in an extremity, from our veteran competitor, at so cheap a rate.

The next stand was Columbus on November 9th, 10th, and 11th. The Howes show, in an effort to repeat the triumph, did not perform on the first night, intending, as they had in Macon, to come in fresh and garner the rewards. Not willing to be stung a second time, Thayer & Noyes charged their standard admission prices for the 9th, taking in $2,300, but lowered them competitively with the Howes show on the other two days and received a larger number of patrons. "As we still kept the United States flag and preserved the title of the United States Circus," they continued, "politics evidently had nothing to do with this result."[29]

The two companies traveled to Montgomery on the same railroad train for a stand there on the 13th, 14th, and 15th. On arrival, they were requested by the authorities to forfeit the dates because of a small pox epidemic. Thayer and Noyes complied, jumping instead to Mobile; whereas Howes & Castello played the stand to poor business.

A general view of the success of both circuses can be had by looking at the figures kept by the assessor and collector of the 2% tax on the gross receipts by the United States Revenue Office in Mobile. The books revealed that Thayer & Noyes paid tax on a gross of $15,453 for five days commencing November 14. Howes-Castello was assessed on a gross of $8,813.55 for two weeks commencing November 20.[30]

But the war of the sawdust circle did not end here. These two parties faced off again with New Orleans as the field of battle. Thayer & Noyes opened at the Academy of Music on November 20; Howes-Castello arrived two weeks later with Dan Rice as the feature card. The citizenry, still smarting from the memory of Rice's speeches in the North, were not enthusiastic about giving him a "welcoming home." This lack of civic hospitality signaled to the proprietors that it was more profitable to move on and leave the Crescent City to Thayer & Noyes.

The intended stay was cut short after five days, the stakes pulled up, and the show sent on to greener pastures—Baton Rouge, Natchez, Vicksburg, etc. By December 24 the Howes & Castello party arrived in Memphis for a two-week stand. The company at this time was composed of Dan Rice, James and Josephine DeMott, Thomas and Edwin Watson, Herr Lengel, Theodore Tourniaire, Charles Parker, John Barklay, Lucy Watson, Ted Holloway, Horace Nichols, etc.

After his shipwrecked company disembarked in New Orleans, James M. Nixon went to Memphis, arriving during the Howes & Castello engagement there, intending to negotiate with the two men for putting a trick on the road the coming season. He arrived on the 4th of January. The following day the Howes-owned equipment was shipped to Little Rock and on the 6th the Howes/Castello partnership was terminated. Then, on January 11, after joining with Castello to purchase the Howes outfit, Nixon proceeded to Little Rock to retrieve it.[31] The show was put on the road under Castello's name, with Castello as the manager and drawing card and Nixon the contracting agent. Later, probably the following year, Egbert Howes was added to the partnership. This marked the beginning of an association between these men that would continue for the next three years and carry the showmen from the East coast to the Pacific Ocean.[32]

Flush with victory, Thayer and Noyes organized two circus companies, incorporating the best elements of Nixon's shipwrecked troupe. One unit, under the management of C. W. Noyes, remained in New Orleans in the French Quarter until the 20th of December; after which, it left for Galveston, Houston, etc. The company opened in Houston, December 25, on Main Street, corner of Capital, advertised to remain for "several days." To appease the Texas audiences they operated under the title of "Southern Circus" and pretentiously billed the show as being from the Academy of Music, New Orleans: "This organization comprises exclusively leading artists; a metropolitan troupe on a rural trip, embracing the elite of all the great performers who have this winter made a pilgrimage to New Orleans, that Mecca of all devout Equestrians."[33]

This was strictly a railroad show. It carried no menagerie and no parade equipment. The ads openly stated that it brought no "team horses, comparatively few canvas men, grooms, and laborers, but in their place all the elements of an entertainment seldom witnessed outside the great European capitals or most populous American cities." The classic rationale, stressed that the entertainment was all inside:

> In this trip it was indispensable to disencumber itself of all extraneous material that did not conduce to the entertainment within or discard some of the performers upon which the real merit of the show depended. Therefore, no imposing displays of processions, etc., will be made in the streets. But in weeding out these outside superfluities, it has been impossible to eliminate from the pictorial bills occasional representations of outside displays which will not be exhibited, and must not be expected.[34]

The last ad appeared in the Houston paper on December 31, stating, "Commencing Monday, January 1st, 1866, giving two performances each day, and thereafter in the principal towns in Texas." In addition to Noyes, the performing company consisted of Carlotta DeBerg and husband, James Cooke, the Miaco Brothers, Prof. DeLouis, Master Wooda Cook, Jimmy Reynolds, Thomas Poland, etc. Noyes was manger;

James Cooke, equestrian director; Sidney Webb, ringmaster; C. A. Spalding, treasurer; and Louis Heller, director of the orchestra.

The second unit, under the management of Thayer, chartered the steamboat *Ida May* and sailed toward Shreveport on December 17 and thence to the principal towns on the Red, Ouchita, and Mississippi Rivers. This troupe included the Stickney family, Tom King and wife, Charles Burrows, George Kelley, Sig. Faranti, William Burke, Archie Campbell, John Saunders, etc. Bad fortune hit when the boat sank near the mouth of the Loggy Bayou; but somehow the circus property was recovered. The company then returned to New Orleans and thence worked its way up the Mississippi to rendezvous with the Noyes party at St. Louis.

An era in circus history came to an end with the death of Isaac VanAmburgh on November 29. This circus giant had been connected with menageries since 1833, but his seven year trip to Europe magnified his name and popularized the image of "wild beast tamer" for all time. On his return to America in 1845, proprietors June and Titus established a new show with his name which was identified with both circus and menagerie until 1921. Through his performing, the style of animal acts changed from displays of docility to blatant challenges by man and beast. Never married, he died at circus-friendly Sam Miller's Hotel, Philadelphia.

With the smell of horses cleared from New Orleans' Academy of Music, the Rolland Brothers, gymnasts and acrobats, commenced a memorable engagement of some three weeks. Although a brothers act, the men were not related but were in fact William Holland and Henry Keyes. They began as a team with John Robinson's circus in 1862 and later joined the Hanlon Brothers for a tour. This year they organized a special company and moved down the Mississippi, playing towns along the way, before establishing themselves at the Academy of Music.

The Rollands were famous for their act called *alitora volante*, a feat developed in this country. The act consisted of a series of swings, leaps, and somersaults in midair; after which, one of the brothers hung by his legs from the bar, head downward, and caught the other by his wrists or ankles after a leap of ten or twelve feet, who was then thrown some thirty feet to the stage, alighting in an upright position.

They were well received by the New Orleans press, lauded for their charm, grace, agility and ease of movement, and for a freshness of style; all of which was enhanced by the use of elegant wardrobe and the acrobatic appliances which decorated the stage. It was suggested that aside from the Hanlons there were no other such performers who could wear so well and elicit such cheers from the audiences night after night. It was even doubted that any two of the Hanlons could compete with them, a huge tribute to say the least. Their appearance on December 31 concluded circus activity for 1865.

With the last of the war years at an end, so ends our narrative. We can now examine the limited role circus people had in its outcome. It is not surprising that so few were involved in the fighting of it. Many were not members of a community and therefore not subjected to the local pressures of enlistment. Some were not United States citizens, although, eventually, non-citizens were allowed to enlist. Others, constantly on the move, may have eluded the conscription officers. In any case, it appears that the majority of circus artists and associates were more concerned with professional survival than politics.

In the winter of 1862-63, sixteen men in Girard, PA, were required to fill the draft quota, half being connected with show business—James Thayer, William C. Crum, William Smith, John G. Glenroy, William Kirkwood, James Howland, and James Wadsworth. Thayer and Glenroy went to Erie to seek a settlement; for, as Glenroy stated, "neither of us wanted to go to the war." Glenroy was exempted because of an arm ailment:

> What I therefore had at one time considered a serious and detrimental injury to me, turned out for my good; as, if I had went into active service during the war, the chances are that I never would have served forty-two years in the circus ring.[35]

Thayer, being of good health, hired a substitute. It might be noted that the surrogate, upon arriving at Pittsburgh for induction, was declared physically unfit; thereby, earning for himself the sum of money at no risk to his person.

Some time later, Thayer and Glenroy received draft notices again. Glenroy merely demonstrated to the authorities that he had been previously exempted for a physical disability. The going rate for purchasing a substitute having increased since the first notice, Dr. Thayer paid up and still felt himself lucky to escape the service.[36] These incidents serve to exemplify the ludicrous nature of the induction process.

Still, there were those who either volunteered or were drafted. The future sideshow oddity, Martin VanBuren Bates, the Kentucky

Giant, joined the Confederate 5th Kentucky Infantry in 1861. He later was transferred to the cavalry and was eventually elevated to the level of captain. In the fall and winter of 1862-63, his unit was instrumental in breaking up the lawless guerrilla bands that were a menace to the mountain regions. He was a mere sixteen years of age at the time he joined; nevertheless, he must have been issued a huge horse. Later, under Humphrey Marshall's command, he was captured in a raid at Pound Gap. When, as a prisoner of war being taken through the town of Louisa, KY, en route to Camp Chase, OH, he was observed astride a small army mule, his feet sweeping the ground as he rode.[37]

Others recorded as serving their country include Thomas A. Edwards, who began his circus career as business manager for Spalding & Rogers in 1849 and remained with the firm until 1857, before leaving to join an expedition with Gen. Albert Sidney Johnson against the Mormons as scout and dispatch bearer. After serving in the war, he returned to scouting for Indian fighters. Frank Hyatt was attached to the Duryea Zouaves before taking his first circus employment with Van-Amburgh & Co. in 1863. Burr Robbins, rider and circus manager, joined the Union army for the duration, beginning as wagon boss with Gen. George B. McClellan's brigade, where he worked his way up to becoming a colonel. Clown Archie Campbell, after being captured by the Confederates at the Stoneman raid in 1864, spent some time in Andersonville prison. Richard Guy Ball, contracting agent, saw service with Company D, 1st Michigan Cavalry until 1865. Herr Elijah Lengel was a volunteer in the 19th Regiment National Guards of Philadelphia, which were encamped around Ft. McHenry near Baltimore in June of 1861. George W. Archer, globe performer, was drafted in January, 1864, and died the following year. Charles J. Melville, later one of the champion bareback riders of the world, served in the 52nd Ohio Regiment until he was wounded and sent home. Agent Giles Pullman enlisted in Co. A, 117th New York Volunteers and served through the war. J. B. Gaylord, agent, enlisted in the Union Army in 1861 and remained throughout as well. John Fulton, who had traveled with several circuses before he enlisted, was sent home after an injury from falling off a horse, an embarrassing fate for an equestrian. John Mackley (real name Terrance John McGannon), clown and vaudevillian, was present at the Appomatox Court House in Virginia when Lee surrendered to Grant. William Stanhope, later connected in the management with W. W. Cole and John B. Doris, served in an Ohio regiment. Capt. E. H. Sawyer of the 4th

New York Cavalry, formerly with Franconi's Amphitheatre, was taken prisoner in September of 1864. Showman George Middleton saw action with the 39th Indiana Regiment. He was captured and sent to Libby and later Belle Isle prisons. Some time after he had enjoyed professional success, he gave a Civil War monument to Jefferson County, IN, which was erected at Madison.

Not everyone performed with distinction. James Erwin, sideshow manager, was twice sentenced to be shot for desertion. The first time, as a mere boy, he was pardoned by President Lincoln; the second time he succeeded in escaping.

Justice was served in full view of the public at S. O. Wheeler's circus in Boston on the evening of January 27. While two workmen were engaged in laying down a carpet for one of the acts, a brace of policemen entered the ring and escorted one to the lockup. He had been recognized as a bounty jumper.

Although not a part of the fighting forces, M. M. Hilliard, a showman from Vermont, was in Vicksburg, MS, in 1863, active in the buying of cotton on the Yazoo River. He was captured by the Confederates and imprisoned for nine months at Demopolis and Mobile. On being moved to Meridian, MS, he escaped and persevered for eleven days as a hunted man, subsisting on green corn and anything else the land could provide before reaching Vicksburg and safety.

The circus, as a national institution, came through the conflict unscathed and unchanged. Of the managements on the road at the start of the war, nearly half were active at its finish—George F. Bailey & Co., Gardner & Hemmings, Spalding & Rogers, George W. DeHaven, L. B. Lent, John Robinson, John Wilson, William Lake, James M. Nixon, and VanAmburgh & Co. (the Dan Rice title was managed by O'Brien and Forepaugh). These proprietors and some new ones entering the field exhibited a resiliency in the face of the many obstacles the fighting had engendered, as well as an ability to adapt to the limited territory available to them and the crowded conditions created by it.[38]

Circuses would now enter a new era. Opposition wars—the use of "rag sheets," price cutting, and "day and dating"—would become more pronounced. New and dynamic management would enter the field and some of the present ones would enlarge their properties. The use of rail travel would increase along with the expansion of track mileage and with longer jumps between major cities becoming more profitable. By the end of the 1860s, the American circus was ready to enter a new epoch of innovation and growth, following the pattern set by other elements in national culture and commerce, a time that would, in a matter of a few years, lead to its "golden period."

> **CIRCUSES AND MENAGERIES, 1865:** George F. Bailey; Dan Castello; Castello & Howes; Chiarini; George W. DeHaven; Gardner & Hemmings; Great Union Combination (John Robinson); Holland & Madden; Howes European; Frank J. Howes; Lake's Hippo-Olympiad; Lee & Ryland; L. B. Lent; National Circus (Cincinnati, winter); New American Theatre (Philadelphia, winter); New York *Champs Élyées*; Nixon's Amphitheatre (Washington, DC, winter); Orrin & Sebastian (California); Orton Bros.; Palmer; Dan Rice (Dr. Gilbert R. Spalding); Robinson & Deery; Yankee Robinson; Ross & Carlo (California); Stone, Rosston & Co.; Thayer & Noyes; S. O. Wheeler; Whitmore, Thompson & Co.; Wilson & Zoyara (California)

NOTES

[1] Burt, p. 163.
[2] Glenroy, p. 140.
[3] New York *Clipper*, June 17, 1865, p. 78.
[4] New York *Clipper*, April 15, 1865, p. 7.
[5] They were in Louisville, KY, for the 4th of July week, followed by Shelbyville, 11th; Frankfort, 12th; Georgetown, 13th; Cynthiana, 14th; Paris, 15th; Winchester, 17th; Lexington, 18th and 19th; Richmond, IN, 20th; Nicholsville, 21st; Versailles, 22nd; Harrodsburg, 24th; Danville, 25th; Lebanon, 26th; Springfield, IL, 27th; Beardstown, 28th; Mt. Washington, 29th; Elizabethtown, KY, August 1st. Baltimorians did not enjoy another circus this year until George F. Bailey's aggregation arrived on Monday, September 11, for five days. They advertised the Mellville family, Sands, Nathans & Co.'s performing elephants, and the now famous hippopotamus. Music was provided by J. Withers' Brass Band. Along with the Melvilles in the arena were James Ward, Philo Nathans, Shappee & Whitney, William Kincade (the Baltimorean), etc. C. H. Farnsworth was the agent. A special exhibition was given at 10:00 a.m. on Wednesday, Thursday and Friday, showing the hippo, the elephants and the Herr Driesbach menagerie under the charge of Prof. Langworthy. "Liberal deductions" were made to attending groups from schools.
[6] King, p. 71.
[7] *Ibid.*
[8] *Ibid.*
[9] *Ibid.*, p. 72.
[10] Glenroy, 141.
[11] *Ibid.*, pp. 141-42.

[12] New York *Clipper*, September 2, 1865, p. 166.

[13] From a member of the company writing on August 16, New York *Clipper*, September 2, 1865, p. 166.

[14] Stover, p. 61.

[15] *Ibid*, pp. 61-2.

[16] The circus was in Belleville, IL, May 8; Decatur, May 15; Monticello, 16; Danville, May 22.

[17] Information submitted to the author by Stuart Thayer. The item appeared in the paper on April 15, 1893. Presumably this was Masillon, OH.

[18] New York *Clipper*, February 24, 1866, p. 367. Quote from advertisement in the Galveston *Daily News*, running from June 5 through 12, 1866.

[19] New York *Clipper*, April 7, 1866, p. 415. The route included Shreveport, April 25-28; Marshall, April 30-May 1; Elysian Fields, May 2; Mt. Enterprise, May 8; Linn Flat, May 9; Nacodoches, May 10; Douglas, May 11; Alto, May 12; San Antonio, June 22-26; Austin, July?

[20] Barnum, pp. 639-46.

[21] Nixon did take a show into Texas later, an effort that was unsuccessful. He left on December 7, 1870, but within a month word came back that salaries had not been paid and that the outfit had been attached.

[22] After Rice received compensation for his steamer that Gen. Fremont had seized in St. Louis during the war, the award of $32,000 was returned to the government for the care of wounded soldiers and their families. He also established a series of church houses for southern slaves and contributed to most any charity for which he was solicited.

[23] Galveston *Daily News*, December 2, 1865, p. 2.

[24] New York *Clipper*, March 10, 1866, p. 383. The letter was dated Red River, February 15, 1866..

[25] *Ibid*.

[26] *Ibid*. The roster included Barney and Mrs. Carroll, Marie Maginley, Master Willie, Burdeau, Carr, Naylor brothers, Bliss family, P. H. Seaman, Sam Lathrop, and Cary (clowns), Billy Manning, Harry Blood, Alex Prentice, John Somers, Master Hubert, Master Jimmy, W. A. Johnson.

[27] New York *Clipper*, October 25, 1865, p. 263.

[28] New York *Clipper*, January 6, 1866, p. 311.

[29] *Ibid*.

[30] *Ibid*.

[31] New York *Clipper*, January 13, 1866, p. 318; January 20, 1866, p. 327; January 27, 1866, p. 335.

[32] Stuart Thayer submitted this solution to the show's purchase in an e-mail dated December 1, 1996: "In the Clipper for 2 March 1867 is a comment that in forming the 1867 show Castello, Nixon and Egbert Howes would contribute their circus company, including the equipment that they bought from Seth B Howes on January 4 1866. The Castello show moved almost entirely by boat and rail in 1866. This reinforces my statements that Egbert owned nothing. It was all

Seth B's in 1865. Egbert moved the equipment from Memphis to Little Rock in January, 1866, then Nixon and Castello bought it and Nixon went to Little Rock to bring it back to Memphis."

[33] Advertising in the Galveston *Daily News*, beginning December 29, 31, 1865.

[34] *Ibid.*

[35] Glenroy, pp. 128-29.

[36] *Ibid.*

[37] "The Kentucky Giant," etc. p. 9-10.

[38] The partnership of Spalding & Rogers was dissolved on October 7, 1865, after seventeen years. Rogers sold his interest in the Academy of Music, New Orleans, to Spalding. They had previously divided their other real estate properties. Some of their ring horses were sold in Havana to Cuban circus manager Signor Albisu. Rogers retired well off and well liked. Spalding's last venture into management was in 1874-75 when he was co-proprietor with John O'Brien and Ben Maginley in Melville, Maginley & Cooke's Continental Circus and Thespian Company. The Gardner & Hemmings title went through a gradual change. As we have seen, John O'Brien's interest was taken over by James E. Cooper. In 1866, the year the firm engaged Dan Rice at $1,000 a week, Gardner sold his share of the show to Cooper over an altercation with Rice. In 1868 the ownership became Hemmings, Cooper & Whitby until the fall of 1870, when Harry Whitby was shot and killed during a front-door riot in Mississippi. Following this tragedy, the show went out as Hemmings & Cooper for two seasons, with James A. Bailey as advertising agent. Hemmings sold out to Cooper at the end of the 1872 season. With the names of both Gardner and Hemmings cleared from the title, for 1873 it became Cooper & Bailey. Of the managers that entered the business after the start of the war, Adam Forepaugh became the most successful, beholden to no man and solidly active until his death in 1890. John O'Brien managed to inveigle his way along until he sold out in 1887. George K. Goodwin had disappeared from circus management by 1865; his partner, James W. Wilder, was in and out of it until 1876; Thayer & Noyes ended their partnership after disaster struck the show in 1869.

DEATHS IN 1865: Globe performer, **George W. Archer**, in Baltimore, MD, February 7; **Fred Ashley**, gymnast and fancy dancer, from performance injuries, in Boston, March 1, age 29; the elephant **Hannibal**, on May 7 in Centerville, MD; **James Crockett**, lion tamer, of heat prostration in Cincinnati, July 6; **Charles Warner**, at Sam Miller's Hotel, Philadelphia, age 34, on August 30; **Abner W. Pell**, advertiser, later keeper of the Cottage Place Hotel, Chicago, age 45, September 27; **Lloyd Howes**, brother of Seth B., drowned on August 1 while crossing a swollen stream near Elmira, MO; **Benoit Tourniaire**, rider and juggler, in Havana, Cuba, September 13; **Old Dice**, "The Gypsy Queen," curiosity, September 28 in New York City, age 45; **Archie Campbell**, clown, in New Orleans, October 4; **Thomas L. Huntley**, tight-rope walker, while performing in Wilmington, NC, November 27; **Isaac VanAmburgh**, lion tamer, November 29, at Sam Miller's Hotel, Philadelphia; **Charles Johnson**, forty-horse driver, December 18, age 33.

BIBLIOGRAPHY

BOOKS

Angle, Paul M. and Earl Schenck Miers. *Tragic Years, 1860-1865,* TwoVolumes. New York: Simon and Schuster, 1960.

Barnum, P. T. *Struggles and Triumphs; or Forty Years' Recollections.* Hartford., J. B. Burr & Co., 1870.

Boatner, Mark Mayo, III. *The Civil War Dictionary.* New York: David McKay Company, Inc., 1959.

Brown, Col. T. Allston (edited by William L. Slout). *Amphitheatres and Circuses.* San Bernardino, CA: The Borgo Press, 1994. Book publication of "A Complete History of the Amphitheatre and Circus," serialized in the New York *Clipper* from December 22, 1860, through February 9, 1861.

_____. *History of the American Stage.* New York, Benjamin Blom (reissue), 1969.

_____. *History of the New York Stage,* 3 vols. New York: Benjamin Blom (reissue), 1964.

Chindahl, George L. *A History of the Circus in America.* Caldwell, Idaho: Caxion Printers, 1959.

Clapp, William A. *A Record of The Boston Stage.* New York: Greenwood Press (reissue), 1969.

Coup, W. C. *Sawdust & Spangles.* Washington, DC: Paul A. Ruddell, reissue, 1961.

Day, Charles H. (edited by William L. Slout). *Ink from a Circus Press Agent.* San Bernardino, CA: The Borgo Press, 1995.

Frost, Thomas. *Circus Life and Circus Celebrities.* London: Tinsley Brothers, 1875.

Glenroy, John H. *Ins and Outs of Circus Life.* Boston: M. M. Wing & Co., 1885.

Gossard, Steve. *A Reckless Era of Aerial Performance, the Evolution of Trapeze.* Self published, 1994.

Howes, Jeanne Chretien. *The Howes Circus Story.* Weston, CT, 1990.

Kendall, John S. *The Golden Age of the New Orleans Theatre.* Baton Rouge: Louisiana State University Press, 1952.

Leavitt, M. B. *Fifty Years in Theatrical Management*. New York: Broadway Publishing Co., 1912.

Ludlow, Noah Miller. *Dramatic Life as I Found It: A Record of Personal Experiences*. St. Louis: G. I. Jones & Company, 1880.

MacAllister, Copeland. *People of the Early Circus*. Framingham, MA: Salem House, 1989.

_____. *Uncle Gus and the Circus*. Framingham, MA: Self-published, 1984.

MacMinn, George R. *The Theatre of the Golden Era of California*. Caldwell, ID: Caxton Press, Ltd., 1941.

Odell, George C. D. *Annals of the New York Stage*, Vols. 1-8. New York: Columbia University Press, 1927-1931.

Picton, Col. Tom (edited by William L. Slout). *Old Gotham Theatricals*. San Bernardino, CA: The Borgo Press, 1995.

Reynolds, Chang. *Pioneer Circuses of the West*. Los Angeles: Westernlore Press, 1966.

Robinson, Josephine DeMott. *The Circus Lady*. New York: Thomas Y. Crowell Co., 1925.

Ropes, John Codman. *The Story of the Civil War*, Parts I, II. New York: G. P. Putman's Sons, 1894.

Shannon, Fred A. *The Farmer's Last Frontier: Agriculture, 1860-1897*. New York: Harper & Row, 1945.

Slout, William L., ed. *Broadway Below the Sidewalk*. San Bernardino, CA: The Borgo Press, 1994.

_____. *Theatre in a Tent*. Bowling Green, OH: Bowling Green University Popular Press, 1972.

Smith, George Winston, and Charles Judah. *Life in the North During the Civil War*. Albuquerque, NM: University of New Mexico Press, 1966.

Smith, Solomon Franklin. *Theatrical Management* in the *West and South for Thirty Years*. New York: Harper & Brothers, 1868.

Smither, Nelle Kroger. *A History of the English Theatre in New Orleans*. New York: Benjamin Blom (reissue), 1967.

Speaight, George. *A History of the Circus*. London: The Tantivy Press, 1980.

Stover, John F. *American Railroads*. Chicago: University of Chicago Press, 1961.

Thayer, Stuart. *Annals of the American Circus*, Vol. III, 1848-1860. Seattle, WA: Dauven & Thayer, 1992.

ARTICLES

"Among the Wild-Beast Tamers," *New York Clipper,* December 15, 1877.

Andress Charles, "The Circus of Yesterday, the Circus of Today and the Circus of Tomorrow," *New York Clipper,* December 19, 1914.

Berliner, Lawrence, "Press Agents and What They Accomplish," *Billboard,* August 25, 1906.

Bernard, Charles, "Circusiana," *Hobbies,* January, 1938, p. 32.

_____,"Old-Time Showmen," *Billboard,* December 31, 1932, pp. 64, 77; January 26, 1935.

Bowen, Albert R. "The Circus in Early Rural Missouri," *Missouri Historical Review,* XLVII (October, 1952), pp. 1-17.

Braathen, Sverre O., "Circus Days in Madison, Wisconsin," *The White Tops,* September/October, 1948, pp. 5-6.

Briarmead, Chess L. "The American Circus," *New York Clipper,* April 17, 1875.

"The Broadway Circus," *New York Clipper,* November 30, 1878.

Burt, Eliza Logan [as told to Mr. and Mrs. James R. Harvey], "Recollections of the Early Theatre," *The Colorado Magazine,* September, 1940, pp. 161-67.

Carey, John D., "The Circus Press Agent," *Billboard,* April 15, 1911.

Chindahl, George, "The Circus in Early Chicago," *The White Tops,* November/December, 1954, pp. 3-7.

"Circus in the War, The," unidentified clipping (Cincinnati Special to New York *Sun.*).

"Circus Tragedy of 1867," *Hobby-Bandwagon,* May, 1948, pp. 9-10.

Clarke, Birkit, "Among the Showmen"" *New York Clipper,* March 18, May 6, December 2, December 16, December 23, 1871; January 20, 1872.

Cole, George S., "Circus Recollections," *Billboard,* July 11, 1908.

Conklin, Peter, "Adventures of Pete Conklin," *Billboard,* March 22, 1913, p. 24-8, 153.

_____,"Showing Under Two Flags," *Barnum & Bailey Annual Route Book and Illustrated Tours,* 1906.

Conley, Dr. H. H., "Circus History of Midwest During the Civil War," *The White Tops,* February/March, 1942, pp. 7-9.

Dahlinger, Fred, Jr., "The Development of the Railroad Circus," Part One, *Bandwagon,* November/December, 1983, pp. 6-11.

Davies, Ayres, "Wisconsin, Incubator of the American Circus," *Wisconsin Magazine of History,* XXV (March, 1942), pp. 283-96.
Day, Charles H., "History of American Circus and Tented Exhibitions," *Billboard,* December 29, 1906; January 5, 1907.
_____, "The Press Agent's Antiquity," New York *Dramatic Mirror,* November 25, 1905.
DeHaven; Claude, "Remarks From An Advance Agent," *New York Clipper,* April 6, 1872.
Draper, John Daniel, "Madame Louise Tourniaire and Her Family," *Bandwagon,* September/October, 1986, pp. 22-26.
Durand, W. W., "The Late Andrew Haight," New York *Clipper,* February 20, 1886, p. 770.
"Fans Visit Delavan, Wis., Cemetery," *The White Tops,* September/October, 1962, pp. 11-13.
Fostell, Al, "Richard Hemmings, the Oldest Living Showman," New York *Clipper,* December 25, 1915,
Garvie, Billy S., "Civil War Circus Days at Hartford, Connecticut," *The White Tops,* June/July/August, 1943, p. 11.
Gossard, Steve, "When Galesburg Was a Circus Town, 1867-1872," *Bandwagon,* September/October, 1988, pp. 23-29.
Grace, John P., "The Circus of 1868," *The White Tops,* Christmas, 1941, pp. 9-10.
"Great Show Celebrities and the Thrilling Stories of Their Adventures," reprinted from clippings fron the New York *Mercury,* 1873, from the files of C. G. Sturtevant, *The White Tops,* August/September, 1940, pp. 13-14.
Heck, Will S., "Chats With an Old Circus Man," *Billboard,* March 21, 1908, pp. 45, 48.
Hemmings, Richard, "A Circus Man's Reminiscences" *Billboard,* June 6. 1908.
Henderson, John M., "Winning Wealth with Wind," *Billboard,* September 7, 1907, pp. 17, 28.
Hubbard, Kin, "Old Overland Circus Days," *The Saturday Evening Post,* December 8, 1923, pp. 53-54, 56.
"Interview With Dan Castello," Denver *Times,* March 17, 1902, p. 10.
James, Theodore, Jr., "Giant Wedding of the Little People," *The White Tops,* January/February, 1975, pp. 9-13.
_____,"What the Press Agent Represents," *Billboard,* March 22, 1913.

Keeler, Ralph, "Three Years as a Negro Minstrel," part three, *New York Clipper*, August 15, 1874.

"Kentucky Giant, World Wonder, The," *The White Tops*, July August, 1951, pp. 9-10, reprinted from the *Daily Independent*, Ashland, KY.

King, Orin C., "Only Big Coming," *Bandwagon*, May/June, 1987, p. 4-17.

_____, "Only Big Show Coming," Supplement, *Bandwagon*, November/December, 1996, pp. 68-73.

Kunzog, John C., "Circus Hardships of a Century," *Bandwagon*, November/December, 1958, pp. 15-16.

_____, "A Civil War Incident with a Circus Flavor," *Bandwagon*, October/November, 1954, pp. 3-5.

Loeffler, Dr. Robert J., "Biographies of Some of the Early Singing Clowns," *Bandwagon*, September/October, 1969, pp. 16-23.

MacAllister, Copeland, "The Fist Successful Railroad Circus Was in 1866," *Bandwagon*, July/August, 1975, pp. 14-16.

Macrosson, Isaac F., "Sawdust and the Gold Dust, the Earnings of the Circus People," *Bookman*, June, 1910.

Moore, Theodore A., "Recollections of the Season of '69 With the Forepaugh Aggregation," *The White Tops*, May, 1944, p. 23.

"A Nestor of Clowns, Old Dan Castello Talks of His Experiences of Long Ago." Probably from the Syracuse *Standard*. Date unknown.

"Old Days of Sawdust and Spangles," *Literary Digest,* August 18, 1917.

Parkinson, Bob, "John Robinson Circus," *Bandwagon*, March/April, 1962, pp. 4-8.

Parkinson, Tom, "Yankee Robinson Circus—Season 1866," *Bandwagon*, February, 1943.

Phillips, Fred H., "A Circus in Charlottetown," *The White Tops*, March/April, 1964, pp. 23-24.

_____, "The Circus Goes to Canada," *The White Tops*, December/January, 1936/1937.

Polacsek, John F., "The Circus in New Orleans, 1861-1865," *Bandwagon*, September-October, 1976, pp. 4-7.

Robinson, Fayette Lodawick, "Dilly Fay, the Clown," New York *Clipper*, February 17, 1872.

Robinson, Gil,,"The Circus Life in Early Days," *Billboard,* December 9, 1911.

Sharpe, Adrian D., "The Orton Circus," *Bandwagon*, July/August, 1969, pp. 4-8.

Stallings, Roy, "The Drama in Southern Illinois, 1865-90," *Journal of the Illinois State Historical Society*, June, 1940, pp. 190-202.

Sturtevant, C. G. "The Circus in America During the Civil War," *The White Tops*, November/December, pp. 3-6.

_____, "The Stickney Family," *The White Tops*, April/May, 1938, pp. 3-5, 28-29.

Tedford, Harold C., "Circuses in Northwest Arkansas Before the Civil War," *Arkansas Historical Quarterly*, Autumn, 1967.

_____, "Circuses in Northwest Arkansas, 1865-1889," *Arkansas Historical Quarterly*, Summer, 1973.

Thayer, Stuart, "The Belair Lot in Baltimore," researched by James F. Stegall, pp. 1-5.

_____, "John O'Brien's Winter Quarters, Frankford, PA," *Bandwagon*, January/February, 1995.

_____, "Legislating the Shows: Vermont, 1824-1933," *Bandwagon*, July/August, 1981, pp. 20-22.

_____, "One Sheet" column, *Bandwagon*, November/December, 1974, p. 21.

Walsh, Townsend, "The Grand Old Lady of the Circus," *Billboard*, March 24, 1928, p. 59.

_____, "Oldest Living Bareback Rider," *Billboard*, March 23, 1929, p. 65.

Wamack, Thomas, "Some Observations About Press Agents," *Billboard*, April 3, 1909.

OBITUARIES

Austin, Nat, New York *Clipper*, June 11, 1892.
Aymar, Walter B., New York *Clipper*, June 20, 1891.
Aymar, William T., New York *Clipper*, March 24, 1883.
Bancker, James W., New York *Clipper*, March 3, 1866.
Barnum, P. T., New York *Times*, April 8, 1891.
Barry, Tom, New York *Clipper*, January 23, 1909.
Bidwell, David, New York *Clipper*, December 28, 1889.
Buckley, Harry, New York *Clipper*, September 27, 1884.
Carlo, William, New York *Clipper*, October 4, 1879.
Carroll, William B., New York *Clipper*, July 20, 1889.
Castello, Dan, *Billboard*, August 7, 1909.
Costello, William, New York *Clipper*, February 22, 1890.
Crockett, James, New York *Clipper*, July 15, 1865.

DeBerg, Carlotta, New York *Clipper*, December 4, 1915.
DeHaven, Claude, New York *Clipper*, June 9, 1888.
DeHaven, George W., New York *Clipper*, September 6, 1902.
DeMott, James H., *Billboard*, October 18, 1902.
Derious, Edwin, New York *Clipper*, July 28, 1888.
Doris, John B., New York *Clipper*, February 24, 1912.
Dunbar, George, New York *Clipper*, October 4, 1884.
Forepaugh, Adam, New York *Clipper*,February 1, 1890.
Foster, John, New York *Clipper*, June 30, 1906.
Fuller, Charles W., New York Clipper, April 14, 1888.
Howes, Lloyd, New York *Clipper*, August 19, 1865.
Howes, Seth B., New York *Clipper*, May 25, 1901.
Hyatt, Frank, New York *Clipper*, March 16, 1889.
Gardner, William H., New York *Clipper*,February 23, 1889.
Gardner, Dan, New York *Clipper*, October 16, 1880.
Glenroy, John, New York *Clipper*, May 24, 1902.
Haight, Andrew, New York *Clipper*, February 13, 1886.
Howes, Egbert Crosby, New York *Clipper*, April 23, 1892.
Howes, Frank J., New York *Clipper*, October 30, 1880.
Jones, Richard P., New York *Clipper*, May 15, 1869.
June, Lewis, New York *Clipper*, February 4, 1888.
Lake, Agnes, New York *Clipper*, September 7, 1907.
Langworthy, J. M., New York *Clipper*, June 3, 1871.
Lent, Lewis B., New York *Clipper*, June 4, 1887.
Long, Samuel, New York *Clipper*, May 23, 1891.
Lowlow, John, New York *Clipper*, October 29, 1910.
Lusbie, Ben, New York *Clipper*, July 19, 1884.
Marks, Hiram, New York *Clipper*, July 23, 1910.
Melville, Frank, New York *Clipper*, December 5, 1908.
Murray, John Hayes, New York *Clipper*, January 7, 1882.
Nathans, J. J., New York *Clipper*, October 21, 1893.
Nichols, Horace F., New York *Clipper*, January 23, 1886.
Nichols, William W., New York *Clipper*, December 24, 1887.
North, Levi J., New York *Clipper*, July 11, 1885.
Noyes, Charles W., New York *Clipper*, November 21, 1885.
O'Brien, John V., New York *Clipper*, September 14, 1889.
Pastor, William H., New York *Clipper*, November 3, 1877.
Pell, Abner, New York *Clipper*, October 13, 1865.
Rivers, Frank, New York *Clipper*, February 26, 1887.

Rivers, Richard, New York *Clipper*, September 7, 1901.
Rinehart, Sam, New York *Clipper*, November 22, 1890.
Risley, Prof. Richard, New York *Clipper*, June 6, 1874.
Rivers, Frank, New York *Clipper*, February 26, 1887.
Robinson, Frank M., New York *Clipper*, March 4, 1882.
Robinson, James H., New York *Clipper*, October 9, 1880.
Robinson, John, New York *Clipper*, August 18, 1888.
Robinson, Yankee, New York *Clipper*, September 13, 1884.
Rosston, Frank H., New York *Clipper*, March 7, 1874.
Sears, William H., New York *Clipper*, June 27, 1874.
Sherwood, Charles E., New York *Clipper*, December 25, 1875.
Sherwood, Virginia, New York *Clipper*, September 13, 1884.
Showles, Jacob, New York *Clipper*, January 6, 1912.
Smith, Avery, New York *Clipper*, January 6, 1877.
Spalding, Dr. Gilbert R., New York *Clipper*, April 17, 1880.
Stickney, Emma, *Billboard*, July 14, 1923.
Stickney, Sallie, New York *Clipper*, January 16, 1886.
Stickney, S. P., New York *Clipper*, March 31, 1877.
Stone, Dennison W., New York *Clipper*, April 30, 1892.
Stow, Charles, *Billboard*, August 31, 1907.
Warner, Charles, New York *Clipper*, September 9, 1865.
Waterman, Walter, New York *Clipper*, October 30, 1880.
Wells, Louisa, New York *Clipper*, September 20, 1873.
Whitney, Charles, New York *Clipper*, May 26, 1894.
Whittaker, Francis W., New York *Clipper*, February 19, 1887.
Worrell, William, New York *Clipper*, August 21, 1897.

SHORT BIOGRAPHIES
Batcheller, George F., New York *Clipper*, July 9, 1881.
Batcheller, W. H., New York *Clipper*, February 11, 1882.
Brown, Col. T. Allston, New York *Clipper*, March 3, 1900.
Conklin, Peter, New York *Clipper*, June 2, 1866.
Crockett, James, New York *Clipper*, December 24, 1864.
D'Atalie, Mons., New York *Clipper*, May 24, 1873, p. 57.
DeMott, James, New York *Clipper*, October 23, 1880.
Gardner, William H., New York *Clipper*, February 23, 1889.
Lent, Lewis B., *Billboard*, September 26, 1910.
Nichols, Horace, New York *Clipper*, April 15, 1876.
Nixon, Adelaide, New York *Clipper*, July 21, 1866.

Noyes, Charles W., New York *Clipper*, December 13, 1879.
O'Brien, John V., New York *Clipper*, December 3, 1881.
Pastor, Frank, New York *Clipper*, October 27, 1866.
Pastor, Tony, New York *Clipper*, September 17, 1864; March 11, 1876.
Rivers, Eddie, New York *Clipper*, March 18, 1865.
Robinson, James, New York *Clipper*, August 13, 1864.
Robinson, Yankee, New York *Clipper*, December 30, 1865.
Stickney, Robert, New York *Clipper*, April 21, 1866.
Stokes, Spencer Q., New York *Clipper*, October 4, 1879.
Stone, Dennison W., New York *Clipper*, April 27, 1878.
Thayer, James L., New York *Clipper*, January 28, 1882.
Wallett, William F., New York *Clipper*, January 20, 1866.
Warner, Joel E., New York *Clipper*, May 10, 1879.
Welch, Rufus, New York *Clipper*, May 3, 1862.
Wilder, James W., New York *Clipper*, November 25, 1882.

PERIODICALS
Augusta (ME) *Kennebec Journal*, 1860-1869.
Baltimore *American and Commercial Advertiser*, 1862; July-December, 1863; 1865
Cincinnati *Daily Commercial*, April 1861 through October 1861; July 1863 through April 1865.
Cincinnati *Daily Enquirer*, April 1853; May 1853.
Frank Leslie's *Illustrated Newspaper*, October 6, 1866.
Galveston *Dailey News*, November, 1865-August, 1866.
Memphis *Daily Bulletin*, July 1862 through June 1865.
Nashville *Dispatch*, April 1862 through September 1865.
New York *Clipper*, 1860-70.
New York *Times*, 1860-70.
San Francisco *Daily Dramatic Chronicle*, January-December 1865.
Spirit of the Times, December 1831 through February 1861.

PAPERS
Draper, J. D., "Wheeling, West Virginia Circus History," Robert L. Parkinson Library and Research Center collection.
Ladwig, Ronald V., "'Goodness Gracious' Grady's Unprecedented Old Fashioned American Circus," Robert L. Parkinson Library and Research Center collection.

Webster, Edwin C., "Col. J. H. Wood, Joseph H. Wood, and John Harvey Wood, Showmen," 1994, Robert L. Parkinson Library and Research Center collection.

MISCELLANEOUS

Bailey, James A. Personal diary, 1863. J. T. McCaddon Collection, Princeton University Library.

Brown, Campbell H., Tennessee State Library and Archives, Nashville, TN, letter to Thomas P. Parkinson, dated August 9, 1967.

Carlyon, David James. Dissertation. *Dan Rice's Aspirational Project: The Nineteenth-Century Circus Clown and Middle-Class Formation.* Dissertation, Northwestern University, Evanston, IL, 1993.

CD-ROM, *America's Civil War, A Nation Divided.* Phoenix: Software Marketing Corporation.

Conover, Richard E. *Give 'Em.* Self published, 1965, p. 20-21.

Dahlinger, Jr., Fred. Personal scrapbook.

Dingess, Robert S. Unpublished observations of the circus world as he knew it, generally referred to as the Dingess Manuscript, a copy of which is in the Robert L. Parkinson Library and Research Center, Circus World Museum, Baraboo, WI.

Durang, Charles, "The Philadelphia Stage from the Year 1794 to the Year 1855," Philadelphia *Weekly Dispatch,* 1854-1860. Microfilm in three parts, beginning with issue of May 7, 1854.

Langley, William O. *The Theatre in Columbus, Georgia, from 1828 to 1878.* Unpublished MA Thesis, Alabama Polytechnic Institute.

Lowlow, John, unidentified clipping in the New York *Sun,* "The Circus in the War," from the files of Stuart Thayer.

Thayer, Stuart, letter to author, May 4, 1995.

INDEX

Academy Hall, Baton Rouge, LA, 87
Academy of Music, Boston, 10, 45, 87
Academy of Music, New Orleans, 36, 45, 55, 158, 204, 208, 210, 211, 212, 218
Academy of Music, NYC, 75
Adams, James Capen "Grizzly", 14, 15, 38
Albino Family, 114, 154
Albisu, Signor, 218
Alex Robinson's Circus, 63
Alhambra, 146, 148, 151
Ali, 18, 138
Allen, John, 160
American Theatre, San Francisco, 32
Anderson, Major, 35, 47
Anderson, or, the Patriots at Sumter in '61, 53
Anderson, the Hero of Fort Sumter, 53
Andrews, 36
Antony and Cleopatra (elephants), 64, 103
Antonio & Wilder, 87
Antonio Bros., 13, 76, 121
Appomattox Court House, 181
Arch Street Theatre, Philadelphia, 51
Archer, George W., 214, 219
Armstrong, Thomas, 114
Army of Northern Virginia, 127
Army of the North, 51
Ashley, Fred, 219
Ashley, H., 70
Ashton, Frank, 189, 203
Ashton, William, 189
Astley's Amphitheatre, London, 4, 94, 141, 157
Athenaeum, Cairo, IL, 87
Atwood, A. D., 138
Augusta, Mlle., 114
Austin, Nat, 107, 157, 163, 174, 189, 203
Austin, William, 107
Aymar, Albert, 175, 190
Aymar, Mrs. William, 147
Aymar, Walter, 32, 160
Ayres, David D., 180
Bailey & Co., 76, 121, 153, 179
Bailey, Fred H., 186
Bailey, George F., 6, 216
Bailey, Hachaliah, 164
Bailey, James A., 153, 218
Baker, Thomas, 101
Baldwin, Sam, 180
Ball, Richard Guy, 214
Ballard, Bailey & Co.'s French Circus, 78
Banjo, 85
Banks, Gen. Nathaniel P., 127
Baptiste, Mons., 174
Barclay, Estelle, 25

Barclay, Fred, 25, 37, 171
Barnum, P. T., 6, 14, 15, 53, 67, 114, 115, 116, 138, 154, 164, 202
Barnum's Museum, 67, 83, 202
Barnum's Museum, Circus and Mammoth Amphitheatre, 114, 116
Baron Munchausen, 89
Barry, Frank, 18
Barry, John, 107
Barry, Thomas, 53
Barry, Tom, 18
Bartholomew circus, 121
Bartholomew, George, 31
Barton, Thaddeus, 16, 141
Bassett, Charles H. "Doc", 32, 76, 122
Batchelder, Sarah, 122
Batcheller, George, 174
Bates, Martin VanBuren, 213
Beauregard, Gen. Pierre, 47, 49, 99
Bedouin Arabs, 148, 152, 198
Bell, Oliver, 20, 133
Benshaw, J., 121
Benton, James, 154
Bernard, Harry, 203
Black Squall,, 54
Blake, William, 160
Blanche, Irene, 121
Bliss family, 170, 190, 217
Bliss, Signor, 190, 194, 207
Blondin, Mons., 24, 25
Blood, Harry, 217
Blue Beard, 11
Booth, John Wilkes, 153
Boswold, Charles, 104

Boulware, Mark, 30
Bowery Amphitheatre, 77
Boyzenarius, Mlle. Ella Zoyara, 13
Bragg, Gen. Braxton, 118, 151
Brewer, Joseph W., 38
Bristol, Charles, 18
British First Royal Dragoons, 53
Britton, A. T., 190
Broadway Amphitheatre, 152
Broadway Theatre, 152
Bronze Horse, The, 11
Brooklyn Arena, 153
Brown, Campbell H., 180
Brown, J. Purdy, 85
Brown, John, 3
Brown, S. E., 167
Brown, T. Allston, 24, 37, 64, 77, 94, 101, 111, 162
Bryan's Great Show and Tom King's Excelsior Circus, 170
Bryan's National Circus with Mrs. Dan Rice, 132
Bryant's Minstrels, 4
Buchanan, James, 3, 35
Bucheet, 18
Buckley, Harry, 154
Buell, General D. C., 99
Bull Run, 59, 65, 111
Burdeau & Peppers, 160
Burdeau, Henry, 190, 217
Burgess, Tom, 134, 190
Burke, Ella, 121
Burke, L. Nicholas, 104
Burke, William, 212
Burnell, George, 154
Burns, John, 134
Burnside, John, 121
Burnside, General Ambrose E., 118

Burrows and Kelley, 160, 208
Burrows, Charles S., 134, 175, 186, 212
Burt, Jim, 160
Burt, Sam, 138
California Menagerie, 15
Cameron, James V., 163, 174
Campbell, Archie, 29, 184, 212, 214, 219
Canham, Thomas, 137, 186
Carlisle, James, 180
Carpenter, Frank, 187, 203
Carr, Louis B., 190, 217
Carroll, Barney, 114, 117, 141, 142, 147, 170, 217
Carroll, Marie, 114, 117, 141, 142, 148, 207
Carroll, Mrs. Barney, 147, 170, 217
Carroll, Willie, 217
Carter, James, 167
Cary, 217
Cary, Miss Carrie, 170
Cary, V., 170
Castello & Howes, 216
Castello & VanVleck, 134, 153
Castello circus, 86, 168, 179, 197, 205, 216
Castello, Dan, 44, 134, 168, 197, 199, 208, 217
Castello, Frances, 134
Castello-Howes circus, 208, 210
Castilla, Mlle., 75, 190
Castle, Charles H., 132, 159
Chaillu, Dr., 10
Chambers, Doc, 205
Chambers, Washington, 79
Champs Élysées, Paris, 157

Chancellorsville, 125, 126
Charlton, Mr., 7, 15, 16
Chiarini, Angelo, 79
Chiarini's Italian Circus, 78
Chichester, E., 95
Children of Cypress, 202
Childs, Joe, 154
Christie, Frankie, 143
Cinderella, 11, 47
Cirque Français, 36
Cirque Napoleon, 133
Clark, J. C., 171, 195
Clark, John, 121, 180
Clarke, Philo A., 64
Clermont, Henri Clarence, 154
Cline, Herr Andre, 75, 141-142
Cole, Johnny, 154
Cole, W. W., 214
Comac's Woods, Philadelphia, 21-22
concert saloons, 4, 89, 91
Conklin, Pete, 86, 128, 166-168, 180, 184, 198
Connecticut Giantess, 83
Conover, Richard E., 131
Conrad Brothers, 101, 114, 117, 132, 163, 186
Conrad, Charles, 101
Conrad, William, 101, 116
Continental Circus, Philadelphia, 53
Continental Theatre, Philadelphia, 44
Cook, Wooda, 211
Cooke & Adams, 16
Cooke, Henry, 157, 171, 175
Cooke, John, 16
Cooke, Thomas, 4
Cooke, William, 4, 6
Cooke's Circus, 10
Cooke's Equestrian Troupe, 4, 10, 44
Cooke's Royal Circus, 15, 16

Cooper & Bailey, 218
Cooper, James E., 117, 132, 141, 147, 157, 160, 174, 197, 198, 211, 218
Cornelius & Baker, 95
Couldock, F. L., 163
Coup, W. C., 154
Courier of St. Petersburg, The, 94
Course, Abijah, 153
Cowell, Joe, 154
Coyle, Henry, 190
Cremorne Gardens, London, 101
Cremorne Gardens, NYC, 101, 102
Crescent City Circus, 104
Crockett, James, 167, 198, 199, 219
Cross of Gold, The, 203
Croueste, Edwin, 198
Crum, William C., 213
Cubas, Isabel, 102, 114, 116, 180
Cullen's Iroquois Indian troupe, 187
Cushing, Joseph, 17, 103, 129, 153, 164
Cutler, George, 131
Dan Rice's Great Show, 25, 35, 44, 50, 67, 78, 103, 107, 132, 139, 145, 171, 190
Dan Rice's Menagerie, 189
Dan Rice's Zouaves, 54
D'Atalie, Madame, 203
Davenport, John, 16, 36, 160, 175, 186
Davis, Barney, 133
Davis, Hiram, 133
Davis, Jefferson, 40
Davis, Mons., 174
Dawson, Col., 208
Day, Charles H., 36, 103
Days of '76, or, The Struggle for the Union, The, 145
Days of '76, The, 107
De'Auley, Mlle., 190
DeBach, Mons., 7, 15, 16, 36, 122
DeBerg, Carlotta, 197, 198, 211
de Carno, Señor Carlos, 159
Deery & Robinson's Metropolitan Circus, 195
DeFabier, Louis, 186
DeForrest & Teesdale, 101
DeForrest, C. V., 101
DeHaven & Co.'s United States, 190, 193, 194
DeHaven circus, 76, 216
DeHaven, George W., 20, 21, 190, 194, 205, 215
Delevanti Brothers, 117, 184, 203
DeLorme, Eugenie, 30
DeLouis, Prof., 211
DeMott, Garry, 104, 154
DeMott, James, 138, 197, 198
DeMott, Josephine, 197, 198
Denzer Brothers, 138, 154, 187
Denzer, Jacob, 154
Derious, George, 108, 160
Derious, Master, 36
Devere, Charles, 72, 114, 203, 204
Devinier, Josephine, 142, 143
Dick Turpin, the Bold Highwayman, 142, 143
Dingess, Robert S., 99, 163
Dockrill & Leon, 36
Dodsworth, Henry, 101
Donavan, C., 134

Donovan, William, 180
Doris, John B., 214
Dougherty, Henry, 95
Drew, Billy, 154
Drew, Frank, 25, 26, 37
Drexel, W., 187
Driesbach, Herr, 137
Ducrow, Andrew, 94
Ducrow, Gustave, 154
Ducrow, William, 104, 152
Durand, Frank, 31
Dutton, William, 186
Duval, Mme., 121
Duverney, William, 7, 15, 16, 159
Dwange, the Arab; or, The Fairy Guardian of the Well, 203
E. F. & J. Mabie's Circus, 145
E. F. & J. Mabie's Menagerie and J. J. Nathans' American Circus Combined, 60
Eaton, Gil, 139
Edward and Brownell, 87
Edwards, Thomas A., 214
El Nino Eddie, 187, 203
Elixir of Life, or, the Birth of Harlequin, The, 175
Elizabeth, Mlle., 121
Ellinger & Foote Moral Exhibition, 184
Ellingham, Robert, 16, 36, 138
Ellsler, Jeanette, 107, 163, 189, 203
Eloise, Mlle., 36
Erwin, James, 215
Everett, Edward, 153
Ewell, Gen. Richard S., 127

Fairy Prince O'Donohue, The, 175
Faranti, Signor, 212
Farini, Mme., 122
Farnsworth, C. H., 138, 216
Farragut, Commander David G., 99
Farragut, Flag Officer, 87
Felicei, Ariana, 104
Ferdinand, Signor, 187
Field of the Cloth of Gold, The, 26, 116
First National Union Circus, 58
Fish, Charles, 20, 44, 159, 175
Fitzgerald, James Michael, 106
Floating Palace, 18, 84, 85, 86
Fogg & Howes, 41
Fogg, Jeremiah, 72
Foote, Commodore (midget), 101, 114
Foote, Flag Officer, 87, 89, 95, 99
Ford, J. T., 92
Ford's Theatre, Washington, 92, 181
Forepaugh, Adam, 6, 170, 189, 215, 218
Forrest, Edwin, 16
Forrest, Fannie, 11
Forrest, Hubert, 121
Fort Donelson, 89
Fort Sumter, 47, 181
Foshay, James W., 146
Foster, J. C., 89
Foster, James C., 95
Foster, John, 36, 108, 117, 189, 202
Four Lovers, The, 203
Fox, George L., 51, 65
Francis, Millie, 153
Franconi's Hippodrome, 43, 78, 104, 116, 147, 164
Franklin, William, 121

Fredericksburg, 118, 125
Freeman, Gen., 96
Fremont, Gen., 217
French Spy, The, 92, 102
Front Street Theatre, Baltimore, 26
Frost, Hyatt, 173
Fuller, H. H., 77
Fulton, John, 214
G. F. Bailey & Co.'s Circus, 13, 60, 77, 103, 137, 154, 158, 215
Gagliani, Mlle. Josephine, 25
Gaiety Theatre, Wheeling, WV, 87
Gambati, 5
Gardner & Hemmings, 63, 76, 108, 113, 114, 121, 144, 145, 153, 154, 179, 190, 215, 216, 218
Gardner, Camilla, 108
Gardner, Dan, 21, 108, 114, 117, 157, 218
Gardner, Eliza, 94, 108, 117
Gardner, Hemmings & Co.'s American Circus, 77
Gardner, William, 21
Gayler, Charles, 53, 65, 167
Gaylord, J. B., 214
George K. Goodwin & Co., 63, 78
George W. DeHaven's Circus, 20, 60, 196
Gettysburg, 125, 127
Gibbonoise, Signor, 152
Gifford, James, 92
Glenroy, John, 21, 48, 106, 121, 134, 175, 180, 183, 194, 213

"Glory, Glory, Hallelujah!",, 39
Goffe's Monkey Ballet, 21
Golden Egg, The, 101
Goldie, George, 189
Gonzales, Adolph, 104, 160
Goodwin & Wilder, 76, 87-88, 106, 121, 133, 160, 179
Goodwin, George K., 16, 70, 87, 132, 218
Gordon, Capt. Nathaniel, 83
Gossin, John, 106
Grant, Gen. U. S., 70, 87, 89, 95, 99, 125, 127, 151, 157, 181, 214
Grant, Jesse, 70
Great Orion Circus, 70
Great Union (John Robinson), 179, 186, 216
Green, William H., 171, 195
Grizzly Adam's bears, 69
Hahn, Michael, 159
Haight & DeHaven's Circus, 190
Haight, Andrew, 190, 205, 206, 207
Haight's United States Circus, 205
"Hail Columbia", 29
Haines, J. T., 102
Hall, Charles Henry, 5
Hall, George W., 64, 121
Halleck, Gen. Henry, 87, 155, 175
Haller, Prof., 116
Hamlet, 16
Hammon, Richard, 134
Hankins, James R., 139
Hanlon Brothers, 6, 11, 15, 16, 17, 75, 76, 159, 212, 213
Hanlon, Alfred, 16
Hanlon, Edward, 16
Hanlon, Frederick, 16
Hanlon, George, 16
Hanlon, Thomas, 7, 16, 44

Hanlon, William, 16, 36, 75, 76
Hannibal (elephant), 10, 187, 189, 219
Hardee, Gen. William J., 179
Harlequin Bluebeard, 175
Harlequin Mother Goose, 175
Harper's Ferry, 3
Harrison, W. B., 203
Hart, Billy, 154
Haslett, Joseph, 186
Hatch, J. A., 173
Heenan, John C., 11
Heller, Louis, 212
Heller, Robert, 36
Heloise, Mlle., 7, 45
Hemmings, Cooper & Whitby, 218
Hemmings, Mrs. Richard, 114
Hemmings, Richard, 21, 22, 108, 110, 113, 114, 117, 157, 218
Henderson, David, 180
Hendrickson, William, 174
Hernandez, James, 79
Hernandez, Richard, 104
Hilliard, M. M., 215
Hippotheatron, 157, 159, 161, 171, 174, 203
Hippozoonomadon, 103
Hitchcock, Lyman A., 173
Hoey, Patrick, 141
Hogle, William, 67, 72, 75, 106
Holland, William, 212
Holliday Street Theatre, Baltimore, 92
Holmes, Billy, 153
Hood, Gen., 177, 179
Hough, W. H., 186
Howard, Frank, 104

Howard's Athenaeum, Boston, 76, 87
Howe, Julia Ward, 83
Howes & Castello, 199, 208, 209-210
Howes & Cushing's United States Circus, 6, 18
Howes & Norton, 175, 179
Howes & Turner, 164
Howes, Cady, 153
Howes, Ebenetiz, 180
Howes, Egbert, 198, 217
Howes, Frank, 18, 36, 67, 103, 154, 157, 160, 177, 216
Howes, Lloyd, 219
Howes, Nathan, 78, 164
Howes, Seth B., 78, 145, 164, 167, 199, 208, 217
Howes' European Circus, 164, 167-168, 179, 190, 198-199, 205, 208, 210
Howes Olympian Circus, 194-195
Howland, James, 213
Hubbell, Alonzo, 75
Hubert, Master, 217
Hunt, William, 180
Huntington, Harry, 38
Huntley, Thomas L., 219
Hutchinson, George P., 187
Hyatt, Frank, 214
Hyman, Spaf, 64
"I Wish I Was in Dixie,", 3
I. R. and W. Howes' menagerie, 152
Ingalls, Judge, 107, 154
Irish Beauty, The, 92
Iron Amphitheatre, Havana, 36
Island No. 10, 95
Jackson, Stonewall, 111, 127
James M. June & Co.'s Oriental Circus, 78
James Myers' circus, 6

James Raymond, 18, 29, 55, 85, 86
James West's circus company, 41
Jennings, Charles, 121
Jenny Lind (elephant), 198
Jerry Mabie menagerie, 189
Jim Myers' Circus, 18
Jimmy, Master, 217
Joe Pentland Circus, 44, 78
Joe Pentland's Great New York Circus, 92
John T. Potter's Victory Arena and Great Western Circus, 78
John Wilson's Mammoth Circus, 146
Johnson, Charles, 180, 219
Johnson, Gen. Albert Sidney, 214
Johnson, Jean, 18
Johnson, Robert, 168
Johnson, Vice-President, 177
Johnson, W. A., 217
Johnston, Gen. Joseph E., 95, 164
Johnston, General Albert S., 99
Jones, Dr. Richard P., 67, 118, 132
Jones, Joseph J., 154
June, James M., 122
June, John J., 122
June, Lewis, 122
June, Stebbins B., 79, 122
June, Titus, Angevine & Co., 77, 152
Justice, J. J., 175
Keefe, John, 20, 67, 72, 75, 106

Keeler, F. A., 163
Keeler, Ralph, 86, 121
Keene, Laura, 181, 182
Kelley & Burrows, 208
Kelley, George M., 134, 175, 212
Kemp, William H., 6
Kendall, Ned, 79
Kennedy, William, 104, 195, 203
Kent, Julian, 44, 101
Keys, Harry, 30, 212
Kincade, William, 16, 45, 157, 187, 216
Kincades, 117
King, Capt. H. W., 54
King, Tom, 22, 26, 43, 45, 75, 76, 94, 104, 117, 121, 134, 143, 170, 171, 179, 186, 187, 208, 212
King, Virginia, 26, 43, 104, 171, 186, 208, 212
Kingsley, Omar Samuel, 9, 25
Kirkwood, William, 180, 213
Knott, George P., 199
Kopp, Herr, 16
Ku Klux Klan, 181
Kunzog, John, 77
La Petite Camille, 108
La Petite Flora, 154
Lake & Co., 77, 131, 153, 179
Lake family, 175
Lake, Agnes, 29, 131
Lake, Alice, 29, 131, 180
Lake, William, 29, 30, 131, 215
Lake's Hippo-Olympiad, 216
Lalla Rookh (elephant), 29, 104
Langworthy, Prof., 10, 202, 216
Lathrop, Peoples, Franklin & Co., 31
Lathrop, Sam, 89, 141, 142, 157, 207, 217
Laura Keene's Theatre, NYC, 101

Lazelle Brothers, 131
Lechler, J. E., 175
Lee & Ryland, 179
Lee, Gen. Robert E., 36, 111, 118, 157, 181, 214
Lee, H. C., 146
Lee, Worrell & Sebastian, 146, 153
Lehman, Augustus, 154
Lengel, Herr Elijah, 214
Lent circus, 76, 78, 103, 121, 129, 134, 152, 153, 179, 216
Lent, L. B., 34, 103, 104, 152, 160, 164, 215
Lenton, Nichols & Co.'s Circus, 34
Leotard, 75
Leslie, E. M., 53
Lester, William, 131, 160, 175
Libby, Hercules, 20
Lincoln, Abraham, 13, 34, 35, 39, 51, 96, 111, 153, 177, 181, 182, 215
Lincoln, Mary Todd, 182
Lindsay, Hugh, 38
Little Gemma, 72, 75
Logan, Eliza, 182
Loisset, François, 36
London Zoological Gardens, 18
Long, Daniel, 121
Long, Sam, 29, 44, 59, 146, 154, 157
Longstreet, Gen., 111
Lord, W. G., 157
Louise, Mlle., 153, 190
Lowlow, John, 175, 180
Loyale, Mlle. Caroline, 36
Lum, Frank, 154

Lyon, Capt. Nathaniel, 40
Mabie brothers, 78
Mabie circus, 76, 121
Mabie, Jerry, 145, 154
Mabie's Menagerie, 145, 153, 163, 168
MacAllister, Copeland, 132
Macarte, Marie, 142, 143, 151, 157, 203
Macarte's Grand European Circus Combined with Nixon's Great Cremorne Troupe, 141
Macarthy, Marian, 11
"Macbeth, or, the Downfall of Gilson's Beanery", 11
Mackley, John, 214
Madden, Archie, 21
Madden, George P., 154
Madigan & Carroll, 121
Madigan & Gardner's Circus, 24
Madigan family, 122
Madigan, Charles, 114, 134, 175
Madigan, Eliza, 22
Madigan, Henry P., 76, 122
Madigan, James, 22, 72, 134, 160, 175, 203
Madigan, Rose, 44
Madigan's Great Show, 64
Magic Statue, The, 203
Maginley & Bell, 179
Maginley & VanVleck, 153
Maginley, Ben, 132, 133, 134, 205, 218
Maginley, Black & Co., 179
Maginley, Marie, 217
Maginley's Cosmopolitan Circus, 133, 134
Major Brown's Mammoth Coliseum, 167

Mann, John, 86
Manning, Billy, 217
Marble Heart, The, 153
Marquez, Señor Don Antonio, 159
"Marseillaise Hymn, The", 29
Marshall, Polly, 15
Martin, Agrippa, 106
"Maryland! My Maryland!",, 39
Mason, Madame, 59
Massett, Stephen C., 53
Matty Brothers, 75
McArthur, W., 190
McClellan, Gen. George B., 69, 111, 214
McCollum, Natt, 134
McCord, Alexander, 122
McCracken, William, 86
McCulloch's Invasion of Missouri, 89
McDonough's Olympic concert saloon, 53
McDowell, Gen., 65
McFarland, James, 44, 180
McKnight, Capt. James, 48
McMullin, Capt. Bill, 53
Mechanics Pavilion, 184
Mellville family, 216
Melville & Co., 179
Melville family, 146, 152, 174
Melville, Charles J., 214
Melville, James, 152, 163, 174
Melville, Louise, 163
Melville, Maginley & Co.'s Great Eastern Circus, 154
Melville, Maginley & Cooke's Continental Circus and Thespian Company, 218
Melville's Australian Circus, 159, 163, 168
Menken, Ada Isaacs, 11
"Merry Sports of England", 11
Metcalf, George, 148
Metropolitan (M. J. Robinson), 31, 179
Metropolitan Garden, 7
Metropolitan Theatre, San Francisco, 146
Miaco Brothers, 203, 211
Middleton, George, 215
Miles' Circus Royale, 151, 153
Miller, John, 164
Miller, Sam, 67, 212
Miller, Yale & Howes' Circus, 164
Miller, Yankee, 170
Minute Men of Virginia, 51
Monroe, Charles, 187
Monster of St. Michael, or Harlequin and the Golden Sprite of the Sulphur Mines, The, 45
Montgomery Queen's Circus, 203
Moreste, Henry, 24, 108, 186
Morgan, Frank, 153
Morgan, Gen. John H., 144
Morgan, Julia, 153
Morgan, William, 195
Morgan's Raiders, 143
Morris Bros., Pell & Trowbridge's Minstrels, 4, 11
Mother Goose, or, The Man Who Lost His Wife, 20
Motley Brothers, 137
Mount Pitt Circus, 21
Murphy, J. R., 134
Murray & Hutchinson, 187
Murray, John, 187

Myers, James, 43
Myers, Virginia, 26
Nagel, 36
Nathans, J. J., 168, 195
Nathans, Philo, 138, 216
National Circus, 77
National Circus, Cincinnati, 179, 216
National Hall, Washington, 116
Naylor, John, 171, 217
Naylor, William, 114, 171, 190, 217
Nellis, J. S. K., 121
Nelson Sisters, 15
Nelson, William, 40
New American Theatre, Philadelphia, 216
New Bowery Theatre, 51, 65, 148
New York *Champs Élyées*, 190, 216
Niblo & Sloat, 14, 87
Niblo, Thomas, 34
Niblo, William, 5
Niblo's Garden, 4-7, 10, 15, 25, 44-45, 106, 183
Niblo's Saloon, 4, 15, 76
Nichols, Horace, 101, 143, 147, 157, 197
Nichols, W. W., 160, 184, 203
Nicolo, Bobby, 147, 148, 158, 174
Nicolo, George, 147
Nicolo, James, 147
Nicolo, Prof., 158
Nicolo, Thomas, 147
Nixon & Adams, 16
Nixon & Co., 78
Nixon & Kemp, 78

Nixon Cremorne Garden Circus, 116
Nixon, Caroline, 36, 160, 180
Nixon, Frank, 160
Nixon, James M., 6, 9, 14, 15, 17, 45, 54, 63, 69, 76, 101, 102, 114, 115, 116, 117, 141, 143, 146, 151, 159, 174, 184, 203, 204, 211, 215, 217
Nixon, William, 16, 54
Nixon/Cooke circus, 106
Nixon's Alhambra, 153
Nixon's Royal Circus, 58
Nixon-Macarte, 153
Nixon's Amphitheatre, Washington, DC, 216
Nixon's Cremorne Garden Circus, 113, 117, 121
Nixon's Hippotheatron, 179
Nixon's Royal Circus, 16, 17, 69
North & Co., 60, 75, 76, 78
North, Levi J., 44, 131, 154, 190
North, Levi J. Jr., 190
Norton, Horace, 175
Noyes, Charles, 29, 98, 104, 106, 186, 211
Nutt, Commodore (midget), 114, 116, 202
O'Brien & King's Excelsior Circus, 171
O'Brien, John, 63, 108, 117, 132, 153, 170, 171, 179, 189, 215, 218
Odell, George C. D., 5
Odell, William, 147, 174, 203
O'Donoghue, or, the White Horse of Killarney, 89
Old Bowery Theatre, 41, 44, 70, 75, 89
Old Cary, 121, 153, 179

Old Cary's Great World Circus, 170
Old Dice, 219
Olympic Circus, 77
"Oriental Festival, The", 15
Ormond, Francelia Delsmore, 43
Ormond, Kate, 18, 43, 44, 89, 154, 159, 171
Orrin & Sebastian, 216
Orrin family, 92
Orton Bros.' Great Circus, 196
Otto, Madame, 5
Our American Cousin, 181
Owens, J. H., 190, 193
P. H. Nichols' Grecian Arena and Classic Circus, 77
P. T. Barnum's Asiatic Caravan, Museum and Menagerie, 78, 164
Painter, 32
Palace Garden, NYC, 101
Palmer, H., 195
Palmer's Western Circus, 195
Paris Hippodrome, 43
Parker, Charles W., 108, 142, 147, 157, 163, 197
Parkinson, Thomas P., 180
Pastor, Tony, 26
Pastor, William, 159
Patience and Perseverence, 10
Patti, Carlotta, 101
Peasley, Flint, 160
Pell, Abner W., 219
Pell, Charles, 20
Pemberton, Gen. John C., 127
Penny, H. W., 189
Pentland, Joe, 7, 11, 15, 69, 75, 92, 152
Pentland's Dramatic Equestrian Establishment, 78
Peoples, George, 92
Peoples, John, 32
Pepin & Barnet, 85
Pepin, Victor, 85
Pepper, Tom, 67
Perkins, J. H., 190
Perry, E. W., 131
Perry, Jennie, 131
Perry, Master Thomas, 131
Phelps, Frank, 67, 117
Phelps, Mary, 121
Pierce, Alviza, 199
Platt, Richard, 184, 203
Poland, Thomas, 134, 211
Polk, Gen., 70
Pope, Gen., 95, 99, 111
Powell, J. C. M., 60
Powell, Lee, 72
Pratt, G. A., 87
Prentice, Alex, 217
Preston, William C., 154
Price & Simpson, 41, 72
Pridham, William, 94
Prince of Wales, 3
Pullman, Giles, 214
Putnam, 45
Quaglieni, Sebastian, 11, 15, 36
Queen, Frank, 208
Quick & Mead, 41
Quick, E., 154
Quick, Gerard, 17, 129, 138
R. Sands & Co., 59, 63, 76, 146
R. Sands and G. C. Quick & Co., 78
Rarey, John S., 189, 191, 192
Reed, Charles, 25, 122, 186

Reynolds, Jimmy, 106, 116, 141, 142, 143, 147, 152, 171, 186, 208, 211
Rice circus, 76, 121, 140, 153, 216
Rice, Catherine Ann, 106
Rice, Dan, 20, 25, 26, 29, 31, 54, 56, 58, 85, 89, 92, 94, 95, 96, 104, 107, 147, 171, 189, 204, 210, 215, 217, 218
Rice, Elizabeth Margaret, 106
Rice, Mrs. Dan, 26, 107, 121, 132, 153
Richards, 36
Richardson, Omar T., 104
Ridgeway Brothers, 147
Ridgeway, John, 147
Rinehart, Sam, 160
Ringgold Flying Artillery, 47
Risley's Royal Pavilion, 79
Rivers & Derious, 78, 159
Rivers' Melodeon, 11
Rivers, Charles, 36, 117, 138, 190
Rivers, Eddie, 36, 187, 203
Rivers, J. C., 107
Rivers, Luke, 75, 117
Rivers, Richard, 203
Robbins, Burr, 214
Robinson & Bros., 131
Robinson & Deery, 77, 153, 169, 179, 216
Robinson & Howes, 153, 158, 159, 175
Robinson & Lake, 29-30, 76, 121, 131
Robinson & Toole, 121
Robinson, Alexander, 121, 169
Robinson, G. N., 186
Robinson, Jack, 30
Robinson, James, 6, 11, 15, 44, 106, 137, 157, 160, 165, 168, 175, 203
Robinson, John, 6, 29, 30, 72, 106, 131, 153, 154, 215, 216
Robinson, John Jr., 186
Robinson, Yankee, 76, 107, 109, 121, 153, 168, 179, 216
Robinson's Great Combined Circus and Menagerie, 50, 212
Rochelle, Mons., 104, 117, 171, 195
Rochford, R. C., 121
Rockwell & Stone, 78
Rockwell, Alex, 79
Rockwell, Henry, 85
Rocky Mountain Circus, 31, 37
Rodney, William, 147
Rogers, Charles J., 41, 43, 95, 218
Rogers, John, 41
Rolland brothers, 159, 212, 213
Rolland, Henry, 159
Rolland, William, 159
Ronzani ballet, 45
Rosecrans, Gen. William S., 87, 118, 151
Ross & Carlo, 216
Ross, George, 16, 77
Rosston, Frank, 187
Rowe, Joseph, 14, 37
Royce, Al, 154
Ruggles, Henry W., 36, 159
Runnells, Burnell, 85
Russell, Mr., 139
Rynar, Mrs., 36
Sabastian, Signor, 72
Sagrino, Sophie, 151
Sam H. Nichols' circus, 41, 78

Sandford's Opera Troupe, 4
Sands & Lent's Circus, 152
Sands, Maurice, 121
Sands, Nathans & Co., 121, 137, 153, 179
Sands, Nathans & Co.'s performing elephants, 32, 216
Sands, Richard, 79
Satan in Paris, 11
Satterlee, Bell & Co., 20
Satterlee, R. G., 20
Saunders, John, 186, 208, 212
Sawyer, Capt. E. H., 214
Sayers, Tom, 11
Sbriglia, Sig., 101
Scott, Gen., 59
Seaman, P. H., 190, 217
Seamon, Annette, 190
Sears, John, 63, 145, 163
Sebastian, Romeo, 36
Sebastian, Signor, 16, 45, 75, 92, 146
Seeley, Charles, 106
Self-Propelling Road Carriage, 173
Seward, William H., 13
Shappee & Whitney, 216
Shay, Charles, 107, 134
Shelley, Thomas Jefferson, 154
Shepherd, Mme., 122
Sherman, Gen. William T., 164, 174, 179, 181, 183, 196
Sherman, Robert L., 167
Sherwood family, 116, 157, 173, 174, 184
Sherwood, Charles, 173, 184, 189, 202
Sherwood, Charles Jr., 189, 202
Sherwood, Ida, 173
Sherwood, Virginia, 202
Shield of the Cloth of Gold, The, 15
Shiloh, 99
Showles, Jacob, 107, 173
Showles, Mrs. Jacob, 107, 173
Siegrist Brothers, 44
Siegrist family, 187
Siegrist, Auguste, 43
Siegrist, François, 43, 174
Silloway, Prof., 160
Simpson & Price, 154
Simpson, Samuel, 70
Slaymaker & Nichols, 159, 160, 179
Sliter, Richard, 79
Sloat, J. G., 34
Sloat's New York Circus, 58, 69
Small, Colonel (midget), 101, 114
Smith, Avery, 129, 167
Smith, Gen. Morgan L., 87, 168
Smith, Quick, and Nathans, 199
Smith, William, 22, 44, 75, 117, 134, 171, 174, 184, 195, 213
Snow Brothers, 106, 107, 160
Somers, John, 217
Spalding & Rogers, 18, 29, 41, 43, 44, 45, 59, 76, 78, 85, 87, 95, 121, 153, 159, 171, 179, 214, 215, 218
Spalding & Rogers museum, 18
Spalding & Rogers' Two Circuses, 78
Spalding, C. A., 212
Spalding, Dr. Gilbert R., 41, 85, 86, 95, 103, 145, 216, 218
Spalding, James, 121
Spalding's North American Circus, 78

Spanola Brothers, 152
Sparks, William, 170
Spirit of the Flood, 101
Split Fire, 65
Sporrer, Michael, 37
Springer, Andy, 174, 186
St. Charles Theatre, New Orleans, 17
St. Louis Theatre, 79
Stanhope, William, 214
Stark, Frank, 16
Stars and Stripes, The, 53
Stebbins, H. L., 139
Steele, Gen., 169
Steeple-Chase; or Life in Merry England, The, 15
Stickney, Emma, 72, 104
Stickney family, 208, 212
Stickney, Mrs. S. P., 72
Stickney, Robert, 72, 104, 134, 152, 175
Stickney, Rosaline, 72
Stickney, S. P., 7, 36, 72, 75, 85, 89, 94, 104, 175, 185
Stickney, Sallie, 7, 72, 75, 152
Stickney, Sam, Jr., 72, 139
Stickney's Calisthenics Exhibition, 72
Stickney's National Circus, 72
Stickney's New Orleans Circus, 72
Stokes' circus, 139
Stokes, Emma, 171
Stokes, S. Q., 9, 121, 171
Stone, Den, 187
Stone, Eaton, 36, 69, 75, 89, 106, 116, 141, 142, 147, 157, 174, 189, 202
Stone, Mrs. C. I., 37
Stone, Rosston & Co., 179, 184, 187, 188, 200, 205, 216
Stone, Rosston & Murray, 196, 200
Stone, Rosston & Murray's Great Southern Circus, 200
Stout, William H., 168
Stowe, Harriet Beecher, 94
Straight, Charley, 154, 170
Straight, Ned, 154, 170
Strakosch, Mme., 101
Stratton, Sherwood, 164
Stuart, Thomas, 159
Sturtevant, C. G., 77
Swann, Tom, 154
Sweeney, Joe, 38
Sylvester, Jennie, 147
Syro-Arabic Troupe, 141, 142
Tacon Theatre, 18
Talleen Brothers, 147, 174
Taylor, J. H., 154
Teal, William, 20
Terror of the Road, or, the Race for Life, The, 45
Thayer & Noyes, 50, 77, 103, 104, 106, 121, 137, 153, 154, 157, 173, 179, 186-187, 189, 196, 199, 204-205, 208, 209, 210, 211, 216, 218
Thayer, Dr. James L., 67, 76, 97, 104, 106, 114, 116, 173, 186, 213
Thayer, Sallie, 154
Thayer, Stuart, 17, 37, 55, 117, 180, 217
Theatre San Souci, 5
Thomas, B. F., 10
Thomas, Gen., 177, 179
Thompson, Frank, 154
Thompson, J. W., 121

Thompson, Master, 173
Thumb, Gen. Tom, 11, 114, 116, 164
Thumb, Mrs. Tom, 86
Tidmarsh, Capt. Thomas, 16, 200
Tilghman, Sig., 122
Tilton, E. L., 70
Tinkham, John, 134
Tinkham, Joseph, 170
Tippoo Saib, or, the Storming of Seringgapatam, 45
Tobbin & Tavier, 158
Tolliday, Thomas, 147
Tourniaire, Benoit, 133, 219
Tourniaire, Ferdinand, 133, 159, 171, 197
Tourniaire, François, 133
Tourniaire, Louise, 89, 101, 133, 152, 171, 175, 203
Tourniaire, Theodore, 133, 159
Townsend, J., 154
Tremaine, Le Sieur, 154
Tryon, John, 72
Turner brothers, 77
Turner, Aaron, 6
Uncle Tom's Cabin, 94
Usher, Dicky, 18
"Vacant Chair, or We Shall Meet but We Shall Miss Him, The", 39
VanAmburgh & Co., 10, 60, 63, 76, 78, 103, 121, 128, 145, 153, 171, 173, 179, 186, 215
VanAmburgh, Isaac, 70, 105, 167, 212, 219
VanOrden, Wessell T. B., 77
VanVleck, 134

VanVolkenburg, Richard, 134
Vauxhall Garden's Winter Circus, 21
Verrecke, Mons., 147, 148, 175
Vicksburg, 125, 127, 128
Victoria and Albert (elephants), 32, 38, 64, 103
Victory on Victory; or, the Capture of Fort Donelson, 89
Villanueva Theatre, Havana, 17
Volk, Lawrence , 157, 205
Wadsworth, James, 213
Walker, Lizzie, 154
Walker, Robert, 95
Wallace Brothers, 108
Wallace's performing bears, 134, 152
Wallack's Theatre, NYC, 152
Wallett, William F., 141
Walnut Street Theatre, Philadelphia, 95
Walsh, Townsend, 37
Wambold & Whitby, 76
Wambold, George, 171, 195
Ward, James, 16, 138, 171, 216
Ward's Mission to China, 26
Warlock of the Glen, The, 45
Warner, Charles, 107, 132, 219
Warner, Hannaford A., 133
Warner, Mrs. Charles, 132, 153, 179
Warren, Lavinia, 86
Washington Hall, Wheeling, WV, 87
Watson, Charles, 79, 122
Watson, Lucille, 198
Watson, Tom, 18, 20
Waugh, Henry W. (Dilly Fay), 63
Weaver, Sam, 76
Webb, Josephine, 143
Webb, Sid, 114, 203, 212
Welch & Brothers, 54

Welch & Lent, 78
Welch, Rufus, 7, 36
Welch"s Grand National Circus, 78
Wells, Louisa, 147
Wellsler, Sam, 173
Western, Lucille, 92
"What Is It?", 154
Wheatley Guard, 51
Wheatley, William, 51
Wheeler, Gen. Joseph, 151
Wheeler, Hatch & Hitchcock, 179
Wheeler, S. O., 132, 133, 153, 172-173, 189, 215, 216
Wheeler's International Circus, 132, 154, 189
Whitby, Elvira, 114, 195
Whitby Family, 132, 195
Whitby, Harry, 36, 114, 195, 218
Whitby, Johnny, 114
Whitby, Rosa, 195
Whitby, Willie, 114, 195
White, Alexander, 157
White, W. W., 76
Whitmore, Thompson & Co., 216
Whitney & Shappee, 216
Whitney Brothers, 107
Whittaker, Frank, 22, 117
Whittaker, Marie, 117
Whittaker's Amphitheatre, 153
Wilcox, Johnny, 153
Wild Men of Borneo, 133
Wilder, James W., 87, 218

Williams, Bobby, 107, 173
Williams, Mr. & Mrs. Barney, 10
Wilson & Zoyara, 216
Wilson, Gen., 177, 180
Wilson, Honorable J. M., 158
Wilson, John, 31, 34, 37, 76, 92, 121, 153, 174, 184
Wilson, John, 93, 215
Wilson, Zoyara & Carlos, 179
Wilson's Hippodrome, San Francisco, 184
Winter Garden Theatre, NYC, 102
Withers, J., 216
Wizard Skiff, The, 102
Wolf, Christiana (Mrs. S. P. Stickney), 72
Wood, Col. Joseph H., 86
Worland, Annie, 159
Worland, Jenny, 186
Worland, Jerry, 159, 180
Worland, Mrs. Jerry, 159
Wright, Charles, 122
Yale, Enoch, 164
"Yankee Doodle", 51, 86
Yankee Robinson's Triad, 145, 196
Young, W. H., 203
Young, William, 187
Zanfretta, Louis, 171, 195
Zanfretta, Marietta, 43, 174
Zara, Mlle., 143
Zoological Hall, 10
Zoyara Circus, 139
Zoyara, Ella, 7-11, 15-17, 25, 26, 45, 56, 69, 72, 75, 104, 121, 139, 184
Zoyara, Madame, 26

www.ingramcontent.com/pod-product-compliance
Lightning Source LLC
Chambersburg PA
CBHW030920090426
42737CB00007B/255